Yale Language Series

SPEAK MANDARIN

A Beginning Text in Spoken Chinese

Henry C. Fenn
M. Gardner Tewksbury

Yale University Press, New Haven and London

Set in Documentary type, and printed in the United States of America by The Murray Printing Co., Westford, Mass.

Library of Congress catalog card number: 67–24499
ISBN: 0–300–00453–2 (cloth), 0–300–00084–7 (paper)

This work was developed pursuant to a contract between the United States Office of Education and Yale University and is published with the permission of the United States Office of Education, Department of Health, Education and Welfare.

20   19   18   17   16   15   14   13

FOREWORD

Background

Speak Chinese, compiled in 1943–45, published in 1948, has served as a basic textbook in spoken Chinese (Mandarin) for a majority of students in the United States and for a considerable number in other countries over a period of more than two decades. Its use at home port, the Institute of Far Eastern Languages (Yale University), has engendered continual faculty discussions of the problems arising in the classroom, the result of which was a plan for the present revision, called Speak Mandarin.

The changes embodied in this thoroughgoing revision do not express any new theory of teaching approach; they represent an effort to improve the effectiveness of the tool. The original Speak Chinese (1948) included a small amount of drill material with each lesson. Because this proved inadequate, our teachers built up a mass of supplementary exercises, some to help the student prepare his lesson, some to save the teacher's time in classroom drills and written assignments. The new Student's Workbook, used with the twenty lessons of the basic text, functions as a directive to the student, the Teacher's Manual as a guide to the inexperienced teacher.

The very mass of the Workbook materials makes it necessary to tailor its use to the time allotment of the program, and Chinese language programs currently range from the now outmoded three 50–minute periods per week, through a more adequate five periods per week, to the new "intensive" courses requiring from ten to twenty periods per week, variously apportioned between the classroom and the laboratory.

Following the suggestion of students who have used the tentative edition, basic text and workbook have been bound separately, so that both books may be placed side by side on the student's desk, thereby reducing the amount of leafing back and forth required in study.

The Lessons

The twenty-four lessons of the original text have been regrouped into twenty, with some changes in the order in which structural patterns are presented. Each lesson contains:

Dialogue (or narrative) which presents vocabulary and patterns in a natural setting. The student will do well to memorize considerable portions of these dialogues and recite them as a check on pronunciation and rhythm. An English translation is placed at the end of the lesson to serve as a guide in reproducing the Chinese version.

Vocabulary. The original vocabulary of 750 items has been increased to 850 in order to include terms which teachers have told us they would like included. The policy of the authors is to stress mastery of standard speech patterns rather than extensive vocabulary at the initial stage. Several types of current idiom, however, have been added: courtesy expressions, classroom utility expressions, and aphorisms. The last have been selected for their value in typifying structural patterns.

Sentence Patterns. There is no logical or absolute order for presenting speech patterns. The order here used developed out of classroom experience

v

rather than from linguistic theory. In introducing a pattern, we have used the deductive approach, presenting a number of sample sentences and deriving from them a pattern or principle. The number of such examples has been curtailed because extensive additional examples are available in the Workbook.

Notes. Our effort to distinguish patterns and notes has not always met with success. In general, the notes elaborate on and further explain the treatment of the patterns and deal with specific word usage.

What about the Characters?

Chinese characters, like other writing systems, were devised to record speech. Only after a Chinese child learns to speak is he taught the written symbols for his words. Although this order of precedence is not peculiar to the Chinese language, the characters are not a phonetic alphabet and embody ideographic elements and therefore they present a greater learning problem than any alphabet.

Furthermore, the characters are monosyllabic, while the spoken language is polysyllabic. This results in a tendency on the part of Chinese— even when teaching the language— to read characters in a staccato cadence far removed from the rhythmic flow of polysyllabic words. Students who start with the characters have greater difficulty in acquiring a normal speaking rhythm.

At what point should characters be introduced? Users of the Yale Chinese language series of textbooks will find that Read Chinese, Book I (300 characters) assumes a knowledge of the vocabulary of the first half of Speak Mandarin. The student meets no new characters whose meaning and pronunciation are not already familiar. His task is simply to recognize and to write each character. Read Chinese, in order to avoid banality in reading content, uses an admixture of romanization along with characters, the need for which soon disappears. The advantage of this approach lies in the fact that, at the outset, the student concentrates on the mastery of patterns of speech rather than dividing his attention with the complexities of the ideograph. Whether to start characters at Lesson 11 or earlier is not a major issue; the essential principle is an audiolingual approach— speak first; then read and write what you have learned to say.

H. C. F.

ACKNOWLEDGMENTS

In revising a body of materials used over a period of two decades and to which many teachers and students have contributed constructive suggestions, it is a well nigh impossible task to give credit where credit is due.

The present co-authors were greatly helped in making plans for the revision and bringing them to fruition by Gerard P. Kok, Associate Director of the Institute of Far Eastern Languages of Yale University, and by Fang-yu Wang and James J. Wrenn of the Institute Faculty.

Much of the supplementary materials on which the Student's Workbook is based was originally prepared by Linda T. Hsia and Yenchan Wang. The final form of the exercises in both Workbook and Teacher's Manual is the work of Helen T. Lin, Joseph C. Kuo, and Henry T. K. Kuo. Mr. Henry Kuo was further of great help in the final proofreading.

Without the very practical assistance done by the secretarial staff of the Institute, notably Sophie M. O'Neill, Antoinette Ferretti, Harriet Tyska, Doris M. Bovee, and Ida C. Tyrrell, the completion of this work would have been impossible.

To all of the above, and to many more unnamed, go the hearty thanks of the authors.

M. Gardner Tewksbury
Henry C. Fenn

New Haven, Connecticut
September 1966

CONTENTS

Foreword v

Acknowledgments vii

Guide to Pronunciation of Chinese Sounds xi
    The Four Tones xiii
    Checklist of Syllables xv

Abbreviations xix

Lesson 1. Functive and Stative Sentences 1
    Sales Clerk and Customer
    Two Students

Lesson 2. The Indirect Object— Auxiliary Verbs 9
    A Chinese Student and an American Student

Lesson 3. Specifiers— Numbers— Measures 16
    Speaking English

Lesson 4. Equative Sentences 25
    'May I Ask Your Name?'
    Buying a Painting

Lesson 5. Money and Price 39
    Shopping

Lesson 6. Changed Status 52
    What Can You Do?

Lesson 7. Modification 60
    Old Friends and Old Clothes

Lesson 8. Location and Existence 70
    In the Bookstore

Lesson 9. Coverbs of Interest— Indefinites and Inclusives 78
    Going Out to Eat
    Writing Letters

Lesson 10. Movement and Direction 88
    Planning a Trip to the City

Lesson 11. Completed Action— Time When 96
    Report on the Trip to the City

Lesson 12. Time Expressions before and after the Verb 105
    The Calendar
    A Friend's Trip Abroad

Lesson 13. Relative Time— Clock Time 118
    Work Time, Play Time

Lesson 14. Expression of Manner 130
    A Good Story

Lesson 15. Compound Verbs 140
    Planning a New House

Lesson 16. The Bǎ Construction   149
    Starting on a Trip

Lesson 17. Resultative Compound Verbs   159
    About the Chinese Language

Lesson 18. Similarity and Comparison   170
    Having a Table Made
    China and America Compared

Lesson 19. Separation and Distance   183
    Three Routes to China
    A North China Trip

Lesson 20. Coverbs of Agent   194
    The Lost Invitation

Index   203

GUIDE TO PRONUNCIATION OF CHINESE SOUNDS

The Chinese ideographs have standard meanings and (to a large extent) standard usage throughout the Chinese world, but the spoken language shows a multiplicity of dialects, with differences in pronunciation so extreme as to make them 'foreign' languages quite as distinct from each other as the romance languages of Europe. The dialects of China's southern and southeastern coastal regions are not intelligible to the remaining three-fourths of the country. The majority of Chinese, however, speak some variety of what is commonly known as Mandarin Chinese. Gwóyŭ, the National Language, is essentially that variety of Mandarin spoken in the capital, Peking.

Most of the languages of Western Europe are written with the Roman alphabet. The Chinese through the long course of their history have used ideographic rather than phonetic symbols. If the occidental wishes to set down Chinese as he hears it, he must use a phonetic script which will enable him to read back with some degree of accuracy what he sets down. Many systems of romanization have been applied to the Chinese language during the past four centuries. Each has betrayed its limitations as a medium for communicating Chinese sounds. The latest comer among these systems is the Yale romanization, evolved to meet the need for speedy teaching of spoken Chinese to our armed forces during World War II. This system is also imperfect, but it has eliminated a number of the weaknesses of previous systems and has proved effective in speeding up the teaching of Chinese pronunciation.

Chinese Sounds with English Counterparts

Many sounds in Mandarin Chinese are for practical purposes identical with their English counterparts. But in English some sounds, especially the vowels, are represented by more than one spelling. We must therefore determine which of the spellings of a given sound is to be used to record the sounds of Chinese.

The following vowels and vowel combinations present little or no problem:

a	as in father
i	as in machine
e	as in stolen; but after y as in yet
o	as in worn
u	as in rumor
ai	as in aisle
ei	as in eight
ou	as in boulder
au	as in sauerkraut

The following initial consonants have the same value in Chinese as in English:

m-, n-, l-, f-, s-, w-, y-

Final Consonants

Mandarin Chinese uses only -n and -ng as final consonants. The value of the preceding vowel is modified by these finals as follows:

-an has a value between the ohn in John and the an in man

-in and -ing are like English sin and sing

In Peking the final n commonly becomes r.

xi

yan is pronounced between yen and yan

yar is pronounced between the yer in lawyer and the yar in yarrow

Paired Initial Consonants

The initial sounds represented by p-, t-, k- are aspirated (i.e. followed by a puff of breath), as in English pin, tin, kin, but with a stronger puff of breath. The initial sounds represented by b-, d-, g- are unaspirated, do not have this puff of breath, and are not voiced (i.e. the vocal cords do not vibrate as in the production of English b, d, g). The closest English equivalent of Chinese unaspirated b, d, g may be found in words where English p, t, k are preceded by s-, as in spate, state, skate.

Aspirated	Unaspirated	Preceded by s
pate	bate	spate
tate	date	state
kate	gate	skate

The Sounds ts- and dz-

Another unvoiced aspirate and unaspirate pair is represented by ts and dz which occur in English but not initially. Look for them between words, as in:

Aspirated		Unaspirated	
it's high	(tsai)	its eye	(dzai)
it's home	(tsou)	its own	(dzou)
it's hay	(tsei)	its aim	(dzei)

Sibilants

In English we have the sounds s- and sh- as in sin and shin. Chinese has both of these as well as a third sibilant sound represented by sy-. It is pronounced with the flat part of the tongue pressed against the palate. It appears in combination as indicated in the table below:

s-	sy-	sh-
sa	sya	sha
se	sye	she
—	syi	—
su	—	shu
sou	syou	shou
su	syou	shu
sai	—	shai
sei	—	shei
—	syu	—
—	sywe	—

This sound is an s followed by a y as between words in English:

less yet   bless ye
less yarn   less yolk

Retroflex Sounds: ch-, j-, sh-, r-

The sound represented by ch- is aspirated as -ch h- in much hope, and is pronounced with the tongue curled back in the mouth, behind the ridge at the base of the teeth. J- is also retroflex but is unaspirated (and unvoiced). Sh- is pronounced as in English shut, but with the tongue curled far back. R is as in English true but with the tongue curled far back.

When ch- and j- occur before i or y they are pronounced with the flat part of the tongue pressed against the palate.

ji	jyu	jya	jye	jyou	jyau
chi	chu	chya	chye	chyou	chyau

'Zero' Final Sounds

There are two final sounds in Chinese for which it is difficult to find an equivalent in English.

The sound represented by -z may occur after s-, ts-, or dz-, giving the syllables sz, tsz, and dz. To produce the final sound, place the fore part of your tongue close to the roof of your mouth, tense your muscles and draw out the sound.

The sound represented by -r may occur after j-, ch-, and sh-, giving the syllables jr, chr, and shr, or r alone. The sound is a very retroflex r- sound, with the tongue farther back in the mouth than for the production of English r.

The Umlaut yu- (-yw-)

This sound does not exist in English but is common in both German and French. In German it is written ü or ue. In Chinese we spell it yu when it stands alone and yw- when followed by a vowel. Purse your lips as if you were going to say oo (as in loot). With the lips in that position, try to say ee (as in beet) instead. The result— if you obey orders strictly— is yu. (The extreme pursed-lip position will not be necessary after you have learned to make the sound.)

Consonant Clusters

Certain consonant clusters are formed of the initial sounds described above, plus w, y, as in:

chwán	boat	jyāu	to teach
dzwèi	most	sywé	to learn
lyòu	six	chywán	altogether
syǎng	to think		

THE FOUR TONES

In learning to speak Chinese the initial problems seem more difficult than they really are. This is particularly true of pronunciation. As you have seen, the Chinese have very few sounds which cannot be found in the English language. One of the chief differences between the two languages is the characteristic tone, or movement of pitch, associated with each syllable of Chinese. For instance, in English, the word 'fan' means the same thing whether spoken with a rising inflection as in the question 'Do you have a fan?' or with a falling inflection in the statement 'Let me use your fan.' In Chinese, fan pronounced with a rising inflection means 'to be bored, fed up'; with a falling inflection it means 'food' or 'cooked rice.' A Chinese word or syllable that conveys a certain meaning when pronounced with a certain tone will yield either a different meaning or no meaning at all if pronounced with a different tone.

In the Peking dialect there are four tones. These tones vary relative to the range of the speaker's voice. They maintain their distinctive characteristics

whether enunciated by a soprano voice or a bass voice. In combinations of syllables, the tones may vary slightly but are related to the tone which each syllable
has in isolation. The four tones are as follows:

No.	Description	Symbol	Example
1	high and level	ˉ	gāu
2	high and rising	´	máng
3	(a) by itself or at the end of a phrase, low and rising	ˇ	hǎu
	(b) before another syllable with third tone— third tone is modified to second tone pronunciation (pronounced hén hǎu, but written hěn hǎu)		hěn hǎu
	(c) before syllables other than third tone— third tone is pronounced low		nǐ gāu nǐ máng nǐ lèi
4	falling from high to low		lèi

These may be placed on a diagram to indicate the relative position and pattern of the tones with relation to the middle range of the speaker's voice.

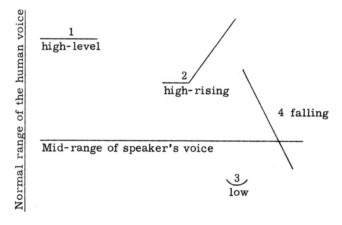

For illustration of the meaning differences which accompany change of tone,
let us take the syllable ma, which may be pronounced in all four of the tones and
with the following differences in meaning:

			Meaning
	mā	pronounced in the high level first tone	mama
	má	pronounced high and with a rising inflection (put a little jerk in that rise)	hemp
	mǎ	at the bottom of your range; may rise slightly	horse
	mà	snapped out, as in giving orders; with a short fall (Go!)	to curse

In the written language, meaning distinctions are clear because the written characters are different. In the spoken language you have only the correct tone and the setting of the word in the sentence to guide your comprehension.

How important these tonal differences are is evident from the two common words: mǎi meaning 'buy' and mài meaning 'sell.'

Vowel Modifications

When y appears initially or between another consonant and the diphthong ou, the value of you changes from the sound of the English word you in the high and high rising tones to the sound of yeo in yeoman in the low and falling tones, thus:

yōu, yóu, yǒu, yòu

CHECKLIST OF SYLLABLES

The Chinese syllable is made up of three elements:

1. An initial or beginning sound
2. A final or ending sound
3. A tone or tonal inflection

Finals

A final may be vowel, consonant, or combination of vowel-plus-vowel or vowel-plus-consonant. Finals may also constitute complete syllables. The following is a list of finals met in the standard Mandarin Chinese of the capital.

Symbol	Description	Example	Meaning
a	as in father, or ma, with mouth wide open	mǎ	horse
an	between ohn in John and an in man, but closer to the former	màn	be slow
ang	as a in father plus ng in song	máng	be busy
ai	as in aisle	mài	sell
au	as ow in how	māu	cat
ar	as ar in car	wár	to play
e	as e in stolen; after y, as e in yet	dé yě	obtain also
o	as o in worn (occurs only after w or before u)	wǒ	I
en	as un in under	kěn	be willing to
eng	as ung in lung	lěng	be cold
ei	as in eight	lèi	be tired
ou	as in low	lóu	building
er	as er in her	èr	two
i	as in machine	pí	skin
in	as in spin	pīn	spell out
ing	as in sing	píng	be level
u	as u in rumor	kū	cry

Symbol	Description	Example	Meaning
ung	as <u>oo</u> in <u>book</u> followed by <u>ng</u>	lúng	dragon
yu	pronounced with tongue in position of <u>i</u> (as in <u>machine</u>) but with lips rounded; as French <u>u</u> or German <u>ü</u>	nyŭ	female
yun	sound described for <u>yu</u> plus <u>n</u>	yùn	to ship (goods)
z	pronounced with the forepart of the tongue close to the roof of the mouth and the muscles of the mouth tense	tsẑ	occasion
r	pronounced as a very retro-flex <u>r</u>-sound, with the tongue farther back in the mouth than for an English <u>r</u>	shŕ	ten

Initials

An initial may be a single consonant or a consonant cluster.

p	as in <u>pun</u>, but with a stronger aspiration (puff of breath) after it	pén	basin
b	as <u>p</u> in <u>spun</u>, without any puff of breath after it	bĕn	volume
t	as in <u>tongue</u>, but with a stronger aspiration	téng	ache
d	as <u>t</u> in <u>stung</u>, without any aspiration	dēng	lamp
k	as in <u>cool</u>, but with a stronger aspiration	kū	to cry
g	as <u>c</u> in <u>scoop</u>, without any aspiration	gù	to hire
m	as in <u>month</u>	mén	door
n	as in <u>none</u>	néng	be able to
f	as in <u>fun</u>	fēn	to divide
l	as in <u>lung</u>	lĕng	be cold
h	a strong <u>h</u> sound as in <u>hot</u> when said emphatically; as German <u>ch</u> in <u>ach</u>	hú	lake
y	as in <u>yet</u>	yĕ	also
w	as in <u>weigh</u>	wèi	to feed
ch	as in <u>chew</u> but with a strong aspiration		
	(1) tip of tongue held in the position it occupies in pronouncing <u>r</u> in <u>true</u>	chū	emerge
	(2) initial pronounced with tip of tongue placed as	chŕ	to eat

Symbol	Description	Example	Meaning
	described in (1) and held there until tone has been completed		
	(3) when followed by i, y, yu, or yw, tip of tongue is held against back of lower teeth	chī chyán chyù chywán	seven money to go altogether
j	as in ch in chew (no aspiration)		
	(1) tongue position same as in (1) under ch	jù	to dwell
	(2) tongue position as in (2) under ch	jř	paper
	(3) tongue position as in (3) under ch	jī jyàn jyù jywé ª	chicken cheap sentence consider
sh	as in shoe		
	(1) tongue position same as in (1) under ch	shū	book
	(2) tongue position as in (2) under ch	shŕ	ten
r	(1) tongue position same as in (1) under ch	rén	man
	(2) tongue position as in (2) under ch	ȓ	sun
ts	(1) like ts-h in it's high, i.e. ts with a strong aspiration	tsài	vegetable
	(2) pronounced with tip of tongue held in position of an s until tone has been completed	tsż	occasion
dz	(1) like dz in cod's eye	dzài	again
	(2) tongue position as in (2) under ts	dż	character
s	(1) as in sight	sài	to compete
	(2) tongue position as in (2) under ts		
	(3) when followed by y, yu, or yw, tip of tongue is held against back of lower teeth	syī	west

ABBREVIATIONS

The following abbreviations are used in referring to word classifications and elements of sentence structure. References are to places in lesson materials where each is defined or illustrated:

A	adverb	1-N8
AV	auxiliary verb	2-N6
BF	bound form	4-N8
CV	coverb	8-N2
DO	direct object	1-V
EV	equative verb	4-C, N2
EX	expression	2-A
FV	functive verb	1-N6
IO	indirect object	2-N1
L	localizer	8-N1c
M	measure	3-N2
MA	movable adverb	3-N6
N	noun	1-N3
NU	number	3-N1
O	object	1
P	particle	1-N9
PN	pronoun	1-N4
PW	place word	8-N1
QW	question word	1-C3
RE	resultative ending	17-N2
RV	resultative (compound) verb	17-A, N2
RVE	resultative verb ending	17-N1
S	subject	1
SP	specifier	3-N7
SV	stative verb	1-N7
T	(prestated) topic	4-D
TW	time word (or expression)	12-N1
V	verb	1-N5
VO	verb-object	6-N2

References: The first figure indicates the Lesson. After the hyphen, the capital letters A, B, C, D indicate divisions of the section on Sentence Patterns. Capital N refers to Notes, followed by the number of the specific note.

SPEAK MANDARIN!

Let the title of this textbook be the theme-song for the course. Use Chinese in the classroom the very first day.

Tīng!	Listen!
Shwō!	Speak! Say (it)!
Dwèi!	Correct!
Búdwèi!	Wrong!
Dwèi budwèi?	Is it correct?

FUNCTIVE AND STATIVE SENTENCES

TWO DIALOGUES

1. Sales Clerk and Customer

S: Nín hǎu a?
C: Hǎu. Nǐ máng ma?

S: Bùmáng. Nín mǎi shémma?
C: Wǒ mǎi bǐ. Nǐmen mài bǐ ma?

5 S: Wǒmen búmài bǐ.
C: Nǐmen búmài bǐ ma?

S: Búmài.
C: Nǐmen mài shémma?

S: Wǒmen mài shū, mài bàu.
10 Nín kàn bàu búkàn?
C: Kàn. Bàu hǎu ma?

S: Bàu hěn hǎu.
C: Gwèi búgwèi?

S: Bàu búgwèi. Nín kàn shū ma?
15 C: Wǒ kàn. Nǐmen mài shū ma?

S: Mài.
C: Shū gwèi ma?

S: Bùhěn gwèi.
C: Shū hǎu ma?

20 S: Hěn hǎu.
C: Wǒ bùmǎi shū, bùmǎi bàu.
Wǒ mǎi bǐ. Shéi mài bǐ?

S: Tāmen mài bǐ.
C: Bǐ gwèi búgwèi?

25 S: Bùhěn gwèi.

2. Two Students

A: Nǐ hǎu a?
B: Hǎu. Nǐ hǎu a?

A: Hěn hǎu. Máng bùmáng?
B: Bùmáng.

5 A: Nǐ mǎi shémma?
B: Wǒ mǎi bàu.

A: Nǐ kàn bàu ma?
B: Kàn. Nǐ búkàn bàu ma?

A: Wǒ búkàn. Bàu bùhǎu.
10 B: Nǐ kàn shémma?

A: Wǒ kàn shū.
B: Shū hǎu ma?

A: Shū hěn hǎu.
B: Gwèi búgwèi?

15 A: Búgwèi.
B: Shéi mài shū?

A: Tāmen mài shū.
B: Tāmen mài bàu ma?

A: Tāmen búmài bàu.
20 B: Tāmen mài bǐ búmài?

A: Tāmen mài bǐ.
B: Bǐ hǎu ma?

A: Hěn hǎu.
B: Gwèi búgwèi?

25 A: Bùhěn gwèi.

VOCABULARY

Nouns (N)

wǒ	I, me
nǐ	you (singular)
nín	(singular form used in polite speech)
tā	he, him; she, her
wǒmen	we, us
nǐmen	you (plural)
tāmen	they, them

shū		book
bàu		newspaper
bǐ		pen, pencil, writing instrument
shéi?		who? whom?
shémma?		what?

Verbs (V)

kàn	FV:	look, look at; read
mǎi	FV:	buy
mài	FV:	sell
gāu	SV:	be tall, high
máng	SV:	be busy
hǎu	SV:	be good, well
gwèi	SV:	be expensive
lèi	SV:	be tired
ǎi	SV:	be short, low

Adverbs (A)

| bù-, bú-, bu- | | not |
| hěn | | very, quite, very much |

Participles (P)

| ma? | | (interrogative sentence particle used to form simple questions; see Sentence Pattern C) |
| a | | (semi-interrogative particle used in greetings) |

Expressions

(Note: These are to be memorized rather than analyzed. They will frequently exceed the vocabulary bounds.)

Nín hǎu a?	How do you do? How are you?
Dzǎu!	Good morning! (lit. 'It is early.')
Dzàijyàn!	Goodbye! (lit. 'See you again.')
Chǐng	Please

SENTENCE PATTERNS

A. Simple Functive Sentence (S FV O)

Wǒ mǎi bàu.	I am buying a newspaper.
Tāmen kàn shū.	They are reading books.
Wǒmen mài bǐ.	We sell pens.
Tā búkàn shū.	He doesn't read books.
Tāmen búmài bǐ.	They don't sell pens.

The functive sentence consists of a subject (S), a functive verb (FV), and an object (O), in the pattern:

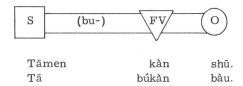

| Tāmen | kàn | shū. |
| Tā | búkàn | bàu. |

B. Simple Stative Sentence (S SV)

Tā hěn lèi.	He is very tired.
Wǒ bugāu.	I am not tall.
Shū hěn gwèi.	Books are very expensive.
Bǐ búgwèi.	Pens are not expensive.
Bàu buhěn hǎu.	The newspaper isn't very good.
Shéi máng.	Who is busy?

The stative sentence consists of a subject (S) and a stative verb (SV):

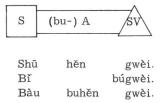

Shū	hěn	gwèi.
Bǐ		búgwèi.
Bàu	buhěn	gwèi.

C. Three Types of Questions

1. Simple Questions with the Interrogative Particle ma

Tā kàn bàu ma?	Does he read the newspaper?
Nǐmen búmài bǐ ma?	Don't you sell pens?
Nín máng ma?	Are you busy?
Shū búgwèi ma?	Isn't the book expensive?

Simple questions are formed by adding the interrogative particle ma to statements, without change in word order:

Functive
Sentence

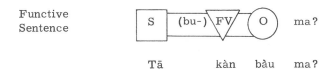

| Tā | kàn | bàu | ma? |

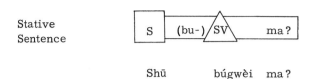

Stative
Sentence

          Shū   búgwèi ma?

2. Choice-Type Questions

Tā mǎi shū bumai?   Is he buying books (or isn't he)?

Tā kàn bàu bukan?   Does he read newspapers (or doesn't he)?

Shū gwèi bugwei?   Are books expensive (or aren't they)?

Nín máng bumang?   Are you busy (or aren't you)?

Choice-type questions are formed by adding to a positive statement the negative form of the verb. A positive-negative choice is thus presented. No interrogative particle is used.

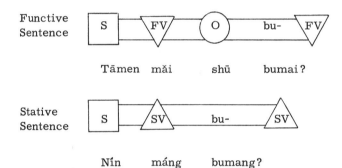

Functive
Sentence

          Tāmen mǎi   shū   bumai?

Stative
Sentence

          Nín   máng   bumang?

3. Question-Word Questions

Shéi mài bǐ?   Who sells pens?

Shémma búgwèi?   What is not expensive?

Nín kàn shéi?   Who are you looking at?

Nǐ mǎi shémma?   What are you buying?

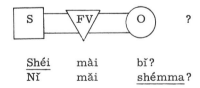

          Shéi   mài   bǐ?
          Nǐ   mǎi   shémma?

The question words shéi and shémma may stand either before or after the
verb. Shémma hǎu? 'What is good?' Nǐ mǎi shémma? 'What are you buying?'

NOTES

1. Tone on the Negative bu-

    The negative adverb bu- is normally pronounced with the falling tone, except when it is immediately followed by another falling tone, in which case it is replaced by the rising tone:

bùgāu		búlèi
bùmáng	but	búgwèi
bùhǎu		
bùǎi		

    In rapid speech the tone of unstressed bu- is seldom identifiable. Hence no tone is marked on bu- unless the word is stressed.

2. Successive Low Tones

    When a low tone is followed immediately by another low tone, the first one is replaced by the rising tone. Thus Nǐ hǎu is pronounced Ní hǎu; similarly, Wǒ mǎi bǐ is pronounced Wó mái bǐ. Stress or pause will modify this general rule and the original tones will be retained.

3. Nouns (N)

    Chinese nouns function essentially as do their counterparts in English, i.e., as subject and object. They are not specific with respect to number, so that for example shū may stand for 'a book' or 'books,' bǐ may refer to 'a pen' or 'pens.'

4. Pronouns (PN)

    Pronouns are a type of noun and are used as substitutes for nouns. The ending -men is added to singular pronouns (and, occasionally, to a few personal nouns) as a pluralizer: e.g., Tā 'he,' tāmen 'they,' wǒ 'I,' wǒmen 'we.'

5. Verbs (V)

    Chinese verbs, unlike English verbs, are unspecific with respect to person, number, or tense. A Chinese verb may correspond to a variety of English verb forms:

Wǒ kàn bàu.	I (customarily) read newspapers.
	I am (now) reading the newspaper.
	I am going to read the newspaper.
	(etc.)

    The adverb bu- is affixed to the verb to negate it.

Wǒ bukàn bàu.	I don't (customarily) read the newspaper.
	I am not (now) reading the newspaper.
	I'm not going to read the newspaper.
	(etc.)

    The pronoun subject is often omitted if it is easily understandable from the context.

a. Functive Verbs (FV)

Functive verbs may be used in the pattern S V, as: wǒ kàn 'I'm reading,' or in the pattern S V O, as: wǒ kàn bàu 'I'm reading the newspaper.'

b. Stative Verbs (SV)

Stative verbs describe a state of being, and often correspond to English 'be' plus an adjective, as: Hǎu '(It) is good,' Gwèi '(It) is expensive.'

Stative verbs can be modified by a word meaning 'very.'

An unmodified stative verb in a positive statement may imply comparison, as: Tā gāu 'He (as compared with someone else) is tall.' With the addition of an adverb such as hěn (a weak 'very'), however, such a sentence does not have a comparative sense, but is an absolute statement.

6. Adverbs (A)

Adverbs modify verbs and other adverbs and always precede them. Negatives are a type of adverb.

7. Particles (P)

Particles following a word or statement modify the meaning, e.g., ma changes a statement to a question, a changes a statement to a polite command, suggestion, or presumption.

8. Answers to Questions

Questions calling for 'yes' or 'no' answers are answered by repeating the verb of the question in its positive or negative form. Inclusion of elements other than the verb is optional. (Chinese has no exact counterparts of 'yes' and 'no.') In question-word questions, the minimal reply is the word which answers the question.

Questions	Answers
Tā kàn shū ma?	Tā kàn shu.
	Kàn shū.
	Tā kàn.
	Kàn.
Nín máng bumang?	Wǒ bùhěn máng.
	Bùhěn máng.
	Hěn máng.
	Bùmáng.
	Máng.
Shéi mǎi bàu?	Tā mǎi bàu.
	Tā mǎi.
	Tā.
Nǐ mài shémma?	Wǒ mài bǐ.
	Mài bǐ.
	Bǐ.

9. Compound Sentences

Compound sentences are made up of a series of closely related statements or questions:

Tā gāu, wǒ bùgāu.	He is tall, (but) I am not.
Tā mǎi shū, wǒ mǎi bàu.	He is buying a book, I am buying a newspaper.
Tā bùmǎi bàu, wǒ mǎi bàu.	He isn't buying a paper, (but) I am.
Shéi kàn shū, shéi kàn bàu?	Who reads books, (and) who reads the newspaper?
Shéi máng, shéi bùmáng?	Who is busy (and) who isn't?

A compound sentence may consist of a subject with more than one predicate:

Tāmen mài shū, mài bàu.	They sell books (and) sell newspapers.
Tāmen mài shū, búmài bàu.	They sell books (but) not newspapers.
but: Tāmen búmài bàu, tāmen mài shū, mài bǐ.	They don't sell papers, they sell books and pens.

The juxtaposition itself corresponds to the English 'but' or 'and.'

10. Omission of Tone Marks

Every Chinese syllable has tone. However, in normal speech, the tone of an unstressed syllable may be lost. Tone marks can be a guide to rhythm as well as to meaning. Note that:

1. The tone of a particle is not sounded in context. The tone it has when pronounced in isolation can be ascertained only by consulting a character dictionary or by hearing it pronounced in isolation.

2. The tone of the negative adverb bu- (normally bù-) appears only when the word is stressed (Tā bùgāu 'He is not tall'), and when it is replaced by bú- before a falling tone (Shū búgwèi).

3. Normal speech is characterized by a sentence rhythm of stressed and unstressed syllables in which, on the average, fewer than half the syllables are stressed. As a consequence, a considerable proportion of the tones are not sounded. To retain all tone marks in a written notation of spoken sentences would be misleading.

4. In some cases the normal stress pattern for a word is modified by its position to such an extent that its tone is completely lost or is barely audible. In the question Nǐ yàu buyau? the major stress is on the first yàu, and the second yau has a secondary stress or none at all. To say Nǐ yàu buyau? is the equivalent of saying in English, 'Now do you or don't you want it?' The milder question 'Do you want it?' is expressed either by Nǐ yàu ma? or by Nǐ yàu buyau? As a visual aid to correct pronunciation, the tone mark has been dropped in this book from the negative verb in a positive-negative choice-type question.

TRANSLATION OF THE INTRODUCTORY DIALOGUES

Note: These translations avoid as far as possible mere word-for-word rendering; they try to give English counterparts for Chinese speech — what would be said in a similar situation. They are placed at the end of each lesson to encourage the student to grasp Chinese sentences as entire units rather than as individual words.

1. Sales Clerk and Customer

S: How are you, (sir)?
C: Fine. Are you busy?

S: No. What are you buying, (sir)?
5 C: I'm buying a pen. Do you sell pens?

S: No, we don't sell pens.
C: You don't sell pens?

S: No, we don't.
10 C: What do you sell?

S: We sell books and newspapers. Do you read newspapers (sir)?
C: Yes, I do. Is it a good
15   paper?

S: It's a very good paper.
C: Is it expensive?

S: No, it isn't. Do you read books (sir)?
20 C: Yes, do you sell books?

S: We do.
C: Are they expensive?

S: Not very expensive.
C: Are they good?

25 S: Excellent.
C: I'm not buying books or newspapers. I'm buying a pen. Who sells pens?

S: They sell pens.
30 C: Are pens expensive?

S: Not so expensive.

2. Two Students

A: How are you?
B: Fine. How are you?

A: Fine. Are you busy?
B: No.

5 A: What are you buying?
B: I'm buying a newspaper.

A: Do you read the paper?
B: Yes, I do. Don't you?

A: No, I don't. Newspapers are
10   no good.
B: What do you read?

A: I read books.
B: Are they good?

A: Books are fine.
15 B: Are they expensive?

A: No.
B: Who sells books?

A: They sell books.
B: Do they sell newspapers?

20 A: No, they don't.
B: Do they sell pens?

A: They do.
B: Are the pens (any) good?

A: Very good.
25 B: Are they expensive?

A: Not very.

Lesson 2

THE INDIRECT OBJECT—AUXILIARY VERBS

DIALOGUE

Conversation between a Chinese Student and an American Student

(Chinese student's name is Hán,
American student's name is Méi.)

	Méi:	Tāmen gěi nǐ shémma?
	Hán:	Tāmen gěi wǒ chyán.
	Méi:	Nǐ méiyou chyán ma?
	Hán:	Yǒu, wǒ yǒu Jūnggwo chyán, méiyou Měigwo chyán.
5	Méi:	Nǐ yǒu byǎu méiyǒu?
	Hán:	Wǒ méiyou byǎu. Byǎu tài gwèi.
	Méi:	Nǐ yǒu jūng ma?
	Hán:	Wǒ méiyou jūng. Jūng tài dà, bùhǎukàn.
	Méi:	Měigwo jūng bùdōu dà. Nǐ kàn, wǒde jūng bútài dà.
10	Hán:	Nǐde jēn hǎukàn. Nǐ yàu mài ma?
	Méi:	Wǒ búmài.
	Hán:	Wǒ hěn syǐhwan nǐde byǎu. Nǐde byǎu hěn gwèi ma?
	Méi:	Wǒde dà byǎu búgwèi, syǎu byǎu hěn gwèi.
	Hán:	Syǎu byǎu dōu gwèi ma?
15	Méi:	Bùdōu gwèi.
	Hán:	Wǒ yàu mǎi bǐ. Shéi mài?
	Méi:	Tāmen mài.
	Hán:	Tāmen yǒu shémma bǐ?
	Méi:	Tāmen yǒu Měigwo bǐ, méiyou Jūnggwo bǐ. Tāmende chyānbǐ, gāngbǐ
20		dōu bútài hǎukàn. Nǐ byé mǎi tāmende bǐ.
	Hán:	Wǒ yàu mǎi ywándzbǐ. Tāmen mài ma?
	Méi:	Mài. Tāmende ywándzbǐ hěn gwèi. Tāmende shū búgwèi. Nǐ syǐhwan
		kàn shū ma?
	Hán:	Wǒ hěn syǐhwan kàn.
25	Méi:	Wǒ gěi nǐ Jūnggwo shū, chǐng nǐ kàn.
	Hán:	Syèsye.

VOCABULARY

Nouns (N)

jūng	clock
byǎu	watch

chyānbǐ	(lead) pencil
gāngbǐ	pen
ywándzbǐ	ball-point pen
fěnbǐ	chalk
chyán	money
wǒde	my, mine
nǐde, nínde	your, yours
tāde	his, her, hers
wǒmende	our, ours
nǐmende	your, yours
tāmende	their, theirs
shéide?	whose?
Jūnggwo	China, Chinese (see Note 2)
Měigwo	America (USA), American (see Note 2)
wàigwo	foreign country, foreign (see Note 2)

Verbs (V)

yǒu	FV:	have, has
méiyǒu, méi(yǒu)		have not, has not (negative for yǒu is méi-, see Note 4)

gěi   FV: give, give to

Wǒ gěi ta chyānbǐ, bugěi ta gāngbǐ.
'I'm giving him a pencil, not a pen.'

Tā gěi ni shémma?
'What is he giving you?'

yàu   FV/AV: want; going to, want to

Nǐ yàu chyānbǐ ma? Búyàu.
'Do you want a pencil?' 'No.'

Nǐ yàu kàn bàu ma? Yàu.
'Do you want to read the paper?' 'Yes.'

syǐhwan   FV/AV: like, prefer, enjoy; like to

Wǒ hěn syǐhwan ta.
'I like him very much.'

Tā syǐhwan kàn bàu.
'He likes to read the paper.'

byé	AV:	don't (imperative)
dà	SV:	be large, big
syǎu	SV:	be small, little

Jūng dà, byǎu syǎu.
'Clocks are large, watches are small.'

Wǒ yàu dà byǎu, búyàu syǎu byǎu.
'I want a large watch, not a small watch.'

hăukàn	SV: be good-looking, handsome

Nĭde jūng jēn hăukàn.
'Your clock is really handsome.'

Adverbs (A)

méi	not (negative for yŏu)
dōu	all, both (see Sentence Pattern 5)
budōu	not all (of)
dōu bu-	none

Shū dōu hěn gwèi.
'All the books are quite expensive.'

Tāmen dōu bumáng.
'None of them are busy.'

Wŏmen budōu măi byău.
'Not all of us are buying watches.'

tài	too, excessively, too much

Měigwo shū tài gwèi.
'American books are too expensive.'

Jūng bútài hăukàn.
'The clock is not too good-looking.'

jēn	really, quite

Měigwo gāngbĭ jēn hău.
'American pens are quite good.'

Wŏ jēn buyàu!
'I really don't want it!'

Expressions

Chĭng gěi wo shū.	Please give me the book.
Syèsye!	Thanks! Thank (you)!
Búkèchi!	You're welcome! (lit. 'Don't be ceremonious!')

SENTENCE PATTERNS

A. Indirect Objects (See Note 5.)

Tā bugěi women bàu.	He isn't giving us (any) newspapers.
Shéi yàu gěi ta chyán?	Who is going to give him money?
Tā gěi women shū.	He (will) give us (some) books.
Nĭ gěi ta byău bugei?	Are you giving him a watch?

An indirect object precedes a direct object (see Note 1).

Pattern:

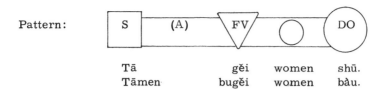

Tā   gěi   women   shū.
Tāmen   bugěi   women   bàu.

B. Auxiliary Verbs (AV)

Tāmen hěn syǐhwan kàn shū.   They enjoy reading very much.

Tā yàu mǎi chyānbǐ.   He is going to buy a pencil.

Wǒmen bútài syǐhwan kàn bàu.   We are not too fond of reading news-
                                    papers.

Shéi syǐhwan kàn shū?   Who likes to read books?

The auxiliary verb (AV) may take for its object either a functive verb (with or without its object), or (in many cases) a simple noun.

Pattern:

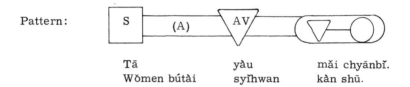

Tā   yàu   mǎi chyānbǐ.
Wǒmen bútài   syǐhwan   kàn shū.

C. Questions and Answers with Auxiliary Verbs

Questions	Answers
Nǐ yàu mǎi chyānbǐ búyàu?	Wǒ yàu mǎi chyānbǐ.
	Yàu mǎi.
	Yàu.
Nín syǐhwan kàn shū ma?	Wǒ syǐhwan kàn shū.
	Syǐhwan kàn.
	Syǐhwan.

Note that in answering questions involving auxiliary verbs, it is the auxiliary verb, not the functive verb, which is repeated as counterpart of the English 'yes' or 'no.'

D. The Totalizing Adverb dōu

Tāmen dōu kàn bàu.   They all read newspapers.

Shū dōu hěn hǎu.   The books are all fine.

Tāmen dōu bumáng.   None of them are busy.

Bǐ, bàu, shū, dōu búgwèi.   Pens, newspapers, and books are all
                                    inexpensive.

Jūnggwo shū budōu gwèi.   Not all Chinese books are expensive.

Nǐmen budōu kàn shū ma?   Don't all of you read (books)?

Tāmen budōu yǒu shū.   Not all of them have books.

Dōu, being an adverb, may be followed only by a verb or another adverb. Its meaning effect, however, is to totalize a plural or collective noun or series of nouns occurring before it. Whether the negative stands before or after dōu makes for marked differences in translation. Compare:

Gāngbǐ dōu hǎukàn.	The pens are all good-looking.
Chyānbǐ budōu hǎukàn.	Not all the pencils are good-looking.
Fěnbǐ dōu buhǎukàn.	None of the chalk is good-looking.
Wǒmen dōu yǒu chyānbǐ.	All of us have pencils.
Wǒmen budōu yǒu ywándzbǐ.	Not all of us have ball-point pens.
Wǒmen dōu méiyou fěnbǐ.	None of us have chalk.

E. More Choice-Type Questions

In Lesson 1 we noted a type of question in which a positive-negative choice (concerned with the action) was offered, and a yes-or-no answer expected. The choice may also be between different subjects or objects (nouns):

1. Choice between Subjects:

Nǐ gāu, tā gāu?	Are you the taller, or is he?
Tāmen yǒu chyán, nǐmen yǒu chyán?	Do they have the money, or do you?

2. Choice between Objects:

Nǐ kàn shū, kàn bàu?	Do you read books or newspapers?
Tā mài jūng, mài byǎu?	Does he sell clocks or watches?

Note that in Chinese the verb must be repeated. Choice-type questions do not use the interrogative particle ma: the question is implied by the offering of alternatives. The sentence Tā kàn shū, kàn bàu, in isolation, is ambiguous, since it may also be interpreted as a double statement; in practice the meaning is usually clear from the context.

NOTES

1. Indirect Objects

In Chinese, an indirect object precedes a direct object, as in the English sentence 'He gave me the book.' Indirect objects occur most frequently with the verb gěi. Pronouns used as objects of gěi usually are unstressed unless emphasized. However, an unstressed low tone still affects a low tone immediately preceding it. Hence:

Gěi nǐ shū	approximates	Géi ni shū
Gěi wǒ bǐ	approximates	Géi wo bǐ

2. Relation of Nouns to Each Other:

   a. Modification: One noun may stand before another noun to modify it. (The same principle appears in English in such expressions as 'country store' and 'city street.')

Jǔnggwo bǐ	Chinese pen
Měigwo bàu	American newspaper
wàigwo bàu	foreign newspaper
shémma shū?	what book?

b. Coordination: Position does not always indicate modification. Certain nouns are commonly coupled in a coordinate rather than a subordinate relation. No connective is required in Chinese:

Nǐ wǒ, dōu syǐhwan kàn Jǔng-gwo shū.	You and I both enjoy reading Chinese books.
Jǔng, byǎu, dōu hěn gwèi.	Both clocks and watches are quite expensive.

3. Stative Verbs as Modifiers of Nouns

Certain stative verbs (usually monosyllabic) may be used like English adjectives to modify a noun. When a stative verb consists of more than one syllable or is modified by an adverb, the particle -de must be affixed to permit its use as a modifier of a noun. E.g.:

Tā yǒu syǎu byǎu.	He has a small watch.
Byé mǎi dà jūng.	Don't buy a large clock.
Tā mài hǎu shū.	He sells good books.

But: Hǎukànde shū budōu gwèi.	Not all beautiful books are expensive.
Wǒ búyau mǎi hěn gwèide byǎu.	I don't want to buy a very expensive watch.

4. Use of méiyǒu

Méiyǒu at the end of an expression is normally stressed on the second syllable, even when followed by a particle; elsewhere the first syllable is stressed. In the question yǒu meiyou?, the main stress is on yǒu, a secondary stress on the final -yǒu.

Wǒ méiyou chyán.	I have no money.
Nǐ yǒu meiyǒu? Méiyǒu.	Have you any? No.

5. Omission of Tone Marks on Pronoun Objects

Personal pronouns standing as the object of a verb are usually unstressed and the tone mark will be omitted unless to indicate special stress.

Tā gěi wo shū.

Nǐ busyǐhwan ta ma?

but: Tā gěi wǒ, bùgěi nǐ.

6. Auxiliary Verbs (AV)

We commonly refer to certain verbs in Chinese as 'auxiliary' verbs chiefly because their counterparts in English are so labeled. Actually most of the verbs so classified are functive verbs—that is, they may take a nominal object—but have the additional function of taking a verbal object. This verbal object may be either a verb or a verb plus its nominal object. Many auxiliary verbs, including <u>yàu</u> and <u>syǐhwan</u> in this lesson, may be modified by the adverb <u>hěn</u>.

> Wǒ syǐhwan Jūnggwo shū.
> Wǒ hěn syǐhwan Jūnggwo shū.
> Wǒ hěn syǐhwan kàn Jūnggwo shū.

TRANSLATION OF THE INTRODUCTORY DIALOGUE

Conversation between a Chinese Student and an American Student

A: What did they give you?
C: They gave me (some) money.

A: Haven't you any money?
C: I have some Chinese money but no American money.

5 A: Do you have a watch?
C: No, I don't have a watch. Watches are too expensive.

A: Do you have a clock?
C: No, I don't. A clock is too big and unsightly.

A: Not all American clocks are large. Look, my clock isn't too large.
10 C: Yours is certainly good-looking. Do you want to sell it?

A: No, I won't sell it.
C: I like your watch very much. Was it very expensive?

A: My large watch wasn't, (but) the small one was.
C: Are all small watches expensive?

15 A: Not all (of them).
C: I'd like to buy a pen. Who sells (them)?

A: They do.
C: What (sort of) pens do they sell?

A: They have American pens (but) no Chinese pens. None of their pens
20   are too good-looking. Don't buy their pens!

C: I want to buy a ball-point pen. Do they sell them?

A: Yes, their ball-point pens are quite expensive. Their books are not expensive. Do you like to read books?
C: I do, very much.

25 A: I'll give you a Chinese book. Please read it.
C: Thank you.

Lesson 3

SPECIFIERS—NUMBERS—MEASURES

DIALOGUE

<u>Speaking English</u> (A: American; C: Chinese)

    A: Nǐ hwèi shwō Yīngwén ma?
    C: Wǒ búhwèi shwō.

    A: Nèige rén yě búhwèi shwō Yīngwén ma?
    C: Hwèi shwō, kěshr tā búywànyi shwō. Tā bútài syǐhwan shwō hwà.

5 A: Jèilyǎngge Jūnggworen cháng shwō Yīngwén ma?
    C: Cháng shwō. Tāmende Yīngwén yě hěn hǎu. Yīnggwo ren dōu shwō
       Yīngwén ma?

    A: Dōu shwō Yīngwén.
    C: Jūnggwo ren shwō Jūnggwo hwà, Yīnggwo ren shwō Yīngwén, Měigwo
10   ren shwō Měigwo hwà. Dwèi budwèi?

    A: Bútài dwèi. Měigwo ren yě dōu shwō Yīngwén.
    C: Nǐ cháng shwō Jūnggwo hwà ma?

    A: Wǒ bùcháng shwō.
    C: Nǐ buywànyi shwō ma?

15 A: Wǒ hěn ywànyi shwō, kěshr wǒ shwō Jūnggwo hwà, Jūnggwo ren shwō
      tāmen bùdǔng.
    C: Nǐ néng kàn Jūnggwo shū ma?

    A: Wǒ néng kàn. Wǒ cháng kàn Jūnggwo shū.
    C: Nǐ yǒu jèisānběn shū ma?

20 A: Wǒ méiyou. Dōu hǎu ma?
    C: Jèisānběn bùdōu hǎu.

    A: Něiběn hǎu?
    C: Jèilyǎngběn hěn hǎu. Wǒ bútài syǐhwan nèiběn.

    A: Hǎu. Wǒ kàn jèilyǎngběn. Syèsye.

VOCABULARY

Specifiers (SP)

jèi-	this
	Nín kàn jèiben shū.
	'Read this book. (Look at this book.)'
nèi-	that
	Wǒ mǎi nèige gāngbǐ.
	'I'm buying that pen.'

16

nĕi-?   which?

                                  Nĭ syĭhwan nĕige byău?
                                  'Which watch do you like?'

Numbers (NU)

yī   one
èr   two
sān   three
sż   four
wŭ   five
lyòu   six
chī   seven
bā   eight
jyŏu   nine
shŕ   ten

líng   zero (see Note 1), plus, over

lyăng-   two, a couple of (see Note 3)

                                  Wŏ yŏu lyăngge chyānbĭ.
                                  'I have two pencils.'

jĭ-?   how many? (for numbers under ten)

                                  Nĭ yŏu jĭge byău?
                                  'How many watches do you have?'

Measures (M)

-gè   (general measure; see Note 2a)

                                  Wŏ măi sānge jūng.
                                  'I'm buying three clocks.'

-bĕn   volume (for books; see Note 2b)

                                  Tā yŏu lyăngbĕn Jūnggwo shū.
                                  'He has two Chinese books.'

Nouns (N)

jwōdz   table (M: -jāng)
yĭdz   chair (M: -bă)
shūjwōdz, shūjwōr   desk

                                  Wŏ măi yìjāng jwōdz, sżbă yĭdz, yìge shū-
                                      jwōr.
                                  'I'll buy a table, four chairs, and one desk.

rén   person, man, people
hwà   language, (spoken) words (M:-jyù, sentence)

                                  Jūnggwo rén dōu shwō Jūnggwo hwà ma?
                                  'Do all Chinese speak Chinese?'

wèntí   question, problem

Nǐ yǒu shémma wèntí?
'What questions do you have?'

Yīnggwo   England, English (see Note 2, Lesson 1)
Yīngwén   English language

Yīnggwo rén, Měigwo rén, dōu shwō Yingwén
ma?
'Do English and Americans all speak English?'

Adverbs (A)

yě   also, too
yě bu-   and . . . not, not . . . either

Tā gāu, nǐ yě gāu.
'He is tall, and so are you.'

Tāmen búkàn bàu, wōmen yě búkàn bàu.
'They don't read newspapers, nor do we.'

kěshr   MA: but, however (see Note 6)
kě   A: but

Wǒmen mài chyānbǐ, kě(shr) búmài ywándz-
bǐ.
'We sell pencils but not ball-points.'

Tā kàn Jūnggwo bàu, wǒ kě búkàn.
'He reads Chinese newspapers, but I don't.'

Tāmen kě búmài Měigwo bàu.
'But they don't sell American newspapers.'

cháng   A: often, frequently
chángchang   MA: commonly, often, customarily

Tā chángchang gěi rén shū.
'He's always giving people books.'

Tā bucháng gěi rén chyán.
'He doesn't often give people money.'

Verbs (V)

shwō   FV: say, say that; speak
shwō hwà   VO: speak

Tā búhwèi shwō Jūnggwo hwà.
'He can't speak Chinese.'

Tā shwō ta búhwèi shwō Jūnggwo hwà.
'He says that he can't speak Chinese.'

Tā shwō: Wǒ búhwèi shwō Jūnggwo hwà.
'He says: I can't speak Chinese.'

Byé shwō hwà!
'Don't speak!'

dǔng	FV:	understand

Wǒ shwō Jūnggwo hwà. Shéi dǔng?
'I'll speak Chinese. Who understands it?'

wèn(wen)	FV:	ask
néng	AV:	can (in the sense of 'be able to')
hwèi	AV:	can (in the sense of 'know how to')
kéyi	AV:	may, can (in the sense of 'be permitted to')
ywànyi	AV:	wish to, want to

Wǒ bunéng kàn Jūnggwo shū.
'I can't read Chinese books.'

Tā búhwèi shwō Jūnggwo hwà.
'He can't speak Chinese.'

Nǐ bukéyi gěi ta nèige.
'You mustn't give him that.'

Wǒ ywànyi gěi ta sānběn.
'I want to give him three volumes.'

dwèi	SV:	be correct, right

Wǒde Jūnggwo hwà hěn buhǎu, dwèi budwèi?
'My Chinese is very poor, isn't that right?'

Dwèi!
'Right!'

Expressions

Dzài shwō.	Say it again.
Nǐ yíge rén shwō.	You alone say it.
Chǐng wèn?	Please, may I ask?
Dwèile.	That's correct.
Dwèibuchǐ!	I beg your pardon!
Hǎu buhǎu?	Wouldn't it be a good idea?

SENTENCE PATTERNS

A. Quantification of Nouns (NU-M N)

yíge rén	one person
lyǎngge byǎu	two watches
sānge jūng	three clocks
wǔběn	five volumes
báge	eight (of something)

For measuring the number or amount of persons or things, a number (NU)
plus a measure (M) appropriate to the noun measured is used. The sequence
of number and measure (NU-M) is referred to as a 'quantifier.' The noun
quantified is frequently omitted when context permits.

B. Specification of Nouns (SP-NU-M N)

jèi lyǎngge rén	these two persons
nèi sānběn	those three volumes
nèige rén	that person
jèiběn	this volume
něige?	which one?
jèige	this one

When a specifier (SP) stands before a number-measure combination (SP-NU-M), it points specifically to a particular item or group of items. These combinations (with or without the noun specified) form nominal elements which may stand in the subject or object position (see Note 5). The pattern is:

$$\boxed{\text{(SP)} \quad \text{NU-M}} \quad \boxed{\text{N}}$$

(jèi)   sānběn   shū
(these) three   books

C. Verbs Which May Take a Sentence-Object

Tā shwō tā mǎi gāngbǐ.	He says that he is buying a pen.
Tā shwō: Wǒ syǐhwan gāngbǐ.	He says: I like pens.
Wǒ shwō gāngbǐ tài gwèi.	I say that pens are too expensive.
Nǐ shwō gāngbǐ gwèi bugwei?	Would you say that pens are expensive?

Certain verbs (such as shwō) may take a sentence as object. The sentence-object of the verb shwō may either be an indirect or a direct quotation. When there is a pause after shwō, what follows is likely to be a direct quotation (as in the sentence Tā shwō: Wǒ bumǎi gāngbǐ. 'He says: I'm not buying a pen.'). There is no Chinese equivalent for the English relative pronoun 'that' before indirect quotations. The pattern is:

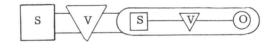

Indirect: Tā   shwō   tā mǎi   gāngbǐ.
          'He says (that) he is buying a pen.'

Direct: Tā   shwō: Wǒ   mǎi   gāngbǐ.
          'He says: I am buying   a pen.'

D. Compound Sentences with yě and kěshr

Wǒ kàn shū, yě kàn bàu.	I read books, and newspapers too.
Tā bumáng, wǒ yě bumáng.	He's not busy, and I'm not either.
Tā hěn hǎu, kěshr tā méiyou chyán.	She's fine, but she has no money.
Tā hwèi mǎi shū, kě(shr) búhwèi mài shū.	He knows how to buy books; but he doesn't know how to sell books.

Compound sentences are formed by combining two or more predicates in a single sentence (see Lesson 1, Note 11). Certain adverbs (such as yĕ and kĕshr) may be used before the predicate of subsequent statements. Kĕshr is a 'movable adverb' (MA), in that it may stand before the subject as well as before the predicate. (See Note 6.)

When the subject of the first clause and the subject of the second clause are identical, kĕshr normally stands before the second subject. This second subject may be dropped:

> Tā hwèi shwō Yīngwén, kĕshr   'He can speak English, but not Chi-
> (ta) búhwèi shwō Jūnggwo hwà.   nese.'

When kĕ is used instead of kĕshr, the second subject is dropped, since a fixed adverb (monosyllable) always stands immediately before the verb it modifies.

> Tā hwèi shwō Yīngwén, kĕ   'He can speak English, but not Chi-
> búhwèi shwō Jūnggwo hwà.   nese.'

NOTES

1. Numbers (NU)

The basic numbers in Chinese are the digits from one through nine. Zero is represented by líng. The basic numbers and líng are used for telephone numbers, simple counting, and mathematical calculations, but they cannot be used alone to measure a quantity of persons or things, in other words, nor for 'quantifying.'

líng-bā	0-8
èr-sż	2-4
sān-líng-wŭ	3-0-5
lyòu-bā-líng-yī	6-8-0-1
jyŏu-líng-sān-chī-líng	9-0-3-7-0
èr-líng-líng-wŭ-líng-líng	2-0-0-5-0-0

2. Measures (M)

A measure is used in Chinese whenever a noun is quantified by a number. It always appears after this number (NU-M). The measure is omitted only when the noun is used generically, to refer to something without regard to quantity: as with sheep, rice, leather, paper, etc., in English:

> Wŏmen mài shū, bumài bàu.   We sell books, not papers.

The English language has many measure words, but they are all limited in use to certain categories of things or to certain types of measurement:

a quart of milk	one piece of candy
a length of string	a couple of slices of bread
a fleet of ships	three suits of clothes
a herd of cattle	a dozen sheets of paper

None of these English measures is 'general' in the sense that it can be applied to practically anything or everything.

a. General Measure -gè: In addition to counterparts of most of the measures
    commonly used in English, Chinese has a general measure (-gè). The M
    -gè literally means 'item,' but it is not readily translated. It is a bound
    form in that it can only be used in combination with another element —
    here a number (NU-M). The measure -ge loses its tone, except in rare
    instances where it is stressed.

b. Specific Measures: While most nouns may be used with -ge, some nouns
    require a specific measure. Shū is one of them, and -běn (volume) is the
    measure:

Wǒ mǎi sānběn shū.	I'm buying three books.
Nín mǎi jǐběn?	How many volumes are you buying?

Specific measures will be noted in the vocabularies when required or preferred. Some nouns may be used either with -ge or with a specific measure.

3. Use of èr and lyǎng-

Èr and lyǎng- are both words for 'two.' Èr is one of the basic digits and its
use is described in Note 1 above. Lyǎng- is a bound form, and is required
for use in the pattern for quantification (NU-M), e.g. lyǎngge rén, lyǎngběn
shū.

4. Unstressed yige

Yige when unstressed corresponds to the indefinite article 'a' or 'an,' in English. (Wǒ yàu mǎi yige chyānbǐ. 'I'm going to buy a pencil.') Unstressed
yige often loses the yi in speaking (an exception to the rule that a measure
always stands after a number). (Tā yǒu ge Yīnggwo byǎu. 'He has an English watch.')

5. Specification (SP-NU-M)

Specifiers (SP) occur in a pattern of specification which is commonly a sequence of specifier, number and measure (SP-NU-M) (as jèi wǔběn 'these
five volumes'). The three elements in combination constitute a nominal expression, and like most nouns may modify other nouns. Specifiers may appear independently, but only in the subject position.

Note the following examples of specification:

Wǒ ywànyi kàn nèilyǎngběn shū.	I'd like to read those two books.
Nèisānge rén dōu hěn gāu.	Those three people are all quite tall.
Jèige hěn hǎu, kěshr nèige buhǎu.	This one is fine, but that one's no good.
Jèi tài dà, nèi tài syǎu.	This is too large, that is too small.
Wǒ yàu jèiyíge, búyàu nèi-lyǎngge.	I want this one, not those two.

Pronouns may also stand before specified and/or numbered nouns to further
modify them.

wǒ jeige gāngbǐ	this pen of mine
tā jeisānge jwōdz	these three tables of his
nín neiwǔběn shū	those five books of yours

6. Movable Adverbs (MA)

Movable adverbs like other adverbs may appear immediately before the verb or another adverb. Unlike other adverbs they may also stand before the subject of the sentence. Kĕshr is one such. Most movable adverbs have more than one syllable:

Wŏ syĭhwan tā, kĕshr tā busyĭhwan wŏ.	I like him, but he doesn't like me.
Wŏ syĭhwan tā. Tā kĕshr busyĭhwan wŏ.	I like him. But he doesn't like me.

7. Change of Tone on Certain Numbers and bù-

Word	Stand-ing Alone	Before High Tone	Before Rising Tone	Before Low Tone	Before Falling Tone
not	bù	bùgāu bùshwō	bùmáng bùnéng	bùhǎu bùdǔng	búgwèi búkàn
one	yī	yìjāng	yìhwéi	yìbĕn	yíwèi
seven	chī	chījāng	chīhwéi	chībĕn	chíwèi chíge
eight	bā	bājāng	bāhwéi	bābĕn	báwèi báge

TRANSLATION OF THE INTRODUCTORY DIALOGUE

Speaking English

    A: Can you speak English?
    C: No, I can't.

    A: Can that man also not speak English? (Can't that man speak English either?)
5 C: He can speak it, but he doesn't wish to. He's not too fond of talking.

    A: Do these two Chinese often speak English?
    C: Yes, they speak it frequently. Their English is very good, too. Do all English people speak English?

    A: Yes, they all speak English.
10 C: The Chinese speak Chinese; the English speak English; and the Americans speak American. Is that right?

    A: No, that's not quite right. Americans all speak English too.
    C: Do you often speak Chinese?

    A: Not often.
15 C: Don't you want to speak it?

    A: I want very much to speak it, but (when) I speak Chinese, the Chinese say they don't understand.
    C: Can you read Chinese books?

    A: Yes, I can. I often read Chinese books.
20 C: Do you have these three books?

A: No, I don't. Are they all good?
C: Not all of the three are good.

A: Which one is the best?
C: These two are excellent. I don't care much for that one.

25   A: Good. I'll read these two. Thank you.

Lesson 4

EQUATIVE SENTENCES

TWO DIALOGUES

1. 'May I Ask Your Name?'

Jāng : Nín gwèisyìng?

Wáng: Wǒ syìng Wáng. Nín gwèisyìng?

Jāng : Wǒ syìng Jāng.

Wáng: Jèiwei syìng shémma?

5 Jāng : Wǒ jeiwei péngyou syìng Lǐ. Lǐ Syansheng, jèi shr Wáng Syansheng.

Wáng: Lǐ Syansheng, nín hǎu a? Nín gwèigwó shr něigwó? Shr Yīnggwo ma?

Lǐ   : Búshr, wǒ shr Fàgwo rén. Kěshr wǒ tàitai shr Yīnggwo rén.

Jāng : Lǐ Syansheng Lǐ Taitai yǒu sānge syǎuhár: lyǎngge nánháidz, yíge
10   nyǔháidz.

Wáng: Chǐng wèn Lǐ Syansheng, nín neisānge háidz dōu jyàu shémma míngdz?

Lǐ   : Nánháidz, yíge jyàu Lǐchá, yíge jyàu Wēilyán.

Wáng: Syáujye jyàu shémma?

15 Lǐ   : Tā jyàu Mǎlì.

Wáng: Jāng Syansheng yǒu jǐge háidz?

Lǐ   : Dwèibuchǐ, Jāng Syansheng méiyou tàitai, kěshr tā yǒu yige nyǔ-
          péngyou, hěn hǎukàn.

Wáng: Shr̀ ma? Nínde nyǔpéngyou syìng shémma?

20 Lǐ   : Jāng Syansheng búgàusung women, kěshr wǒ jr̄dau shr yige sywé-
          sheng.

Jāng : Shéi shwō! Wǒ méiyou nyǔpéngyou. Tā shwō wǒ yǒu, kěshr wǒ jēn
          méiyǒu.

Lǐ   : Jāng Syansheng, wǒ wèn nín: Fàgwo hwà, Yīngwén, Jūnggwo hwà,
25   nín dōu hwèi shwō ma?

Jāng : Budōu hwèi. Wǒ jyòu hwèi shwō Jūnggwo hwà. Yīngwén, Fàgwo hwà,
          wō dōu búhwèi shwō.

Wáng: Hǎu, wǒ hwèi shwō Yīngwén, kě búhwèi shwō Fàgwo hwà. Kěshr
          wǒmen sānge rén dōu hwèi shwō Jūnggwo hwà.

2. Buying a Painting

Wáng: Wǒ yǒu lyǎngge hǎu péngyou: yíge mài jwōdz yǐdz; yíge mài jř, mài
          hwàr.

Lǐ   : Wǒ wèn ni: Jūnggwo hwàr hǎu, Měigwo hwàr hǎu?

Wáng: Hwàr, wǒ bútài dǔng, kěshr wǒ yíge péngyou shwō wàigworén dōu
5   syīhwan Jūnggwo hwàr. Lǐ Syansheng, nín hwèi hwà hwàr búhwèi?

Lǐ   : Wǒ búhwèi hwà hwàr, kěshr wǒ hěn syīhwan kàn hwàr. Jèige rén
         shwō Jūnggwo hwàr hǎu, nèige rén shwō Měigwo hwàr hǎu. Wǒ shwō
         Jūnggwo hwàr, Měigwo hwàr dōu hǎu. Wǒ dōu syīhwan kàn.

Wáng: Wǒ yǒu s̀jāng Jūnggwo hwàr. Chǐng nín kàn něige hǎu?

10 Lǐ   : Jèis̀jāng hwàr nǐ dōu mài ma?

Wáng: Budōu mài.

Lǐ   : Jèilyǎngjāng jēn hǎu. Nǐ mài bumài?

Wáng: Búmài. Wǒ yě hěn syīhwan jèilyǎngjāng. Nèijāng hwàr wǒ mài.
         Nín yàu buyau?

15 Lǐ   : Nèijāng wǒ bútài syīhwan. Wǒ yàu mǎi Měigwo hwàr. Nǐ yǒu meiyou?

Wáng: Měigwo hwàr, wǒ méiyǒu, kěshr wǒde péngyou yǒu. Wǒ wèn tā mài
         bumai.

Lǐ   : Hǎu. Syèsye.

Wáng: Búkèchi. Dzàijyàn.

VOCABULARY

Measures (M)

-jāng   M: sheet (for paper, tables, paintings)

                         Jèijāng jwōdz jēn hǎukàn.
                         'This table is really good-looking.'

-wèi   (polite measure for persons; see Note 4e)

                         Nèiwei yǒu jǐge gāngbǐ?
                         'How many pens does that person have?'

-shŕ   NU/M: a unit of 10 (see Note 1a)

                         èrshrjāng jwōdz
                         'twenty tables'

-bǎi   NU/M: hundred

                         sānbǎiběn shū
                         'three hundred books'

-chyān   NU/M: thousand

                         wǔchyānge chyānbǐ
                         'five thousand pencils'

Nouns (N)

péngyou   friend

Nǐ yǒu jǐge Jūnggwo péngyou?
'How many Chinese friends do you have?'

syìng   surname (see under Verbs)

Nǐ yǒu Jūnggwo syìng meiyǒu?
'Do you have a Chinese surname?'

míngdz   given name; name

Nǐ yǒu Jūnggwo míngdz ma?
'Do you have a Chinese given name?'

syānsheng   gentleman, teacher, husband, Mr., sir
(Lǐ) Syansheng   Mr. (Lǐ)

Nèiwei syānsheng syǐhwan Lǐ Syansheng.
'That gentleman likes Mr. Li.'

Tāde syānsheng méi chyán.
'Her husband doesn't have (any) money.'

Syānsheng, nín mǎi shémma?
'Sir, what are you buying?'

sywésheng   student, pupil

Jūnggwo sywésheng dōu dǔng Yīngwén ma?
'Do all Chinese students understand English?'

tàitai   (married) lady, wife, Mrs.

Tāde tàitai hwèi shwō Yīngwén.
'His wife can speak English.'

syáujye   young lady, girl, daughter
Syaujyě   Miss

Jōu Syaujyě yǒu sɀshrge sywésheng.
'Miss Jōu has forty pupils.'

Nín neilyǎngwei syáujye jēn hǎukàn.
'Your two daughters are really beautiful.'

háidz, syǎuhár,   child, children
  syǎuháidz
                               Nǐmen yǒu jǐge syǎuhár?
                               'How many children do you have?'

Nèige háidz busyǐhwan kàn shū.
'That child doesn't like to read.'

dàren   adult

Dàren dōu syǐhwan syǎuhár ma?
'Do all adults like children?'

nán-   BF: male (of persons)
nyǔ-   BF: female (of persons)
nánde   man, male
nyǔde   woman, female

Nèige sywésheng yǒu lyǎngge nyǔpéngyou.
'That student has two girl friends.'

Wǒmen yǒu sānge syǎuhár: yíge nánde,
  lyǎngge nyǔde.
'We have three children: one boy and two
  girls.'

jǐ   paper (M: -jāng)

Jèige jǐ buhǎu.
'This (sort of) paper is no good.'

Nèijāng jǐ tài syǎu.
'That piece of paper is too small.'

hwàr   picture, painting (M:-jāng)

Wǒmen kéyi mǎi jèijāng Jūnggwo hwàr.
'We might buy this Chinese painting.'

dūngsyi   thing

Jèige dūngsyi tài dà.
'This thing is too large.'

Wàigwo dūngsyi dōu gwèi, dwèi budwei?
'All foreign things are expensive; is that
  right?'

Fàgwo   France
Dégwo   Germany
Yìgwo   Italy

něigwó?   SP-N: which country, nationality?
  gwèigwó
  (see Note 4)   Něigwo byǎu hǎu?
                            'Which country's watches are best?'

-wén   BF: language (as in Jūngwén, Yīngwén, etc.)

dwōshau?   N/NU: how many? how much?

                    N: Nǐ yǒu dwōshau chyán?
                       'How much money do you have?'

                    NU: Nín yǒu dwōshaujāng hwàr?
                        'How many paintings do you have?'

Adverbs (A)

yě . . . yě . . .   both . . . and . . .
yě bù- . . . yě   neither . . . nor . . .
  bù- . . .
                                Tā yě gāu, yě hǎukàn.
                                'He is both tall and handsome.'

                                Wǒ yě bugěi tā, yě bugěi nǐ.
                                'I'm giving it neither to him, nor to you.'

jyòu   only, just

Wǒ jyòu yǒu sānge sywésheng.
'I have only three pupils.'

Wǒde syǎuhár jyòu syǐhwan shwōhwà.
'My children just like to talk.'

Verbs (V)

shr̀   EV: be, am, are, is

Tā shr shéi?
'Who is he?'

Jèi shr nǐde gāngbǐ bushr?
'Is this your pen?'

Tā shr něigwó rén?
'What is his nationality?'

syìng   FV: be (sur)named
gwèisyìng   (used in respectful address; see Note 4)

Nèiwei syānsheng syìng shémma?
'What is that gentleman's name?'

Nín gwèisyìng a?
'May I ask your honorable name?'

jyàu   FV: be called, have as a given name; call, summon

Jèige (dūngsyi) jyàu shémma?
'What is this thing called?'

Nèige háidz jyàu shémma (míngdz)?
'What is that child's name?'

gàusung, gàusu   FV: tell, inform

Tā gàusung wǒ tā péngyou syìng Mǎ.
'He tells me his friend's name is Mǎ.'

Byé gàusu ta!
'Don't tell him!'

chǐng   FV: invite; invite to, ask to; please

Wǒmen yàu chǐng sānge sywésheng.
'We're going to invite three students.'

Chǐng nǐmen búyàu shwō Yīngwén.
'Please don't speak English.'

Chǐng ta hwà yìjāng hwàr.
'Ask him to paint a picture.'

jr̄dau   FV: know, know of, know that

Nǐ jr̄dau jèige rén ma?
'Do you know of this man?'

Tā syìng shémma, nǐ jřdau bùjrdàu? Wǒ bùjrdàu.

'Do you know what his name is?' 'No, I don't.'

hwà   FV: draw, paint (pictures)

Nǐ hwèi hwà hwàr ma?
'Can you paint?'

wár   FV: play, play at or with

Syǎuhár dōu syīhwan wár.
'All children like to play.'

ài   FV/AV: love, like, love to, like to

Tā hěn ài syǎuhár.
'He is very fond of children.'

Tāmen dōu ài kàn shū.
'They all love to read.'

kèchi   SV: be polite, courteous

Nèige sywésheng hěn kèchi.
'That student is very courteous.'

Nín tài kèchi!
'You're being too polite.' 'Don't stand on ceremony.'

Expressions

Dzài shwō yítsż.	Say it once more.
Tswòle.	Wrong.
Nǐ shwōtswòle.	You said it wrong.
Bútswò!	Not bad! Correct!

Common Sayings

Chinese conversation is colored and enlivened by the frequent use of proverbial and concise sayings. Those selected for this textbook may use an occasional unfamiliar term (see Index).

Shwō yī, shr yī;   Say one, it's one; say two, it's two. (Say
   shwō èr, shr èr.   what you mean.)

SENTENCE PATTERNS

A. Counting

1. Numbers 10-99

   a. shŕyī   11   shŕsż   14   shŕjǐ?   how many (between
      shŕèr   12   shŕjyǒu 19   10 and 20)?

The 'teens' follow the pattern: 'ten-one,' 'ten-two,' etc. The stress falls on the digits (as in English, thirteen, nineteen, etc.)

   b. èrshr   20 | wŭshr   50 | jĭshr?   how many tens?
       sānshr 30 | bāshr   80 |

The 'tens' take the form: two-ten, three-ten, etc. In these combinations -shŕ stands for 'a unit of 10,' and is called a numerical measure. The stress is on the digits which stand before shŕ (as in English forty, eighty, etc.).

   c. èrshryī 21 | sɀshrsɀ   44 | jĭshrjĭ?   how many tens and
       èrshrèr 22 | chīshrwŭ 75 | how many units?

Number combinations between any unit of 10 and the next higher are formed by adding the appropriate digit to a 'ten unit': as two-ten-one 21, six-ten-three 63, etc. The stress falls on the digits which precede and follow shŕ (as in English fifty-five, sixty-nine, etc.)

2. <u>Numbers 100–999</u>—introducing two more numerical measures (in addition to shŕ)—bǎi and chyān.

   a. Normal Pattern

	chyān	bǎi	shŕ	(digit)
sānchyan-wúbai-lyòushr-sɀ	3	5	6	4
sɀbai-bàshr-sān		4	8	3

The pattern is composed of a series of number-measure (NU-M) elements ending in a digit.

   b. Zeros

	chyān	bǎi	shŕ	(digit)
yìbai-líng-wǔ		1	0	5
lyǎngchyan-líng-wǔshŕ	2	0	5	0
lyǎngchyan-líng-wǔ	2	0	0	5

Líng 'zero' replaces one or more number-measure elements in the series. No measure is used after líng. In the final digit position, líng is omitted.

   c. Abbreviations

	chyān	bǎi	shŕ	(digit)
èrbai-wǔ(shŕ)		2	5	0
sānchyan-lyòu(bǎi)	3	6	0	0

When a number consisting of two or more number-measure elements ends in a numerical measure, this final numerical measure may be dropped.

B. Quantifying:

shŕjāng hwàr	10 pictures
shŕèrge chyānbĭ	12 pencils
èrshrge rén	20 persons
lyòushrběn shū	60 books
wǔshr-chíge háidz	57 children
chīshr-wǔjāng jř	75 sheets of paper

When quantifying a noun, the number combinations analyzed above are always followed by the measure appropriate to that noun.

C. Equative Sentences with shr̀

Tā shr shéi? Tā shr Chén Syansheng.	Who is he? He is Mr. Chen.
Tā búshr Fàgwo rén ma? Búshr.	Isn't he a Frenchman? No.
Jèi shr shémma? Shr chyānbǐ.	What is this? It's a pencil.
Jèibén shū shr shéide? Shr tāde.	Whose book is this? It's his.
Tā shr̀ bushr nínde sywésheng? Shr̀.	Is she your student? Yes.
Jèi shr̀ tāde bǐ bushr? Búshr.	Is this pen(cil) his? No, it's not.

The verb shr̀ equates two nouns or nominal expressions. It is the core of the equative sentence. The pattern is:

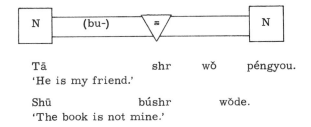

Tā   shr   wǒ   péngyou.
'He is my friend.'

Shū   búshr   wǒde.
'The book is not mine.'

D. Prestatement of Topic

1. a. Jèige byǎu, wǒ bùnéng gěi nǐ.   This watch I can't give you.

   b. Byǎu, wǒ yǒu, jūng wǒ méi-   I have a watch, but not a clock.
      you.

   c. Nín nèilyǎngběn shū, wǒ hěn   Those two books of yours I would very
      ywànyi kàn.   much like to read.

The object of a sentence may be transposed to the 'topic' position at the head of the sentence: (a) for emphasis, or (b) for contrast.

2. a. Jūng, byǎu, chyānbǐ, gāngbǐ,   I sell clocks, watches, pencils and
      wǒ dōu mài.   pens.

   b. Jř, bǐ, wǒmen dōu yǒu.   We each have paper and pen.
                                     or, We have both paper and pen.
                                     or, We each have both paper and pen.

Transposition is required whenever a plural object is totalized with dōu (a). When the subject as well as the transposed object are plural (b), the dōu refers back to either one or both. Context usually indicates which is intended.

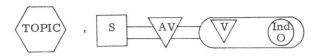

Jèige byǎu,   wǒ   ywànyi   gěi   nǐ
'I'd like to give you this watch.'

NOTES

1. Numbers below 10,000

a.

	NU-NU/M -chyān	NU-NU/M -bǎi	NU-NU/M -shŕ	NU digits
1				yī
2				lyǎng-
10 (b)			shŕ	
12 (b)			shŕ	èr
20			èrshŕ	
63			lyòushr	sān
100		yìbǎi		sż
204 (c)		èrbǎi	líng	wǔ
385		sānbǎi	bāshr	yī
411 (b)		sżbǎi	yīshr	
1,000	yìchyān			lyòu
2,006 (c)	lyǎngchyān	líng	yīshr	chī
2,217 (b)	lyǎngchyān	èrbǎi		
3,090 (c)	sānchyān	líng	jyòushr	
4,300	sżchyān	sān(bǎi) (e)		
9,999	jyǒuchyān	jyǒubǎi	jyǒushr	jyǒu

a) Note that -shŕ, -bǎi and -chyān above function both as numbers and as
   measures. A numerical measure differs from an ordinary measure in that
   it can be followed by another measure. The measure -ge is commonly
   omitted after -chyān, less commonly after -bǎi, but never after -shŕ, e.g.,
   lyǎngchyān rén, sānbǎi sywésheng, but èrshrge jūng.

b) The number yī is usually omitted before shŕ and the 'teens' 11–19 (but
   contrast the Chinese numbers above 100, where yī is usually retained).

c) líng is used in counting and quantifying wherever a column or a sequence
   of columns is skipped. Note that in this use, líng never stands as the
   final element in a number.

d) The measures in the last column (with or without nouns) may be used with
   any numbers appearing in the columns before it.

e) Final numerical measures are frequently dropped.

2. Question Words jǐ-? and dwōshau?

   a. Jǐ-? is an interrogative number, used when the speaker expects an answer
      in which one of the digits or shŕ replaces jǐ-? Jǐ-? always takes a mea-
      sure. Only jǐ- (never dwōshau?) may stand before or after the numerical
      measures (shŕ, bǎi, etc.)

Nǐmen yǒu jǐge háidz? Wǒmen yǒu sānge.	How many children do you have? We have three.
Tāmen chǐng shŕjǐwèi syān-sheng? Shŕwǔwèi.	How many teachers are they inviting? Fifteen.
Nín yàu jǐshrběn Jūnggwo shū? Bāshrběn.	How many Chinese books do you want? Eighty (volumes).
Nǐmen yǒu jǐbǎijāng hwàr? Wǔbǎijāng.	How many hundreds of pictures do you have? Five hundred.

   b. Dwōshau? is an interrogative number when followed by a measure. When
      a measure does follow dwōshau it is usually a specific measure, seldom
      -ge. With dwōshau no expectation is assumed as to the size of the number.
      Dwōshau also functions as a noun, and hence may stand before another
      noun to modify it.

Nǐmen yǒu dwōshau Dégwo sywésheng? Sānshrge.	How many German students do you have? Thirty.
Nín mǎi dwōshaujāng jǐ? Lyòubǎijāng.	How many sheets of paper are you buying? Six hundred sheets.

3. More Verbs Which May Take Sentence-Objects — wèn and gàusung

   The verbs wèn and gàusung are verbs like shwō (see Lesson 3, Pattern C)
   which may take a sentence as object. They differ from shwō in that they may
   also take an indirect object. In this respect they are like gěi, introduced in
   Lesson 2.

Wǒ wèn ta (tā) yǒu gāngbǐ méiyou.	I asked him whether he had a pen or not.
Wǒ wèn ta: Nǐ yǒu gāngbǐ méiyou?	I asked him: Do you have a pen?
Tā gàusung wo (tā) méiyou gāngbǐ.	He told me that he didn't have a pen.
Tā gàusung wo shwō: Wǒ méiyou gāngbǐ.	He told me (saying): I don't have a pen.

   Sentence-object verbs may be distinguished from auxiliary verbs by the fact
   that the object of an auxiliary verb may not contain a subject.

4. Inquiring Name and Nationality

   a. To inquire of a second person directly his surname or nationality, gwèi
      'honorable' is placed before syìng 'surname' or gwó 'country.' Dàmíng
      'great name' may be used in inquiring directly a person's given name.
      The pronoun nín is commonly used in direct inquiry instead of nǐ, especial-
      ly in North China:

Nín gwèisyìng?	What is your surname?
Nín dàmíng shr . . . ?	Your given name is . . . ?
Nín gwèigwó shr něigwó?	What is your nationality?

Titles such as Syānsheng, Tàitai, or Syáujye are often substituted for nín:

Syānsheng gwèisyìng?	Your (the gentleman's) surname is . . . ?
Syáujye gwèigwó shr něigwó?	What is your (the young lady's) nationality?

b. To inquire about another person's name, etc., the verbs syìng and jyàu are used in the functive sentence pattern. The same pattern is used with children and wherever etiquette does not require a more formal form:

Tā (or Nǐ) syìng shémma?	What is his (or your) surname?
Tā (or Nǐ) jyàu shémma míngdz?	What is his (or your) given name?

c. The answers to such inquiries, do not use the courtesy forms gwèisyìng, gwèigwó, and dàmíng.

Wǒ syìng Jāng.	My name is Jāng.
Wǒ jyàu Désyīn, Jāng Désyīn.	I'm called Désyīn, Jāng Désyīn.
Wǒ shr Měigwo rén.	I am an American.

d. Names with titles

Chén Syansheng	Mr. Chén
Chén Jř-ywǎn Syansheng	Mr. Jřywǎn Chén
Chén Jř-ywǎn, Chén Syansheng	Mr. Chén, Jřywǎn Chén

In Chinese, the order for names with titles is: surname, given name, title (the reverse of English). In referring to oneself, the title is omitted.

e. The measure -wèi is more polite than -ge in referring to persons. However, the noun rén by itself (unmodified) cannot take -wèi as measure.

Jèiwei shr Jàu Syansheng.	This is Mr. Jàu.
Tāmen sānwèi dōu shr Fàgwo rén.	All three of them are French.
Yíwèi shr tàitai, yíwèi shr syáujye.	One is a married lady, one is a girl.

f. Note that courtesy expressions do not always fall into regular patterns of sentence structure. They are idioms, not patterns on which to build other sentences.

5. Coordination

It was noted in Lesson 2 that one noun may stand before another noun to modify it. But position alone does not necessarily indicate modification. Successive nouns or nominal elements of kindred meaning may have a coordinate relationship. Note the following:

nǐ wǒ	you and I
nǐde wǒde	yours and mine
jèige nèige	this and that
shū bàu	books and newspapers
jūng byǎu	clocks and watches
jwōdz yǐdz	tables and chairs

The first three examples, however, may be used only in the subject position.

6. <u>Apposition</u>

One noun or other nominal element may stand immediately after another to explain or clarify. The two nouns are said to be in apposition. (Compare English: the chairman, Mr. Smith; Jack Doe, the shoemaker).

wǒmen Měigwo rén	we Americans
nǐmen lyǎngge (rén)	you two
tā neige rén	the person in question

7. Question patterns for equative verbs are in general the same as for functive verbs. There is an additional pattern for positive-negative choice-type which is common with <u>shr̀</u>.

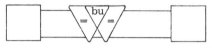

Tā   shr̀ bushr   nǐde péngyǒu?
'Is he your friend?'

Jèige jwōdz shr̀ bushr   tāde?
'Is this table his?'

<u>Shr̀ bushr̀</u> may also be used in the sense of 'Is it or isn't it true that . . . ?'

Shr̀ bushr Jūnggwo rén dōu hwèi hwà hwàr?	'Is it true that all Chinese can paint?'

<u>Shr̀</u> may be used to introduce each of the choices offered in an alternative-choice question:

Tāmen shr Jūnggwo rén, shr Fàgwo rén?	'Are they Chinese or French?'
Jèibĕn shū shr nǐde, shr tāde?	'Is this book yours or his?'

8. Bound forms (BF) are word elements carrying individual meaning and thus are distinct from particles, but they are seldom or never used independently. The terms <u>nán</u>- 'male' and <u>nyŭ</u>- 'female' appear in such combinations as:

nánrén	nánpéngyou	nánháidz	nánsywésheng
nyŭrén	nyŭpéngyou	nyŭháidz	nyŭsywésheng

9. <u>Ambiguous Reference in Use of</u> dōu. Transposition of the object place both subject and object under potential totalization by <u>dōu</u>. If both are plural, totalization may be applied to either or both, as suggested by the context.

Shū, bàu, wǒmen dōu kàn.	We read both books and newspapers. All of us read books and newspapers.
Shū, wǒmen dōu kàn.	(probably implies) We all read books.

TRANSLATION OF THE INTRODUCTORY DIALOGUES

1. <u>'May I Ask Your Name?'</u>

Jāng: May I ask your name?

Wáng: My name is Wáng. And yours?

Jāng : Mine is Jāng.

Wáng: And what is this gentleman's name?

5 Jāng : This friend of mine is named Lǐ. Mr. Lǐ, this is Mr. Wáng.

Wáng: How are you, Mr. Lǐ? What nationality are you? Are you English?

Lǐ   : No, I'm French, but my wife is English.

Jāng : Mr. and Mrs. Lǐ have three children: two boys and a girl.

Wáng: May I ask you, Mr. Lǐ, what the names of your three children are?

10 Lǐ   : One of the boys is named Richard, and one William.

Wáng: What is the girl's name?

Lǐ   : Her name is Mary.

Wáng: How many children does Mr. Jāng have?

Lǐ   : Pardon me, but Mr. Jāng is not married. However, he does have
15   a girl friend who is very good-looking.

Wáng: Is that so? What is your girl friend's name?

Lǐ   : Mr. Jāng won't tell us, but I know that she is a student.

Jāng : Who says so? I have no girl friend. He says I have, but actually I
         don't.

20 Lǐ   : Mr. Jāng, may I inquire: Do you speak French, English and Chi-
         nese—all of them?

Jāng : Not all of them. I speak only Chinese; I don't speak either English
         or French.

Wáng: Well, I can speak English but not French. But all three of us can
25   speak Chinese.

2. Buying a Painting

Wáng: I have two good friends. One sells tables and chairs, one sells
         paper and paintings.

Lǐ   : Let me ask you: which are better, Chinese or American paintings?

Wáng: (As to) paintings, I'm not too knowledgeable, but a friend of mine
5   says that foreigners all like Chinese paintings. Can you paint, Mr.
         Lǐ?

Lǐ   : I can't paint, but I very much enjoy looking at paintings. This per-
         son prefers Chinese paintings, that one prefers American. I say
         both Chinese and American paintings are fine. I enjoy them all.

10 Wáng: I have four Chinese paintings. Please look (at them and tell me)
         which is best?

Lǐ   : Are you selling all four of them?

Wáng: No, not all of them.

Lǐ   :   These two are particularly good. Are you selling them?

15 Wáng: No, I'm very fond of these two. I'll sell that painting. Would you
             like it?

Lǐ   :   I'm not too taken with that one. I'd like to buy (some) American
             paintings. Do you have any?

Wáng: I have no American paintings, but my friend has some. I'll ask him
20   whether they are for sale.

Lǐ   :   Fine. Thank you.

Wáng: You're welcome! Good-bye!

Lesson 5

MONEY AND PRICE

DIALOGUE

Shopping

(Seller: Màidūngsyide; buyer: Mǎidūngsyide)

Mǎi: Yǒu gāngbǐ ma?

Mài: Yǒu. Nín yàu shémma gāngbǐ?

Mǎi: Yīnggwo gāngbǐ, Měigwo gāngbǐ, wǒ dōu kànkàn, hǎu buhǎu?

Mài: Hǎu. Jèilyǎngge shr Yīnggwo gāngbǐ; nèilyǎngge shr Měigwo gāngbǐ—
5   yě pyányi, yě hǎu.

Mǎi: Dwōshau chyán yìjī̌?

Mài: Měigwo gāngbǐ shŕkwai-líng-wǔmáu; Yīnggwode gwèi—shŕèrkwai-
chīmau-wǔ yìjī̌.

Mǎi: Wǒ yàu yìjī̌ Měigwo gāngbǐ. Nǐmen yě mài Jūnggwo shū ma?

10 Mài: Jūnggwo shū yě yǒu, kě budwō. Nín yàu mǎi shémma Jūnggwo shū?

Mǎi: Wǒ děi syǎngsyang . . . Yǒu yìběn shū, míngdz jyàu Jūnggwo Hwàr.
Nǐmen yǒu meiyou?

Mài: Nín kàn, shr̀ bushr jèiběn? Jèiběn děi mài lyòubǎi-líng-bákwai
Jūnggwo chyán, kěshr Měigwo chyán jyòu shr shŕwǔkwai-èrmáu-èr.
15   Jèiběn jēn hǎu.

Mǎi: Hwàr jēn hǎukàn, kěshr tài gwèi. Wǒ jyòu gěi shŕkwai-bàn. Nǐ mài
bumai?

Mài: Shŕkwai-bàn tài shǎu. Nín dwō gěi yidyǎr; wǒ kéyi shǎu swàn yidyǎr.
Shŕszkwai-chīmau-wǔ màigei nín. Nín yàu buyau?

20 Mǎi: Shŕszkwai-chīmau-wǔ? Wǒ yàu. Nèijī̌ bǐ, jèiběn Jūnggwo Hwàr,
yígùng dwōshau chyán?

Mài: (Tā swànyiswan.) Yíge shŕkwai-líng-wǔmáu, yíge shŕszkwai-chīmau-
wǔ; yígùng shr èrshrwǔkwai-bàn. Nín kàn dwèi budwèi?

Mǎi: Èrshrwǔkwai-bàn tài dwō yidyǎr. Chǐng nǐ dzài swànyiswàn. Wǒ
25   syǎng shr èrshrwǔkwai-èrmau-wǔ. Shǎu èrmau-wǔ.

Mài: Wǒ dzài swànyiswàn . . . Nín dwèile, shr lyǎngmau-wǔ, búshr wǔ-
máu. Dwèibuchǐ.

Mǎi: Méi shemma! (Gěi ta chyán.) Jèi shr sānshrkwai chyán. Nǐ jǎu wo
szkwai-chīmau-wǔ.

30 Mài: Dwèile. Jèi shr szkwai-chīmau-wǔfen chyán. Wǒmen yě yǒu Fàgwo
hwàr. Nín kàn. Dōu shr hǎu dūngsyi. Yě jēn búgwèi. Nín dwō mǎi
yì-lyǎngběn, hǎu buhǎu?

39

Măi: Fàgwo hwàr, hău shr hău, kěshr wŏde chyán búgòu. Wŏ jyòu yàu
        jèibĕn <u>Jūnggwo Hwàr</u>.

35 Mài: Syèsye nín. Dzàijyàn.

Măi: Dzàijyàn.

VOCABULARY

Specifiers (SP)—Numbers (NU)—Measures (M)

-kwài	M:	piece, lump (used for dollars)
-máu	M:	(for dimes)
-fēn	M:	(for cents)
-fèr	M:	copy (for newspapers)
-jř	M:	(for pencils)
-syē	M:	(suffix indicating quantity, number)
jèisye	SP-M:	these
nèisye	SP-M:	those
nĕisye?	SP-M:	which ones?
hăusyē	NU:	many, a lot of

Jèisyē jř dōu shr shéide? Shr tāde.
'Whose is all this paper?' 'It's his.'

Nín yàu nĕisye shū? Wŏ yàu nèisye.
'Which lot of books do you want?' 'I want
   that lot.'

-wàn	M:	tens of thousands
-wànwan	M:	hundreds of millions

lyăngwànjāng jř (20,000 sheets of paper)
lyòuwànwan rén (600,000,000 people)

jř- (ji-)	NU:	a few (up to ten), some
háuji-	NU:	several, many

Wŏ jyòu yŏu jijāng jř.
'I have only a few sheets of paper.'

Wŏ yàu măi jijř gāngbĭ.
'I want to buy a few pens.'

Jèisye shū, nín măi nĕijibĕn? Wŏ măi jèi-
   jibĕn.
'Which of this lot of books are you buying?'
   'I'm buying these few volumes.'

Tā yŏu hăujijāng Jūnggwo hwàr. Nín kànkan.
'He has a number of Chinese paintings. Take
   a look.'

-bàn	M:	half, one half
bàn-(M)	NU:	half of a (M)

bànkwai chyán 'half a dollar'
bànjāng jř   'half a sheet of paper'

(NU-M)-bàn   (NU-M)-NU: . . . and a half

                              yíkwai-bàn (chyán) 'a dollar and a half'
                              sānfēn-bàn   'three and a half cents'

yíbàn   NU-M: one half, half of

                              Yíbàn shr nǐde, yíbàn shr wǒde.
                              'Half are yours, half are mine.'

                              Wǒ jyòu dǔng yíbàn.
                              'I understand only half.'

                              Wǒ yǒu jijāng jǐ; wǒ gěi nǐ yíbàn.
                              'I have several sheets of paper; I'll give
                                 you half.'

-dwō   NU: plus, and more, over
  NU-M-dwō   (plus less than another full measure)

                              lyòumau-dwo chyán   (more than six dimes
                                                    —up to 7)
                              lyǎngkwai-dwo chyán (more than $2.00—
                                                    up to $3.00)
                              shŕèrkwai-dwo chyán (more than $12.00—
                                                    up to $13.00)
                              èrshrwǔkwai-dwo chyán (more than $25.00
                                                    —up to $26.00)

  NU-dwō-M   (plus additional full measures)

                              èrshr-dwō-kwài chyán   'twenty-odd dol-
                                                        lars'
                              wǔshr-dwō-wèi syānsheng 'fifty-some
                                                     teachers'
                              sānbai-dwō-gè sywésheng 'over 300 stu-
                                                     dents'

yìdyǎr, yidyǎr   NU-M: a little

                              Wǒ syǎng mǎi yidyǎr táng.
                              'I'm thinking of buying a little candy.'

                              Wǒ jyòu hwèi shwō yidyǎr Jūnggwo hwà.
                              'I can speak only a little Chinese.'

Nouns (N)

fùchin	father
mǔchin	mother
fùmǔ	parents

gēge	older brother
dìdi	younger brother
jyějye	older sister
mèimei	younger sister

                      Wo fùchin hwèi hwà hwàr.
                      'My father can paint pictures.'

Ta mèimei jēn hǎukàn.
'His sister is certainly handsome.'

táng	sugar, candy (M: -kwài)
dzájr̀	magazine (M:-běn)
shwèi	tax
yǒude	some, there are those which . . .
yǒude . . . , yǒude . . .	some . . . , others . . .

Yǒude dzájr̀ wǒ hěn syǐhwan kàn.
'Some magazines I enjoy reading.'

Yǒude rén hwèi hwà hwàr; yǒude rén búhwèi.
'Some people can paint, others can't.'

yǒurén   some people

Yǒurén shwō tā hwèi dzwò Jūnggwo fàn.
'Some people say he can make Chinese
food.'

Adverbs (A)

yígùng   altogether, totaling

Tā yǒu sānběn shū; wǒ yǒu lyǎngběn; wǒmen
yígùng yǒu wǔběn.
'He has three books, I have two; we have
five in all.'

dzài   again, additionally, more

Chǐng nín dzài shwō.
'Please say it again.'

Nǐ dzài gěi ta yìmáu chyán.
'Give him ten cents more.'

gòu   enough, sufficiently (see Verbs also)

Jèige jwōdz gòu dà bugòu dà? Gòu dà, kě
búgòu gāu.
'Is this table large enough? It's large
enough but not high enough.'

dwō	more (see under Verbs also)
shǎu	less (see under Verbs also)

Nín dwō mǎi yidyǎr, hǎu buhǎu?
'Won't you buy a little more?'

Dwō shwō hwà, shǎu kàn shū.
'Speak more and look at the book less.'

Verbs (V)

syǎng   V: think

	FV :	(followed by a noun) think about, miss, long for

Nǐ syǎng shéi?
'Of whom were you thinking?'

Háidz dōu syǎng fùmǔ.
'Children all miss their parents.'

FV : (followed by a sentence) think that . . .

Wǒ syǎng ta hwèi shwō Jūnggwo hwà.
'I think he can speak Chinese.'

Tā syǎng wo bùjrdàu.
'He thought I didn't know.'

syǎng(yàu)   AV : (followed by a verb with or without an object) intend to, be thinking of doing

Wǒ syǎng mǎi nèijang hwàr.
'I'm thinking of buying that picture.'

Tā syǎng hwà yijāng hwàr.
'He is thinking of painting a picture.'

syǎng(yi)syang   FV : think over

Nǐ syǎngyisyang, shr̀ bushr tā?
'Think, is it he?'

Nǐ syǎngyisyang, gàusung wo.
'Think it over and let me know.'

děi   AV : must, have to (cannot take negative bu-)
búbì, búbi?   AV : (used as negative for děi) need not, not have to

Nǐ děi gàusung ni fùchin, kěshŕ búbi gàu-sung ni dìdi.
'You must tell your father, but you don't need to tell your younger brother.'

yǒu   FV : (impersonal) there is, there are
méiyou   FV : (impersonal) there isn't, there aren't

Yǒu rén shwō ta hěn hwèi hwà hwàr.
'There are some who say that he paints well.'

Yǒu yige rén gàusung wo . . .
'Someone told me that . . .'

Méiyou rén hwèi shwō-Jūnggwo hwà.
'There is no one who can speak Chinese.'

Méiyou rén budǔng.
'There is no one who doesn't understand.'

swàn   FV   figure, calculate
swànyiswan

Tài gwèi. Shǎu swàn yidyǎr, hǎu buhau?
'It's too expensive. How about making it a
little less?'

jǎu   FV: give in change

Wǒ jǎu nín lyǎngkwai-èr-mau chyán.
'I'll give you two dollars and twenty cents
change.'

mài   FV: sell for (so much)

Jèige mài dwōshau chyán?
'How much does this sell for?'

Nèige mài yîkwai chyán sānge.
'They sell three for a dollar.'

màigěi   FV: sell to

Wǒ màigei ta sānběn Jūnggwo shū.
'I sold him three Chinese books.'

gòu   SV: be enough, be sufficient

Táng bugòu.
'There's not enough sugar.'

Wǒ chyán bugòu.
'My money is insufficient.'

pyányi   SV: be cheap, be inexpensive

Yǒude shū gwèi, yǒude shū pyányi.
'Some books are expensive, some are
cheap.'

Jèige gāngbǐ jēn bupyányi.
'This pen certainly isn't cheap.'

dwō   SV: be many, much, more (see under Adverbs)
shǎu   SV: be few, scarce (see under Adverbs)
                             (These two verbs cannot modify a noun.)

Rén dwō, shū shǎu.
'There are many people but few books.'
    (lit. 'People are many, books are few.')

hěndwō   SV: be many, a lot
bushǎu   SV: be not a few, quite a few, a good many
                             (These forms may modify a noun.)

Yǒu hěndwō rén busyǐhwan kàn bàu.
'There are many people who don't like to
read newspapers.'

Yǒu bushǎu Jūnggwo rén.
'There are quite a few Chinese.'

Háidz jēn bushǎu.
'There are quite a lot of children.'

Particle (P)

-de   (added to nouns— see Note 8)

Expressions

jèige jyùdz	this sentence
dzwò yige lìdz	make (give) an example
Dìjǐkè? Dìyíkè.	Which lesson? Lesson One.
Dǎkai shū.	Open (your) books.
Héshang shū.	Close (your) books.
(Shr) shémma yìsz?	What is the meaning?
Yìsz shr . . .	The meaning is . . .
Nǐ dwèi tā shwō: . . .	(You) say to him: . . .
Nǐ hwéidá.	You answer.
Chǐng nyàn.	Please read.
Chǐng fānyi.	Please translate.
Méi shemma!	It's nothing. (Don't mention it.)
Hǎu shr hǎu, kěshr . . .	That's true enough, but . . .

SENTENCE PATTERNS

A. Monetary Expressions

1. Monetary Measures

The measures in common use are kwài 'dollar,' máu 'dime,' and fēn 'cent.' Since these measures have other more general uses, it is necessary to specify chyán 'money' unless this is clear from the context.

Yìchyān-sānbai-kwai chyán	$1,300.00
Sānbai-lyòushr-kwai chyán	360.00
yìmáu chyán	.10
Chīmau-wǔfen chyán	.75
Jyǒubai-kwai chyán	900.00

Wǒ yǒu lyǎngchyān-wǔbai-èrshrkwai chyán.	'I have two thousand five hundred and twenty dollars.'
Lyòukwai-wǔmau chyán bugòu.	'Six dollars and fifty cents is not enough.'

2. Concise Forms

The full forms given above are preferred except in reply to questions and in situations where the context has been established, when more concise forms are commonly used, such as:

Wǒ yǒu wǔchyan-sānbai-lyòu(shrkwai chyán).	'I have five thousand three hundred and sixty dollars.'
Yíwàn-èr(chyānkwai chyán) tài shǎu.	'Twelve thousand is too little.'

Tā gěi chīmau-bā(fen chyán).   'He offers seventy-eight (cents).'

In these examples it is assumed that the conversational context makes it clear that it is money which is referred to. In addition, final measures may be omitted when the series of measures makes it obvious what is being omitted.

B. Amount per Unit

Jwōdz dwōshau chyán?   Bákwai chyán
'How much is the table?'   'Eight dollars.'

Bàu dwōshau chyán yífèr?   Yìmau chyán yífèr.
'How much per copy is the   'Ten cents a copy.'
  newspaper?'

Yíge rén jǐjāng jř?   Yíge rén wǔjāng.
'How many sheets of paper   'Five sheets each.'
  apiece?'

Chyānbǐ yìmau chyán yijř;   'Pencils are ten cents apiece, three
  sānjř èrmau-wǔ.   for a quarter.'

Nèisye yǐdz, sānkwai-bàn yigè.   'Those chairs are three-fifty apiece.'

The examples given above show three distinct patterns:

Pattern 1:

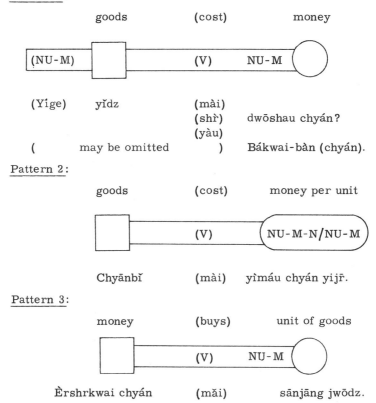

            goods   (cost)   money

(NU-M)   (V)   NU-M

(Yíge)   yǐdz   (mài)
                          (shř)   dwōshau chyán?
                          (yàu)
  (may be omitted   )   Bákwai-bàn (chyán).

Pattern 2:

        goods   (cost)   money per unit

            (V)   NU-M-N/NU-M

Chyānbǐ   (mài)   yìmáu chyán yijř.

Pattern 3:

        money   (buys)   unit of goods

            (V)   NU-M

Èrshrkwai chyán   (mǎi)   sānjāng jwōdz.

Note that in non-monetary situations such as the apportionment of goods among people, the pattern is modified by prestatement of the topic:

goods   unit of people   goods

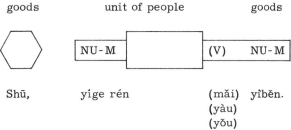

Shū,   yíge rén   (mǎi) yìběn.
                              (yàu)
                              (yǒu)
'Each person (buys, wants, has) one copy.'

C. Uses of -dwō- in Approximations

The use of dwō in approximations, in the meanings 'plus,' 'odd,' or 'more than,' varies depending on the number word. There are two patterns:

1. For numbers which end in zero, the pattern is NU-dwō-M:

èrshrdwō-kwai chyán	more than twenty dollars or twenty-odd dollars
sānshrdwō-běn shū	thirty-some volumes
sżbǎidwō(ge) háidz	more than 400 children

2. For numbers which end in a digit, the pattern is NU-M-dwō:

lyǎngkwai-dwō chyán	over two dollars (but less than three dollars)
shŕsānkwai-dwō chyán	over thirteen dollars (but less than fourteen dollars)
yibàn-dwō	more than a half

NOTES

1. Monetary Measures

The monetary measures where used are used consistently. No numbers above jyǒu 'nine' are used with fēn 'cents.' The pattern is 'one dime three cents' rather than thirteen cents; 'two dimes five cents' rather than twenty-five cents or a quarter; ' one dollar five dimes,' not a dollar and fifty cents.

2. Stative Verbs of Restricted Function

Stative verbs have three potential uses:

a. To predicate: Nèijang hwàr hěn gwèi.
b. To modify a noun: Jèi shr hǎu bǐ.
c. To modify a verb: Jèige hwàr buhǎu hwà.

Not all stative verbs, however, have all three functions. Dwō and shǎu are restricted in that they cannot modify a noun without being prefaced with an adverbial modifier:

<u>Say</u>: hěn dwō rén 'many people'   <u>Not</u>: dwō rén
     hěnshǎu chyán 'very little   shǎu chyán
     money'

Likewise, the stative verb <u>gòu</u> 'be enough' cannot modify a noun. Thus, instead of saying 'I don't have enough money,' the Chinese says 'My money is
not enough.' <u>Wǒde chyán búgòu</u>.

<u>Dwō</u> and <u>shǎu</u> are commonly used adverbially, standing before the verb modi-
fied, while their English equivalents follow the verb as part of its object:

<u>Dwō</u> gěi wo yidyǎr.   Give me a little <u>more</u>.
<u>Shǎu</u> shwō hwà.   Talk <u>less</u>.
Wǒ kéyi <u>shǎu</u> mǎi yidyǎr.   I'll buy a little <u>less</u>.
<u>Dwō</u> gěi yíkwai chyán.   Give a dollar <u>more</u>.

3. Reduplicated Verbs

Functive verbs (particularly monosyllables) are often repeated, with or without the addition of <u>yī</u> 'one.' The verb so repeated loses its tone. A reduplicated verb in a command tends to give a less brusque effect, much as in English. 'Take a look' is milder than 'look,' and 'think it over' is less harsh
than 'think.'

Nǐ kànkan jèifer dzájr̀.   Take a look at this magazine.
Wǒmen wèn(yi)wen syānsheng.   Let's ask the teacher.
Bùjrdàu, wǒ děi syǎng(yi)syang. I don't know, I must think it over.

4. <u>Syǎng</u>

Note that in English we commonly say 'I <u>don't think</u> that he knows how,' meaning rather 'I think that he does <u>not know</u> how.' In Chinese the negative must
stand before the action which is negated. <u>Wǒ syǎng ta búhwèi</u> 'I think he can't.'

5. The Whole before the Part

The whole, of which any part is designated, is stated first; the part follows.
Thus instead of saying as in English, 'six of the ten books are mine,' the
Chinese say in effect, '(as to) the ten books, six are mine.'

Nèisżge sywésheng, lyǎngge gāu, 'Two of those four students are tall,
  lyǎngge ǎi.   two are short.'
Jèisye shū, yǒude gwèi, yǒude   'Some of these books are expensive,
  pyányi.   some are cheap.'

6. 'Some' and 'Any'

The English word 'some' is used in two different senses, usually distinguish-
able by the fact that in one sense the word is stressed while in the other sense
it is not:

a. Unstressed 'some' indicates an indefinite amount. In the negative 'any' is
    used instead of 'some.' In Chinese no word is required to translate either
    term.

Do you want some?   Nǐ yàu buyau?
Don't you want any?   Nǐ búyàu ma?

He doesn't have any.	Tā méiyǒu.
I'm not buying any pictures.	Wǒ bumǎi hwàr.

An indefinite amount may, if desired, be indicated explicitly by the use of ji-M if a number of units are involved, and by yìdyǎr if what is referred to is not readily divided into units.

I have some (a little) money.	Wǒ yǒu yidyǎr chyán.
He has some (a few) books.	Tā yǒu jiběn shū.
Is this little bit enough?	Jèi(yi)dyǎr gòu búgòu?

b. Stressed 'some' usually indicates a part of a larger whole. Since the whole must stand before the part, the Chinese say in effect, 'As for these, some are good,' rather than, 'Some of these are good.'

Some of these books are yours, some are mine.	Jèisye shū, yǒude shr nǐde, yǒude shr wǒde.
Some magazines I often read, others I don't.	Yǒude dzájr̀ wǒ cháng kàn; yǒude wǒ búkàn.

c. Note that while ji-M and yìdyǎr may stand either before or after the verb, yǒude cannot stand after the verb. Hence it must take the topic position at the head of the sentence.

I like some books.	Yǒude shū wǒ syǐhwan.
	(not Wǒ syǐhwan yǒude shū.)

7. Definite and Indefinite Specification

In English the distinction between definite and indefinite specification of a noun is made as follows:

	Definite	Indefinite
a. Articles	the	a, an
b. Numbers	one	a
c. Demonstratives	this, that	the

In Chinese many of these distinctions are made by stress alone. For convenience, lack of stress is here indicated by omission of the tone mark, since the tone usually is indistinguishable in rapid speech.

	Definite		Indefinite	
a. NU-M	yíge	one	(yi)ge	a
b. SP-M	jèige	this (one)	jeige	the
	nèige	that (one)	neige	the
c. NU-M	jǐge	how many?	jige	a few, some

Examples:

Nǐ yàu jǐge?	How many do you want?	Wǒ yàu yíge.	I want one.
Nǐ yàu dwōshau?	How many do you want?		
Nǐ yàu něige?	Which do you want?	Wǒ yàu jèige.	I want this one.
		Wǒ yàu nèige.	I want that one.

Nǐ yàu shémma?	What do you want?	Wǒ yàu bǐ.	I want (some) pens.
		Wǒ yàu yige chyānbǐ.	I want a pencil.
		Wǒ yàu jeige byǎu.	I want the watch.
		Wǒ yàu neiběn shū.	I want the book.
		Wǒ yàu jige chyānbǐ.	I want some pencils.

8. Pronouns Modifying Nouns

While the standard 'possessive' form of a pronoun calls for the suffix -de, in the case of certain personalized nouns the -de is commonly dropped. E.g.: wǒ fùchin, tā dìdi, tā tàitai, wǒ péngyou.

9. Higher Numbers

In the Western world it is customary to point off numbers in excess of 100 in groups of three digits from right to left, giving each group a distinctive label. (The European use of 'billion' is not consistent.) The Chinese point off in groups of four places instead of three, thus:

Chinese			American	
yìchyān	1000	=	1,000	one thousand
yíwàn	1,0000	=	10,000	ten thousand
shŕwàn	10,0000	=	100,000	one hundred thousand
yìbǎiwàn	100,0000	=	1,000,000	one million
yìchyānwàn	1000,0000	=	10,000,000	ten million
yíwànwàn	1,0000,0000	=	100,000,000	one hundred million
shŕwànwàn	10,0000,0000	=	1,000,000,000	one billion

TRANSLATION OF THE INTRODUCTORY DIALOGUE

Shopping

Buyer: Do you have pens?

Seller: Yes, what kind do you want?

Buyer: Let me take a look at both British and American pens.

Seller: Good. These two are English pens; these two are American—
5   they're cheap and they're good.

Buyer: How much are they apiece?

Seller: The American pens are $10.50; the English pens are more expensive, $12.75 each.

Buyer: I'll take an American pen. Do you sell Chinese books too?

10 Seller: We have Chinese books too, but not many. What Chinese book do you want?

Buyer: I'll have to think . . . There's a volume called <u>Chinese Paintings</u>. Do you have it?

15   Seller: Take a look at this; is this it? This has to sell for $608.00 in Chinese money; but in American money it is only $15.22. It's really a fine book.

Buyer: The pictures are certainly beautiful, but it is too expensive. I can't give you more than $10.50 for it. Will you sell?

20   Seller: $10.50 is too little. Make it a little more. I can make it a little less. I'll sell it to you for $14.75. Do you want it?

Buyer: $14.75? I'll take it. That pen and this volume <u>Chinese Paintings</u>: how much is it altogether?

Seller: (He figures.) One item is $10.50 and one is $14.75, (making) $25.50 in all. Does that look right to you?

25   Buyer: $25.50 is a little too much. Please figure it again. I think it's $25.25. Twenty-five cents less.

Seller: I'll figure it again . . . You're right, it's twenty-five cents, not fifty cents. I beg your pardon.

30   Buyer: That's all right. (He hands him money.) Here is thirty dollars. Give me $4.75 in change.

Seller: Correct. Here is $4.75. We have French paintings too. Wouldn't you like to see them? They are all good stuff and quite inexpensive. How about buying one or two more?

35   Buyer: French paintings are very beautiful, it is true, but I'm short of money. I'll just take this book, <u>Chinese Paintings</u>.

Seller: Thank you. Good-bye.

Buyer: Good-bye.

Lesson 6

CHANGED STATUS

DIALOGUE

<u>What Can You Do?</u>

Lǐ : Gāu Syansheng, nín aì chř Jūnggwo fàn ma?

Gāu: Wǒ hěn aì chř. Wǒ tàitai háidz yě dōu aì chř.

Lǐ : Nín tàitai hwèi dzwò Jūnggwo fàn buhwèi?

Gāu: Wǒ tàitai hwèi dzwò Jūnggwo fàn. Háidz yě dōu hwèi dzwò yidyǎr le.
5   Kěshr háidz syǐhwan chř, búda syǐhwan dzwò.

Lǐ : Gāu Syansheng, wǒ jřdau nín hwèi shwō Jūnggwo hwà, nín tàitai yě
     hwèi shwō. Nǐmen háidz yě dōu hwèi shwō ma?

Gāu: Syàndzài hwèi shwō yidyǎr le. Dà háidz yě hwèi chàng jige Jūnggwo
     gēer le. Tā hěn syǐhwan chàng gēer.

10   Lǐ : Wǒ yě syǐhwan chàng gēer. Syàndzài wǒmen chàng yige, hǎu buhǎu?

Gāu: Hǎu. Nín ywànyi chàng shémma gēer?

Lǐ : Yǒu yige Jūnggwo gēer, kěshr wǒ wàngle jyàu shémma míngdz.

Gāu: Nǐ wàngle shr shémma gēer! Nǐ chàng yidyǎr, hǎu buhau?

Lǐ : Syàndzài bunéng chàng le, dōu wàngle.

15   Gāu: Lǐ Syansheng, nǐ neiwei péngyou hái dzwò shř ne ma?

Lǐ : Shéi? Gǔng Syansheng ma?

Gāu: Aì, shr Gǔng Syansheng. Tā hái dzwò mǎimai ma?

Lǐ : Tā syàndzài búdzwò mǎimai le. Mǎimai yǐjing màile.

Gāu: Tsúngchyán tā yě hwà hwàr, shř bushř?

20   Lǐ : Dwèile, kěshr syàndzài tā tài lǎule: yě budzwò mǎimai le, yě buhwà
     hwàr le.

Gāu: Bùnéng dzwò mǎimai, bùnéng hwà hwàr—tā néng dzwò shémma?

Lǐ : Tā jyòu néng chř fàn, hē chá; syàndzài jyǒu yě bunéng hē le.

Gāu: Jēn kěsyī!

VOCABULARY

Nouns (N)

shř(ching)   affair, matter, job, occupation (M: -<u>jyàn</u>)

Wǒ yàu gàusung nǐ yíjyàn shřching.
'I want to tell you something.'

Wǒde péngyou méi shr̀ le.
'My friend is out of work.'

Tā yǒu lyǎngge shr̀ching.
'He has two jobs.'

mǎimai	business (lit. 'buying and selling')
gēer	song
gwógēer	national song
fàn	food, meal (M: -dwùn); cooked rice (M: -wǎn)
dyǎnsyin	cakes, cookies; light refreshments
chá	tea (brewed)
cháyè	tea leaves
shwěi	water
chìshwěi	carbonated drinks
jyǒu	wine, liquor
kāfēi	coffee

Adverbs (A)

yǐjing	A: already
hái	A: still (further), yet (continuing), more

Mǎimai yǐjing màile.
'The business has already been sold.'

Tā hái chr̄ fàn ne.
'He is still eating.'

Wǒ hái yàu lyǎngge.
'I want two more.'

tsúngchyán	MA: formerly, once (in contrast to 'now')
syàndzài	MA: now, at the present time

Tsúngchyán tā syǐhwan hē kāfēi, kěshr
syàndzài (tā) busyǐhwan le.
'He used to like coffee, but he no longer
does.'

hòulái	MA: afterward, later (in past time)
jyou	A: then (introduces subsequent action)

Tsúngchyán tā cháng kàn bàu, hòulái jyou
búkàn le.
'He used to read the paper regularly, but
later he stopped reading it.'

gāngtsái	MA: just now, a short while ago (refers only to very recent time)

Gāngtsái yǒurén shwō nǐ hwèi chàng Jūnggwo
gēer.
'I just heard you can sing Chinese songs.'

búdà, búda	A: not very, not very much

Tā búdà syǐhwan dzwò fàn.
'She doesn't care much for cooking.'

Verbs (V)

dzwò   FV: do, make, engage in

dzwò shr̀   VO: work, engage in an occupation
dzwò mǎimai   VO: engage in business
dzwò fàn   VO: cook, prepare food

Nǐ syàndzài dzwò shémma?
'What are you doing now?'

Wǒ búdzwo mǎimai.
'I am not in business.'

Nǐ hwèi dzwò fàn ma?
'Do you know how to cook?'

chàng   FV: sing
chàng gēer   VO: sing (songs)

Tā hěn aì chàng gēer.
'He loves to sing.'

Yīnggwo gwógēer, nǐmen hwèi chàng ma?
'Can you sing the British national anthem?'

chr̄   FV: eat
chr̄ fàn   VO: eat (a meal)

Wǒmen chr̄ fàn, hǎu buhau?
'How about eating?'

Nǐ syǎng chr̄ Jūnggwo fàn ma?
'Would you like to have some Chinese food?'

Chǐng chr̄ yidyǎr dyǎnsyin.
'Please have some cakes.'

hē   FV: drink

Jūnggwo rén hē chá, Měigwo rén hē kāfēi.
'The Chinese drink tea, Americans drink
     coffee.'

Fàgwo rén hē jyǒu, búai hē shwěi.
'The French drink wine, they don't care for
     water.'

lǎu   SV: be old, elderly

Nèiwei lǎu tàitai shr ta mǔchin ma?
'Is that elderly lady his mother?'

Tā shr wǒ yige lǎu péngyou.
'He is an old friend of mine.'

shūfu   SV: be comfortable, feel well

Jèige yǐdz hěn shūfu.
'This chair is very comfortable.'

Wǒ fùchin búda shūfu.
'My father doesn't feel very well.'

kwùn   SV: be sleepy

Wǒ hěn kwùn, děi hē yidyǎr kāfēi.
'I'm very sleepy, I must have some coffee.'

lǎn   SV: be lazy

Sywésheng budōu lǎn.
'Not all students are lazy.'

hwài   SV: be bad, spoiled, broken

Byé dzwò hwài shr̀.
'Don't do evil things.'

Jèige jyǒu jēn búhwài!
'This wine really isn't bad!'

hǎu-V   SV: (hǎu- before an FV forms a compound which
                              functions as a SV) good to (V), easy to (V)

Jūnggwo fàn hǎuchr̄.
'Chinese food is delicious.'

Jūnggwo gēer bùhǎuchàng.
'Chinese songs are not easy to sing.'

Yīngwén hǎudǔng buhǎudǔng?
'Is English easy to understand?'

wàngle   FV: forget (The form wàng is sometimes heard
                              but is somewhat literary.)

Tā wàngle mǎi shū.
'He forgot to buy any books.'

Nǐ byé wàngle!
'Now don't you forget!'

Particles (P)

le, -le   (indicating change of status; see Pattern A)

ne   (indicating continuing state or action; see
                         Pattern B)

aì!   oh! yes! my goodness!

où!   oh!

Expression

Jēn kěsyī!   That's too bad! It is greatly to be regretted.

Common Sayings

Rén dwō, hǎu dzwó- hwó; rén shǎu, hǎu chr̄fàn.	When people are many, it's good for getting work done; when people are few, its better for eating.
Shǎu shwōhwà, dwō dzwò shr̀.	Talk less! Work more!

SENTENCE PATTERNS

A. Change of Status with the Particle le

Positive Situations:

Tā hěn lèile.	He became quite tired.
Tā hwèi shwō Jūnggwo hwà le.	He can now speak Chinese.
Wǒmen dōu syǐhwan ta le.	We have all come to like him.
Tāmen yǒu háidz le.	They now have children.

Negative Situations:

Wǒ búkwùnle.	I'm no longer sleepy.
Tā búywànyi chàng gēer le.	He doesn't want to sing anymore.
Tā búmài bàu le.	He no longer sells newspapers.

The particle le is placed at the end of a sentence to indicate change in the status of a condition, occurrence, or action. Such changes may be from negative to positive or from positive to negative.

1. The Time Element: Le in itself gives no indication of time (tense). Past, present, and future may be indicated by time words such as tsúngchyán 'formerly,' syàndzài 'now,' and hòulái 'later'; or may be deduced from the context.

Tā tsúngchyán cháng hwà hwàr; syàndzài ta buhwàle.	He used to paint a great deal; now he no longer paints.
Tsúngchyán tā hái néng dzwò- shr̀; hòulái lǎule, bunéng dzwò- shr̀ le.	In those days he still could work; later he grew old and was no longer able to work.
Nǐ búshr syǎuháidz le, shr dàrén le.	You're no longer a child; you've be- come an adult.

2. Status Expressed by Different Types of Verb

Since stative verbs by nature indicate a condition rather than an action or occurrence, it is not difficult to think of change from one quality to a contrasting one. Auxiliary verbs likewise do not involve action, but indicate a state or condition. Even the equative verb shr̀ indicates a state of affairs rather than action, e.g.,

SV : Wǒ búlèile.	I am no longer tired.
AV : Wǒ hwèi hwà hwàr le.	I can now paint.

EV: Jèiběn shū búshr nǐde le.   This book is no longer yours.

3. Change through Starting or Ceasing Action

In the case of functive verbs, the change in status is that of activation or deactivation, hence le indicates that the action or occurrence starts or stops:

Tā búmài bàu le.   He no longer sells newspapers.

Syàndzài tā dzwò mǎimai le.   He has now gone into business.

Wǒ méiyou chyán le.   I have no money left.

4. With or without the assistance of an adverb (kwài 'soon') or an auxiliary verb (yàu 'will'), le sometimes indicates not an accomplished change but one which is imminent or expected:

Tāmen (kwài) chř fàn le.   They are about to eat (their meal).

Wǒ (yàu) dzǒule   I'll be leaving (now).

Chyán (kwài) méiyǒule.   The money will soon be gone.

B. Continuity or Suspense with the Particle ne

Tāmen syàndzài chř fàn ne.   They are now eating.

Syānsheng kàn shū ne.   The teacher is reading.

Tā tàitai dzwò fàn ne.   His wife is getting the meal.

Wǒ hái dzwò mǎimai ne.   I am still in business.

Tā hái yǒu chyán ne.   He still has some money.

Dūngsyi hái hěn pyányi ne.   Things are still quite cheap.

Wǒ hái búlèi ne.   I'm not tired yet.

Wǒ hái búhwèi shwō Jūnggwo   I still can't speak Chinese.
  hwà ne.

Tāmen hái méiyou háidz ne.   They still haven't any children.

1. The final particle ne following a positive verb form indicates continuance of the state or action expressed by the verb. After a negative verb form, it indicates suspense in the state or action, awaiting eventual change.

2. The adverb hái in the sense of 'still' may be introduced before the verb to stress the aspect of continuity.

3. Hái may be omitted without significant change in meaning.

4. In sentences with ne, the negative bu- (or méi- with the verb yǒu) is usually preceded by hái, giving the sense of 'not yet' or 'still not.'

   a. Before stative, auxiliary, and equative verbs and before yǒu, this indicates temporary non-attainment of a condition or state:

Háidz hái bukwùn ne.   The children are not yet sleepy.

Tāmen hái búhwèi chàng ne.	They still haven't learned to sing it.
Nèijāng hwàr hái búshr wǒde ne; wǒ bunéng màigei ta.	That painting isn't mine yet; I can't sell it to him.
Tā hái méiyou chyán ne.	He still hasn't any money.

b. Before functive verbs it may indicate either that no immediate change is expected or deliberate negative intent:

Tāmen hái búchàng gēer ne.	They aren't singing yet. (They haven't yet started to sing.)
Wǒmen hái bùchr̄ fàn ne.	We aren't going to have dinner yet.

NOTES

1. <u>Interrogative Sentences Involving the Particles</u> le <u>and</u> ne

In forming simple questions from statements ending in <u>le</u> or <u>ne</u>, the interrogative particle <u>ma</u>? stands <u>after</u> the aspect particle.

Nínde péngyou hǎule ma?	Is your friend well again?
Tāmen jēn méi chyán le ma?	Have they actually run out of money?
Tā hái méichr̄ fàn ne ma?	Hasn't he eaten yet?
Tā hái chàng gēer ne ma?	Is he still singing?

2. Verb-Object Combinations

Certain Chinese verbs commonly appear with a generalized object which is not required in the English translation.

Chinese Usage	(Literal Translation)	English Usage
shwō hwà	speak speech	speak, talk
chr̄ fàn	eat food	eat, dine
dzwò shr̀	do work	work
kàn shū	read book	read
chàng gēer	sing song	sing
hē jyǒu	drink wine	drink (alcoholic beverages)
hwà hwàr	paint picture	paint, draw
mǎi dūngsyi	buy thing	shop

E.g.:	Chǐng chr̄ fàn.	Please eat.
	Byé shwō hwà.	Don't talk.
	Tā ài dzwò shr̀.	He likes to work.

When a more specific object is used, it takes the place of the general object:
<u>Syǎuhár ai chr̄ táng</u>. 'Children like to eat candy.'

3. Jyou

The connective adverb <u>jyou</u> is commonly used to introduce subsequent or consequent action and may be translated by 'then' or 'thereupon.' But these counterparts are more often omitted than expressed in English, while <u>jyou</u>

is essential in Chinese. <u>Jyou</u> in isolation is pronounced with the falling tone, but in a setting is always neutral so will be written without tone mark.

Nǐ hē yibēi chá jyou hǎule.   'Drink a cup of tea and you'll feel better.'

In a two-clause sentence where the clauses are introduced by <u>tsúngchyán</u>, 'formerly,' and <u>hòulái</u>, 'later,' <u>jyou</u> normally appears in the second clause:

Tsúngchyán tā cháng hwà hwàr;   'Formerly he painted a great deal,
kěshr hòulái jyou buhwàle.   but later he stopped painting.'

TRANSLATION OF THE INTRODUCTORY DIALOGUE

<u>What Can You Do?</u>

Li : Mr. Gau, do you like (to eat) Chinese food?

Gau: Very much. My wife and children like it too.

Li : Does your wife know how to make Chinese food?

Gau: My wife knows how to make it, and the children are learning. (lit.
5 'have come to know how to make it a little.') The children like to eat it, but they are not much interested in making it.

Li : Mr. Gau, I know that you can speak Chinese, and that your wife can speak it. Can all of your children speak it too?

Gau: They can now speak it a little. The oldest child has learned to sing a
10 few Chinese songs too. He enjoys singing very much.

Li : I like to sing too. How about our singing a little now?

Gau: Good, what would you like to sing?

Li : There's a Chinese song, but I have forgotten what it's called.

Gau: You've forgotten what song it is. How about your singing a little?

15 Li : I can't sing it any more. I've forgotten the whole thing.

Gau: Mr. Li, is that friend of yours still working?

Li : Who? Mr. Gung?

Gau: Yes, it's Mr. Gung. Is he still in business?

Li : He's no longer in business. The business has already been sold.

20 Gau: He used to paint too, didn't he?

Li : Right, but he's now too old: he is no longer doing business, and he is no longer painting.

Gau: Can't work, can't paint— what can he do?

Li : All he can do is eat and drink tea; and he can't drink wine any longer.

25 Gau: It's too bad!

MODIFICATION

DIALOGUE

Old Friends and Old Clothes

Wáng: Jōu Syansheng, wǒ tīngshwo nín syǎng sywé yidyar Jūnggwo hwà. Shr̀ ma?

Jones: Shr̀, yǒu yíwèi lǎu syānsheng syìng Chén, syàndzài jyāu wo syě Jūnggwo dz̀ ne; kěshr tā búywànyi jyāu wo shwō Jūnggwo hwà.

5 Wáng: Wǒ jyāu nín shwō Jūnggwo hwà, syíng busyíng?

Jones: Nín ywànyi jyāu wo, tài hǎule! Wǒ wèn nín: Jūnggwo hwà rúngyi sywé, burúngyi sywé?

Wáng: Yě bunéng shwō nán sywé, yě bunéng shwō rúngyi sywé. Wǒ kàn sywé shwō Jūnggwo hwà bunán, kěshr sywé syě Jūnggwo dz̀ burúngyi.

10 Jones: Kàn Jūnggwo shū nán bunán?

Wáng: Jūnggwo rén kàn Jūnggwo shū, bútài nán; wàigwo rén kàn Jūnggwo shū, dōu shwō hěn burúngyi.

Jones: Nín shwō yige gùshr, wǒ tīngyiting, hǎu buhau?

Wáng: Nín byé máng. Wǒ jyāu nín jijyù Jūnggwo hwà, dzài shwō yige gùshr, kànkan nín néng dǔng bunéng dǔng. Syíng busying?

15

Jones: Hǎu, nín jyāu wo ba!

Wáng: Wǒ wèn nín: Nín chwānde jèijyan yīshang shr̀ bushr Fàgwo yīshang?

Jones: Búshr, jèi shr Měigwo yīshang.

Wáng: Kěshr nín dàide neige syǎu màudz shr Fàgwo màudz ba? Wǒ yǒu yige Fàgwo péngyou busyǐhwan dài dà màudz, cháng dài syǎu màudz.

20

Jones: Dwèile, màudz shr Fàgwo màudz, kěshr wo chwānde yīshang shr wǒmen Měigwo rén cháng chwānde yīshang.

Wáng: Où, wǒ míngbaile. Wǒ kàn nín chwānde jeishwāng syé shr syínde ba?

Jones: Búshr syínde, shr jyòude. Syīn yīshang, syīn syé, wǒ bucháng chwān.

25 Wáng: Hǎu. Women Jūnggwo rén yǒu yijyù hwà shwō: Yīshang shr syínde hǎu; péngyou shr jyòude hǎu. Nǐ dǔng budǔng?

Jones: Jèijyu hwà wǒ míngbai, kěshr jyāu wo syě dz̀ de neiwei Chén Syan-sheng shwō wǒmen kéyi shwō 'jyòu dūngsyi,' bùkéyi shwō 'jyòu rén,' 'jyòu péngyou.' Nín shwōde jeijyu, 'Péngyou shr jyòude hǎu,' wǒ kéyi shwō bukéyi shwō?

30

Wáng: Nǐmende syānsheng shwōde hěn dwèi: bùshwō 'jyòu péngyou,' shwō 'lǎu péngyou.' Kěshr wǒ shwōde jeijyu hwà shr Jūnggwode yíjyù súyǔ.

Jones: Où, wǒ míngbaile. Yīngwén yě yǒu yíjyu súyǔ shwō, 'Old friends
35   are best'— yìsz jyòu shr 'Lǎu péngyou dzwèi hǎu.' Jūnggwo ren
        Měigwo ren dōu shwō lǎu péngyou shr dzwèi hǎude.

Wáng: Nǐ shwōde hěn dwèi.

VOCABULARY

Nouns (N)

-jyù   M: (for hwà)

                Nèijyu hwà buhǎudǔng.
                'That sentence is hard to understand.'

jyùdz   N: sentence, phrase (M: -ge)

                Chǐng ni nyàn nèilyǎngge jyùdz.
                'Please read those two sentences.'

yìsz   meaning, idea, intention

dż   word, Chinese character (ideograph)

gùshr   story, tale
shwō gùshr   VO: tell a story

                Hwà hwàr de neiwei Lǐ Syansheng ài shwō
                    gùshr.
                'The Mr. Lǐ who paints likes to tell stories.'

súyǔ   common saying, proverb

yīshang   clothing (M: -jyàn); suit (M: -tàu)
syé   shoe (M: singular -jr̄; pair -shwāng)
màudz   hat, cap

érdz   son
nyǔér   daughter

jǔren   host, hostess
kè (ren)   guest (M: -wèi)
chǐng kè   VO: invite guests

                Wǒmen cháng chǐng kè.
                'We often invite people (to dinner).'

Adverb (A)

dzwèi   the most, -est

                Jūnggwo chá dzwèi hǎuhē.
                'Chinese tea is the most delicious.'

Verbs (V)

sywé   FV/AV: study/learn (how) to
nyàn   FV: read (aloud)
nyàn shū   VO: study

jyāu	FV:	teach
jyāu shū	VO:	teach school

Wǒ syǎng sywé yidyǎr Jūnggwo hwà.
'I'm thinking of studying some Chinese.'

Wǒ yě syǎng sywé shwō Jūnggwo hwà.
'I'm thinking also of learning to speak Chinese.'

Wǒ tsúngchyán jyāu shū, syàndzài wǒ
ywànyi nyàn shū le.
'I formerly taught, now I wish to study.'

míngbai   FV: comprehend, understand (clearly)

Nǐ míngbai wǒde yìsz ma?
'Do you comprehend my meaning?'

chwān	FV:	wear (clothes, shoes), put on
dài	FV:	wear (on head, neck and wrists), put on

Nánháidz busyǐhwan dài màudz.
'Boys don't like to wear hats.'

Nyǔháidz syǐhwan chwān hǎu yīshang.
'Girls like to wear good clothes.'

syě	FV:	write
syě dz̀	VO:	write (characters or words)

Tā ywànyi sywé syě Jūnggwo dz̀.
'He wants to learn to write Chinese characters.'

Yíge rén kàn shū ne, yíge rén syě dz̀ ne.
'One person is reading, one is writing.'

tīng   FV: hear; listen to

Syǎuhár dōu ài tīng gùshr.
'All children love to listen to stories.'

tīngshwō	FV:	hear (it) said, hear tell
tīng . . . shwō		

Wǒ tīngshwō tāmen yǒu jyǒuge érdz!
'I hear that they have nine sons!'

Wǒ tīng Wáng Syansheng shwō nǐ yǒu nyǔpéngyou le.
'I heard Mr. Wang say you have a girl
friend.'

syīn	SV:	be new
jyòu	SV:	be old (worn), used

Wǒ yǒu yige syīn péngyou, syìng Mǎ.
'I have a new friend, named Ma.'

Syīn màudz hǎukàn, jyòu màudz shūfu.
'A new hat is good-looking, an old one comfortable.'

rúngyi	SV: be easy, simple (to do)
nán	SV: be difficult, hard (to do)

Shwō hwà rúngyi, dzwò shr̀ nán.
'To talk is easy; to do is difficult.'

Jèijyan shr̀ching rúngyi shwō, kĕshr hĕn
nán dzwò.
'This matter is easy to talk about but very
hard to do.'

tsūngming	SV: be intelligent
bèn	SV: be stupid, clumsy

Tā hĕn tsūngming, tā hĕn dŭng jèijyan shr̀.
'He is very intelligent, he understands this
matter.'

yŏuyìsz	SV: be meaningful, interesting
méiyìsz	SV: be dull, uninteresting

Tāde hwà hĕn yŏuyìsz kĕshr tā syĕde shū
méiyìsz.
'What he said is interesting, but his books
are dull.'

yŏuchyán	SV: be rich, affluent
méichyán	SV: be poor, destitute

Tā shr yige hĕn yŏuchyánde rén.
'He is a very rich man.'

hăutīng	SV: be good to listen to, tuneful

Yŏude Jūnggwo gēer jēn hăutīng.
'Some Chinese songs are really delightful.'

syíng	SV: be satisfactory, all right

Jèijāng jwōdz syíng busying? Bùsyíng, tài
ăi.
'Will this table do?' 'No, it's too low.'

Nín gĕi bákwai chyán, syíng busying?
Bùsyíng, gĕi nĭ lyòukwai ba!
'Give me $8.00, O.K.?' 'No, I'll give you
$6.00.'

Syíngle.
'That will do.' 'It's all right.'

Particles (P)

de	(added to nouns, phrases or clauses to indi-cate modification; see Note 1)
ba	(sentence final indicating suggestion or prob-ability; see Note 5)

Common Sayings

Kàn shr rúngyi;   To look at a job is easy;
dzwò shr nán.   to do it is hard.

Nánde búhwèi;   What is difficult, one doesn't know how to do;
hwèide bunán.   what one knows how to do is not difficult.

Yǒu yíjyù,   (If you) have one sentence,
shwō yíjyù.   say one sentence. (Don't hide anything.)

SENTENCE PATTERNS

A. Modification of Nouns Indicated by -de:

1. Modification by Pronouns and Nouns

                  nǐde jwōdz   your table
             tāmende shr̀ching   their affair

          syānshengde shū   the teacher's book
          sywéshengde yǐdz   the student's chair

        wǒ péngyoude hwàr   my friend's painting
          tā tàitaide fùmǔ   his wife's parents

     jèisz̀jāng hwàrde yìsz   the meaning of these four paintings
   nèilyǎngge péngyoude míngdz   the names of those two friends

De indicates that the nominal expression standing before it modifies the
nominal expression standing after it. Clusters of nominal forms such as
nǐ neilyǎngge péngyou are treated as if they were a single noun.

2. Modification by Stative Verbs

          yǒuchyán de rén   rich people
           hǎutīng de gēer   tuneful songs

          hěn gwèi de hwàr   very expensive paintings
           buhǎu de jǐ   poor paper
          butài gāu de jwōdz   not very high tables
          hěn rúngyi de shr̀ching   very easy matters

De indicates that an attributive expression consisting of a stative verb,
with or without adverbial modifiers, modifies the noun standing after it
(see Note 5 on limitations).

3. Modification by Clauses

            shwō hwà de rén   the people who are speaking
            kàn shū de sywésheng   the students who are reading

             wǒ mǎi de jwōdz   the table I bought
             tā shwō de hwà   what he says
     nèiwei syáujye chàng de gēer   the songs the young lady sang

     nǐ péngyou gěi wǒ de hwàr   the painting your friend gave me
       tā gàusung wǒ de shr̀ching   the matter he told me of

Thus a complete sentence (subject and object optional) may serve as modifier of a noun. This is simply an extension of the principle that what stands before de modifies what stands after de. In English such clausal modifiers are usually expressed by a relative clause. The three varieties of modifying clauses shown above are:

V-O	de	N	shwō hwà de rén	the people who are speaking
S-V	de	N	tā shwō de hwà	what he says
S-V-O	de	N	tā shwō hwà de yìsz	the meaning of what he says

B. General and Specific Modifying Clauses

1. Ambiguous Situations

Chàng gēer de shr̀ bushr̀ Dégwo rén?	'Are those who sing songs Germans?' 'Is the singer a German?'
Tā chàngde gēer shr Dégwo gēer bushr̀?	'Are the songs he sings German songs?' 'Is the song he is singing a German song?'
Wǒ syǐhwan kàn tā hwàde hwàr.	'I like to look at the pictures he paints.' 'I like to look at the picture he painted.'

There is nothing in the wording of these sentences to indicate whether the application of the modifying clause is intended to be general or specific, singular or plural. The context may or may not give sufficient indication. Offhand, one might guess that in the first two cases the specific interpretation is the correct one, but in the third example preference would be given to the general interpretation.

2. Generalization Indicated by dōu

Chàng gēer de dōu shr Dégwo rén ma?	'Are the singers all Germans?'
Tā chàngde gēer dōu shr Dégwo gēer ma?	'Are all the songs he sings German songs?'
Tā hwàde hwàr wǒ dōu syǐhwan.	'I like all of his paintings.'

Dōu as a totalizer of what precedes it may be inserted before the verb in order to generalize the application of the modifying clause.

3. Specification Indicated by a SP-NU-M Expression

Chàng gēer de neiwei syānsheng shr̀ bushr̀ Dégwo rén?	'Is the gentleman who is singing a German?'
Tā chàngde neilyǎngge Fàgwo gēer jēn hǎutīng.	'The two French songs he sang are really delightful.'
Wǒ dzwèi syǐhwan tā hwàde nei-jāng Jūnggwo hwàr.	'I liked best that Chinese picture he painted.'

C. Uses of the Particle ba

1. Chr̄ fàn ba!   Let's eat!

Gěi wǒ ba!	Let me have it!
Gěi nǐ ba!	Here, take it!
Wèn syānsheng ba!	Better ask the teacher!
Byé gàusung ta ba!	Better not tell him!

In these sentences, the addition of ba! makes the sentence into a mild command or suggestion.

2.
Háidz busyǎu le ba?	The child is quite big now, isn't he?
Nín hěn máng ba?	You're probably quite busy, aren't you?
Nǐmen dōu lèi le ba?	You're all tired out, I presume?

In this use of ba?, the questioner makes a statement with which he presumes the listener will probably agree. Compare the English sentence 'You are ready?' pronounced with a rising inflection at the end to indicate that it is intended as a question rather than a statement of fact.

3. Hǎu ba! is a form of assent or agreement equivalent to the English 'That's fine.' or 'O.K.' The same words however may also be used as a suggestion or half-question, the equivalent of Hǎu buhǎu?

Nín mǎi jèijāng hwàr, hǎu buhǎu? ⎫
Nín mǎi jèijāng hwàr hǎu ba!   ⎬ 'Hadn't you better buy this painting?'
                                   ⎭

The reply may be, Hǎu ba! 'All right.'

NOTES

1. Modification of Nouns with -de

In Lesson 2, Note 2 it was seen that one noun may modify another simply by standing before it (as Jūnggwo bǐ, Měigwo byǎu). The same principle was seen to hold with respect to pronouns before certain personalized nouns (as wǒ péngyou, tā tàitai— Lesson 2). Unmodified monosyllabic stative verbs were seen to function like English adjectives when standing before nouns (as hǎu ren, syǎu byǎu— Lesson 2).

Position alone, however, does not necessarily indicate modification. In Lesson 2 it was shown that some nouns which stand together are related coordinately (as jūng byǎu, shū bàu, jwōdz yǐdz). And again, a noun or nominal element may stand in apposition to the noun before it (as wǒmen Měigwo rén, tāmen lyǎngge).

The distinguishing sign of modification is the particle -de which stands between most nouns— and all phrases and clauses— and the nouns they modify.

2. Modification of Nouns by Phrases with -de

a. When -de appears between a proper geographic name and the noun which it modifies, a change in interpretation is sometimes noted. Compare the following:

Jūnggwo péngyou	Chinese friends
Jūnggwode péngyou	friends of China

b. With respect to most stative verbs of more than one syllable, and all modified stative verbs, the particle -de stands between them and the nouns they modify. (Note that in this position a stative verb functions like an English adjective.) Note the following:

hěn lǎude shū	very old books
yǒuyìszde gùshr	interesting stories
dzwèi tsūngmingde sywésheng	the brightest students
hǎukànde hwàr	beautiful pictures

Exceptions: tsūngming rén 'intelligent people,' pyányi dūngsyi 'cheap things.'

c. Where two or more nominal modifiers stand in sequence before a noun, -de appears after the last element only:

Jūnggwo syǎuhárde màudz	Chinese children's hats
nín neiwei péngyoude míngdz	the name of that friend of yours

d. Numerical expressions followed by de may stand as a modifier of a noun:

yíkwai chyán de táng	a dollar (worth) of candy
sānkwai chyán yìběn de shū	three-dollar (a volume) books
wǔfen chyán yijř de chyānbǐ	five-cent (apiece) pencils

3. Modification of Nouns by Clauses with -de

Modifying clauses on the S-V-O-de pattern are usually expressed in English by relative clauses which follow the noun they modify.

V-O-de-N	hē chá de rén	people who drink tea
S-V-de-N	tāmen hē de chá	the tea which they drink
S-V-O-de-N	háidz gěi wǒmen de dyǎnsyin	the cakes that the children gave us

4. Clausal Expressions Which Have Become Nouns

a. Certain V-O clauses with -de which describe a more or less permanent function have been fused into single words which function as nouns. They correspond to English nouns ending in -er:

màishūde	bookseller
màibàude	newsdealer
dzwòmǎimaide	businessman
dzwòfànde	cook

Since these expressions are equivalent to nouns, they may be specified and/or numbered or otherwise modified:

nèige màibàude	that newsdealer
lyǎngge dzwòfànde	two cooks

b. A stative verb followed by -de may stand alone and function as a noun, or it may be regarded as the modifier of an implied noun.

Wǒ syǐhwan hǎukànde.	I like good-looking ones.
Dàde pyányi, syǎude gwèi.	The large ones are cheap, the small ones expensive.

Nánde búhwèi; hwèide bunán.   What is difficult, one doesn't know
                                                            how to do; what is familiar, is not
                                                            difficult.

Syàndzài chřde, yùngde (dūngsyi)   Now the things you eat and the things
    dōu gwèile.   you use are all more expensive.

5. <u>The Use of Stative Verbs to Modify Nouns</u>

In general, most monosyllabic stative verbs may modify a noun without the
use of <u>de</u>, while most polysyllabic stative verbs require the use of <u>de</u>. Likewise, monosyllabic stative verbs which are modified by adverbs require <u>de</u>.
There are exceptions to this rule, as will appear in the following classifica-
tion of stative verbs which have appeared in Lessons 1-7:

a. May stand alone as modifiers of nouns:

gāu	lǎu	jyòu	tsūngming
hǎu	lǎn	nán	kèchi
dà	syīn	bèn	
syǎu	hwài		

b. Require an adverbial modifier such as <u>hěn</u> and are followed by <u>de</u>:

máng	dwèi	shǎu	kwùn
gwèi		dwō	

c. Require the use of <u>de</u>:

hǎukàn	pyányi	yǒuchyán	méiyìsz
hǎutīng	shūfu	méichyán	yǒuyìsz
hǎudzwò	rúngyi		

TRANSLATION OF THE INTRODUCTORY DIALOGUE

<u>Old Friends and Old Clothes</u>

Wáng :   Mr. Jones, I hear you are thinking of learning a little Chinese. Is
               that so?

Jones: Yes, there's an elderly gentleman by the name of Chén who is teach-
               ing me to write Chinese characters, but he doesn't like to teach me
5   to speak Chinese.

Wáng :   I'll teach you to speak Chinese. How would that be?

Jones: If you'd like to teach me, that would be fine! Let me ask you, is
               Chinese easy to learn?

Wáng :   You can't say it's hard to learn, and you can't say it's easy to learn.
10   I think learning to speak Chinese isn't difficult, but learning to write
               Chinese characters isn't easy.

Jones: Is reading Chinese books hard?

Wáng :   It's not too hard for a Chinese to read Chinese books; but foreigners
               all say they are very hard to read.

15 Jones: How about your telling a story for me to listen to?

Wáng :   Don't be in a hurry! I'll teach you a few sentences of Chinese and
         then tell you a story and see whether you can understand it. How
         is that?

Jones: Good, go ahead and teach me!

20 Wáng :   Let me ask you, are the clothes you are wearing French clothes?

Jones: No, they are American clothes.

Wáng :   But that cap you are wearing is a French cap, right? I have a
         French friend who doesn't like to wear big hats; he always wears
         a small one.

25 Jones: Right, the cap is a French cap, but the clothes I am wearing are
         what we Americans commonly wear.

Wáng :   Oh, now I understand. I guess the shoes you are wearing are new,
         aren't they?

Jones: They're not new, they're old. I don't wear new clothes and new
30   shoes ordinarily.

Wáng :   Good. We Chinese have a saying: 'When it's a matter of clothing,
         the new is best; when it comes to friends, the old are best.' Do you
         understand?

Jones: I understand this sentence, but Mr. Chén who is teaching me to
35   write says that we may say jyòu dūngsyi, but not jyòu rén or jyòu
         péngyou. This expression Péngyou shr jyòude hǎu, which you used
         — can we say it?

Wáng :   What your teacher said is quite right: don't say jyòu péngyou, say
         lǎu péngyou. But the expression I used is one of China's proverbs.

40 Jones: Oh, I understand. In English there is a saying that 'Old friends are
         best,' the meaning of which is Lǎu péngyou dzwèi hǎu. Chinese and
         Americans both regard old friends as the best.

Wáng :   What you say is true.

LOCATION AND EXISTENCE

DIALOGUE

In the Bookstore

Jāng : Wáng Syansheng, nǐ dzai shémma dìfang dzwò shr̀?

Wáng: Wǒ dzai Běijīng dzwò mǎimai.

Jāng : Nǐ dzwò shémma mǎimai?

Wáng: Wǒ yǒu yige syǎu shūpù.

5 Jāng : Dōu mài shémma?

Wáng: Mài shū, mài jř, mài bǐ.

Jāng : Yě mài wàigwo shū ma?

Wáng: Mài. Yīnwei dzai Běijīng yě yǒu rén yàu mǎi wàigwo shū.

Jāng : Nǐ màide shr syīn shū, shr jyòu shū?

10 Wáng: Syīn shū jyòu shū dōu yǒu. Pùdzli syīn shū dōu dzai chyántou, jyòu shū dōu dzai hòutou, yīnwei yàu mǎi jyòu shū de rén butài dwō.

Jāng : Où, pùdz chyántoude shū dōu shr syīnde. Wàigwo shū yě dzai yíkwàr ma?

Wáng: Dōu dzai yíkwàr, dōu dzai pùdz chyántou; kěshr wàigwo shū dzai
15 shàngtou, Jūnggwo shū dzai syàtou.

Jāng : Wèishémma ne?

Wáng: Yīnwei syǎng mǎi wàigwo shū de rén shǎu, syǎng mǎi Jūnggwo shū de rén dwō.

Jāng : Dzai nín jer mǎi shū de rén lǐtou, yǒu sywésheng méiyou?

20 Wáng: Sywésheng hěn dwō.

Jāng : Sywésheng màide dōu shr shémma shū?

Wáng: Yǒuchyánde sywésheng, mǎi wàigwo shū de dwō. Méichyánde sywé-sheng, mǎi wàigwo shū de hěn shǎu. Yīnwei Jūnggwo shū pyányi, wàigwo shū gwèi.

VOCABULARY

Nouns (N)

dìfang PW: place, position, location

Jèi shr shémma dìfang?
'What is this place?'

Nèige dìfang méiyou shwěi.
'There's no water in that place.'

syāngsya   PW: countryside, rural area

chéng   N: city
jyē   N: street (M: -tyáu)
fángdz   N: house, building (M: -swǒ)
wūdz, wū-   N: room (M: -jyān)
ywàndz   N: courtyard

jyā   N: family
                    PW: home

-jyā   M: a family of

pùdz   N: store, shop
-pù   BF: (ending for specific kinds of stores)
shūpù   PW: bookstore

fàngwǎr   PW: restaurant
chágwǎr   PW: teahouse
sywésyàu   PW: school
jyàutáng   PW: church

lóu   N: building (of more than one story)
                       (M: -tséng, a story)
lóushàng   PW: upstairs
lóusyà   PW: downstairs

shàngtou   PW: top, on top of, above (see Note 1b)
syàtou   PW: bottom, below, at the bottom of
chyántou   PW: front, in front of
hòutou   PW: rear, in back of
lǐtou   PW: inside, inside of, among
wàitou   PW: outside, outside of

dāngjūng   PW: middle, in the middle of
dǐsya   PW: underside, underneath

jèr   PW: here
nèr   PW: there
nǎr?   PW: where?

-lǐ   PW: in (localizing suffix to PW; see Note 1)
-shàng   PW: on (localizing suffix to PW; see Note 1)

                    Adverbs (A)

wèishémma?   MA: why?
yīnwei   MA: because
swóyi   MA: therefore, and so

                    Wèishemma jèijyu hwà budwèi?
                    'Why isn't this sentence right?'

                    Yīnwei hòutou méiyou 'le.'
                    'Because there's no le at the end.'

                    Yīnwei ta cháng kàn Jūnggwo shù, swóyi
                       tade Jūnggwo hwà hěn hǎu.
                    'Because he is always reading Chinese
                       books, his Chinese is very good.'

yíkwàr	A:	together
	PW:	(in) one place

Wŏmen yíkwàr chŕ fàn, hău buhău?
'How about eating together?'

Tāmen cháng dzài yíkwàr.
'They are always together.'

gēn   Connective: and (between nominal elements <u>only</u>)

bĭ gēn jŕ
'pen and paper'

wŏ gēn nĭ
'you and I'

Verbs (V)

dzài   FV: be (located) at (see Note 3)

Nĭ gēge dzài năr? Dzài Yīnggwo.
'Where is your brother?' 'In England.'

CV: at

Nĭ dzài shémma dìfang dzwò shŕ?
'Where do you work?'

jù   FV: reside, live

Nín dzai năr jù?
'Where do you live?'

shōushr   FV: put in order

Wŏ tàitai dzai jyā shōushr wūdz ne.
'My wife is at home cleaning house.'

ānjing   SV: be quiet, peaceful
chău   SV: be noisy, clamorous

Syāngsya hěn ānjing; chénglĭtou tài chău.
'It's peaceful in the country, too noisy in
the city.'

Common Sayings

Chyántou yŏu chē,   (If) there are carts ahead,
  hòutou yŏu jé.   there will be ruts behind.

Dzai jyā chyān ŕ hău;   A thousand days at home are good;
  chū wài shŕshŕ nán.   abroad every moment is difficult.

SENTENCE PATTERNS

A.   <u>Location with</u> dzài <u>and a Place Word</u>

The verb <u>dzài</u> 'be (located) at' is used in two ways, as shown in the following pairs of examples:

Wǒ dìdi <u>dzài</u> chénglǐtou ne.	'My younger brother is in town.'
Wǒ dìdi <u>dzài</u> chénglǐtou mǎi dūngsyi ne.	'My younger brother is shopping in town.'
Tā <u>dzài</u> nǎr ne?	'Where is he?'
Tā <u>dzài</u> nǎr dzwò shr̀?	'Where does he work?'
Jāng Syānsheng <u>dzài</u> fàngwǎrli ne.	'Mr. Jang is in the restaurant.'
Jāng Syānsheng <u>dzài</u> fàngwǎr chr̄ fàn ne.	'Mr. Jang is eating at the restaurant.'

1. In the first sentence of each pair, <u>dzài</u> is the main verb and indicates that someone or something is located in or at a given place.

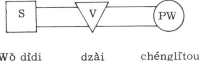

Wǒ dìdi	dzài	chénglǐtou	ne
Tā	dzài	nǎr	ne?
Jāng Ss.	dzài	fàngwǎrli	ne

2. In the second sentence of each pair, <u>dzài</u> and its place word object, form a coverbial expression (CV-O) modifying the main verb.

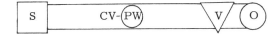

Wǒ dìdi	dzài chénglǐtou	mǎi dūngsyi	ne.
Tā	dzài nǎr	dzwò shr̀?	
Jāng Ss.	dzài fàngwǎr	chr̄ fàn	ne.

In this case <u>dzài</u> functions like a preposition in English (see Note 3).

B. <u>Existence in a Place with a PW and the Verb</u> <u>yǒu</u>

Jwōdzshang yǒu shū.	There are books on the table.
Yǐdz dǐsya yǒu meiyou màudz?	Is there a hat under the chair?
Jèr yǒu hǎu fàngwǎr meiyou?	Is there a good restaurant here?
Wǒmen sywésyàu yǒu Yīnggwo sywésheng ba?	There are English students in our school, aren't there?
Táiwān syàndzài yǒu Měigwo rén ma?	Are there Americans in Taiwan now?

To express the idea that 'at a given place there is someone or something,' a PW stands in the subject position, followed by the verb <u>yǒu</u> in the impersonal sense of 'there is' or 'there are.'

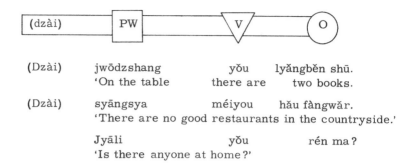

(Dzài)   jwŏdzshang   yŏu   lyăngběn shū.
           'On the table   there are   two books.

(Dzài)   syāngsya   méiyou   hău fàngwăr.
           'There are no good restaurants in the countryside.'

           Jyāli   yŏu   rén ma?
           'Is there anyone at home?'

Note that the CV dzài may stand before the PW at the head of the sentence
but is more commonly omitted.

NOTES

1. Place Words (PW)

Place words are a class of nouns which indicate place or position. All place
words may follow the verb dzài 'be located at' or precede the verb yŏu 'there
is or are.'

Three common types of PWs appear:

a. Proper geographic names which may stand before other nouns (including
   PWs) to modify them (usually without -de). Like pronouns they are them-
   selves not readily modified (see Lesson 7, Note 2a).

b. Positional nouns ending in -tou (such as shàngtou 'on top,' 'above,' lǐtou
   'inside,' 'within,' etc., and jèr, nèr, and năr may stand before other nouns
   to modify them (usually with -de):

   shàngtoude shū   the book(s) on top
   wàitoude jwŏdz   the table(s) outside
   jèrde fàngwăr   the restaurant(s) here
   nărde sywésyàu?   the school in what place?

   They may also stand after certain nouns to point out relative position:

   jwŏdz dǐsya   underneath the table
   chénglǐtou   in(side) the city
   wŏmen jèr   (here) at our place
   wŏ jyějye nèr   over (there) at my elder sister's place
   wŏmen dāngjūng   in the midst of us

   (Note that jèr and nèr are not modified by SV.)

c. Localizers— -lǐ(tou) 'in,' -shàng 'on,' -syà 'down,' -wài(tou) 'outside'

   They are bound forms in that they never stand alone. They may appear
   as endings to nouns to indicate relative position. The noun and the localizer together form a single place word:

   jwŏdzshang   on the table   bàushang   in the newspapers
   shūshang   in the book   jyēshang   on the street

| lóushàng | upstairs | chénglǐ(tou) | in the city |
| lóusyà | downstairs | chéngwài(tou) | outside the city |

A few familiar nouns are PW in their own right: that is, they may stand after <u>dzai</u> without requiring the addition of a localizer.

jyā(li)	at home
sywésyàu(li)	at school
jyàutáng(li)	at church
fàngwǎr(li)	at the restaurant

When <u>dzài</u> is used as a main verb rather than as a coverb, it is customary to add a localizer such as -<u>li</u>, -<u>shang</u>, <u>jer</u>, <u>ner</u>, except in a few cases such as <u>jyā</u> and <u>sywésyàu</u>.

Certain nouns, such as <u>chéng</u>, <u>jyē</u>, <u>lóu</u>, <u>fángdz</u>, <u>wūdz</u> and <u>dìfang</u>, behave like PW when specified and/or numbered:

jèige chéng	this city
nèige lóu	in that building
nèijige dìfang	in those few places
jèityáu jyē	on this street

2. <u>Coverbs (CV)</u>

A coverb with its object may stand before a main verb to modify it. Coverbs do not constitute a distinct and separate class of verbs, but are more often an occasional function of certain regular functive verbs. A coverbial expression functions like an English prepositional phrase.

a. The coverb plus its object (CV-O) functions like a movable adverb as to position in the sentence:

Tā dzài jyā chr̄ fàn.	He eats at home.
<u>Dzài jyā</u>, tā bùhē jyǒu.	At home he does not drink.
Wǒ dzài sywésyàu nyàn shū.	I study at school.
Dzài syāngsya, rén dōu dzwò shémma?	What does everyone do in the country?

b. Either the coverb or the main verb may be negated, depending on whether the action of the verb or the place setting of the action is stressed:

| Tā búdzai jyā nyàn shū. | He doesn't study at home. |
| Dzài jyā tā bunéng nyàn shū. | At home he can't study. |

c. Note that in a choice-type question, the pattern V-bu-V affects the <u>main</u> verb and its object, <u>not</u> the modifying coverbial phrase:

| Nǐ dzai fàngwǎr chr̄ fàn ma? | Do you eat in a restaurant? |
| Dzài Táiwān syǎuhár dài màudz budài? | In Taiwan do the children wear hats? |

3. <u>Translating the English Verb 'Be' into Chinese</u>

a. The English verb 'be' is used in several different senses, each of which has a distinct rendering into Chinese. We have now had four of these:

| Descriptive: | He is tired. | Tā lèi. (SV) |
| Equative: | He is a student. | Tā <u>shr</u> sywésheng. |

Locative: He is at home.   Tā dzài jyā.
Impersonal: There is one.   Yǒu yíge.

b. For the English prepositions 'at,' 'in,' 'on,' 'above,' 'underneath,' 'in front
   of,' 'behind,' etc., the one coverb dzài suffices. The precise relationship
   is indicated in the positional nouns which follow dzài, not in dzài.

dzai chénglǐtou   (be) in the city
dzai jèr   (be) here
dzai jwōdzshang   (be) on the table
dzai fángdz wàitou   (be) outside the house
dzai tāmen ner   (be) at their place

4. The Movable Adverbs: wèishémma?, yīnwei and swóyi

These three are closely related in use: wèishémma introduces a question;
yīnwei introduces the answer. But if there has been no question, yīnwei may
introduce a cause, to be followed by a second statement giving the effect:

Q: Wèishémma nǐ dzài syāng-   'Why do you live in the country?'
   sya jù?
A: Yīnwei chénglǐtou tài chǎu.   'Because it's too noisy in town.'

Cause and effect:

Yīnwei tā syǐhwan ānjing,   'Because he likes quiet, therefore he
   swóyi ta dzai syāngsya jù.   lives in the country.'

In common usage yīnwei is frequently omitted:

Jūngwén tài nán; swóyi ta   'Chinese is too difficult, so he is no
   busywéle.   longer studying it.'

TRANSLATION OF THE INTRODUCTORY DIALOGUE

In the Bookstore

Jāng :   Mr. Wáng, where do you work?

Wáng: I do business in Peking.

Jāng :   What is your business?

Wáng: I have a little bookshop.

5 Jāng :   What all do you sell?

Wáng: I sell books, paper, pens.

Jāng :   Do you sell foreign books too?

Wáng: Yes, because in Peking there are also people who want to buy foreign
         books.

10 Jāng :   Do you sell new books or old?

Wáng: I sell both new and secondhand books. In the store, new books are
         all in front, old ones in the rear, because not many people want to
         buy secondhand books.

Jāng : Oh, the books in the front of the store are all new ones. Are the
15   foreign books also in one place?

Wáng: They're all together in the front of the store, but the foreign books
        are on top (on the upper shelves) and the Chinese books are below.

Jāng : And why is that?

Wáng: Because there are few people who want to buy foreign books and
20   many who want to buy Chinese books.

Jāng : Are there any students among those who buy books at your place?

Wáng: Lots of students.

Jāng : What sort of books do students buy?

Wáng: There are more purchasers of foreign books among the well-to-do
25   students, very few among the less affluent, since Chinese books are
        cheaper and foreign books are more expensive.

Lesson 9

COVERBS OF INTEREST—INDEFINITES AND INCLUSIVES

TWO DIALOGUES

1. Going Out to Eat

Chén: Wŏ syăng chī yidyăr Jūnggwo fàn. Shéi gēn wŏ yíkwàr chī?

Syú : Wŏ gēn ni yíkwàr chī.

Chén: Nĭ hwèi yùng kwàidz ma?

Syú : Yìdyăr dōu buhwèi.

5 Chén: Nĭ syĭhwan yùng dāudz, chādz, fàngwărli dōu yŏu. Nĭ yàu sywé yùng kwàidz, wó kéyi jyāu ni.

Syú : Jèr yŏu hău Jūnggwo fàngwăr ma?

Chén: Chénglĭtou yŏu yige syău fàngwăr, jyàu Syīn Hwà Lóu. Tīngshwō nèrde tsài butswò.

10 Syú : Syīn Hwá Lóu dzai nĕityáu jyēshang?

Chén: Dzai Jūngchéng Lù (Middletown Avenue) lyòushrbáhàu.

Syú : Où, wŏ jīdau neige dìfang. Jèr jyòu yŏu yíge Jūnggwo fàngwăr ma?

Chén: Hái yŏu lyăngge, kĕshr dìfang tài dzāng. Wŏ busyĭhwan chī tāmen dzwòde tsài, yīnwei bugānjing.

(Dzai fàngwărli)

15 Chén: Nĭ syĭhwan chī shémma tsài?

Syú : Wŏ shémma tsài dōu syĭhwan chī.

Chén: Nĭ syăng chī yú ma?

Syú : Hĕn syăng chī.

Chén: Hău, sānge tsài, yíge tāng. Gòu bugou?

20 Syú : Gòule.

Chén: Wŏmen hē yidyăr jyŏu, hău buhau?

Syú : Syèsye, wŏ buhē jyŏu.

Chén: Wŏ gĕi nín dàu yidyăr chá.

Syú : Wŏ dàu ba!

25 Chén: Búkèchi! Jèige cháhú tài dà, buhăudàu. Hău, nín chĭng hē chá!

Syú : Syèsye nín!

2. Writing Letters

Hé : Lău Dù, wŏ syăng gĕi women jyāli syĕ yifēng syìn. Nĭ yŏu syìnjĭ meiyou? Gĕi wo lyăngjāng, syíng busying?

78

     Dù : Syíng! Syìnjř, syìnfēngr dōu yǒu. Chǐng yùng ba! Nǐ yǒu bǐ ma?

     Hé : Bǐ, wǒ yǒule.

5 Dù : Nǐ syě syìn shr yùng máubǐ, shr yùng gāngbǐ?

     Hé : Wǒ buhwèi syě Jūnggwo dž, yě buhwèi yùng Jūnggwo máubǐ. Wǒ jyou hwèi yùng gāngbǐ syě Yīngwén.

     Dù : Nǐmen jyāli cháng gěi ni syě syìn ba?

     Hé : Wǒ tàitai cháng syě syìn. Dà érdz syàndzài nyàn shū ne, hěn máng; 10   bucháng gěi wo syě syìn. Syǎu érdz tài syǎu, hái búhwèi syě dž ne. Tā chǐng ta gēge tì ta syě syìn.

     Dù : Nǐ dōu děi syě hwéisyìn ba?

     Hé : Dwèile! Wǒ busyě hwéisyìn, tāmen jyou bugěi wo syě syìn le. Wǒ jyou bùjrdàu tamen dōu dzwò shémma ne.

15 Dù : Dwèile! Jèr yǒu sānge syìnfēngr, shŕjāng syìnjř. Nǐ kàn gòu bugòu?

     Hé : Gòule. Wǒ méiyou gūngfu syě sānfēng syìn.

     Dù : Hǎu, nǐ syě ba! Wǒ bugēn ni shwō hwà le. Wǒ yě yǒu shr̀.

VOCABULARY

Nouns (N) and Measures (M)

-fēng	M: (for letters)
-wǎn	M: bowl, cup (for tea, rice, etc.)
-hú	M: pot (for tea, water, wine, etc.)
-bēi	M: cup, glass (for drinks)
-hàu	M: a number in a series (for day of month, size, house number, etc.)
yǒusyē	SP: (there are) some (who/which)

         Yǒusyē rén shwō Yīngwen bunánsywé.
         'Some people say English is not hard to learn.'

syìn	letter, mail (M: -fēng)
jyāsyìn	letter (from or to) home
syìnjř	letter paper (M: -jāng)
syìnfēng(r)	envelope
hwéisyìn	letter in reply

         Nǐ cháng syě jyāsyìn ma?
         'Do you write home often?'

         Syě syìn děi yǒu syìnjř syìnfēngr.
         'To write a letter, one must have paper and envelopes.'

gūngfu	time (free or leisure)

         Nín yǒu gūngfu syě hwéisyìn ma?
         'Do you have time to write an answer?'

máubǐ	brush pen (Chinese pen)
tsài	dish of food, course (M: -ge), vegetable
tāng	soup
ròu	meat
jūròu	pork
nyóuròu	beef
yú	fish (M: -tyáu)
kwàidz	chopstick (M: -shwāng)
dāudz	knife
chādz	fork
chŕdz (sháur)	spoon
wǎn	bowl, cup
fànwǎn	rice bowl
cháwǎn (chábēi)	teacup
cháhú	teapot
bēidz	glass
jyǒubēi	wine cup
jyāhwo	utensil, implement, tool
dǎswan	intention, plan

Nǐ yǒu shemma dǎswan méiyou?
'Do you have any plan?'

Verbs (V)

tán, tán hwà	FV, VO:	converse, chat

Wǒ syǎng gēn nín tán yidyǎr shŕching.
'I'd like to talk over something with you.'

Nín syǎng tán shémma shŕching?
'What do you wish to talk over?'

yùng	FV:	use, employ

Nǐmen hwèi yùng kwàidz buhwèi?
'Do you know how to use chopsticks?'

búyùng	AV:	need not, be unnecessary to

Wǒmen búyùng dài màudz ba?
'We don't need to wear hats do we?'

yǒuyùng	SV:	be useful
méiyùng	SV:	be useless
hǎuyùng	SV:	be easy to use

Jèige syǎu jwōdz hěn yǒuyùng.
'This little table is very useful.'

Nèige jūng hwàile, méiyùng le.
'That clock is broken; it's no longer of any use.'

Jūnggwo rén shwō kwàidz hěn hǎuyùng.
'The Chinese say that chopsticks are quite easy to use.'

dàu	FV:	pour
dàule	FV:	pour out, discard

Gěi nín dàu yidyǎr chá ba.
'Let me pour you some tea.'

Nèihú chá buhǎuhē; dàule ba!
'That pot of tea doesn't taste good, throw it out!'

| syǐ | FV: | wash |

Hǎu buhau wǒ gěi nǐmen syǐ wǎn?
'How about my washing dishes for you?'

| gēn | CV: | together with |

Wǒ gēn tāmen hē jyǒu.
'I had a drink with them.'

| gěi | CV: | for (the benefit of), to |

Tā gěi wo mǎi yiběn shū.
'He bought a book for me.'

| tì | CV: | for, in the place of |

Nǐ kéyi bukéyi tì wǒ jyāu shū?
'Can you teach a class for me?'

| yùng | CV: | with, using |

Wàigwo rén buyùng kwàidz chī fàn.
'Foreigners don't use chopsticks to eat.'

| dwèi | CV: | to, toward (lit. 'facing') |

Wǒ dwèi ta shwō: Kàn shr rúngyi, dzwò shr nán.
'I said to him: It's easy to see things but hard to do them.'

| lyán | CV: | even (including), (followed by dōu or yě) |

Lyán tā dōu ài nyàn shū.
'Even he likes to study.'

Tā lyán yìfēn chyán yě méiyǒu.
'He hasn't even one cent.'

| dǎswan | AV: | plan to, expect to, intend to |

Tā dǎswàn syě yìběn shū.
'He intends to write a book.'

| yīngdāng | AV: | ought to, should |

Měigwo sywésheng dōu yīngdāng sywé Jūng-wén.
'All American students should study Chinese.'

Nǐ yīngdāng gàusung tā.
'You ought to tell him.'

bútswò	SV : be not bad (quite good)
	Sywésheng syĕde dż dōu bútswò.
	'The characters the student wrote are not bad!'
gānjing	SV : be clean
dzāng	SV : be dirty

Common Saying

Dwèi nyóu tán chín.   Play a fiddle to an ox. (Cast pearls before swine.)

SENTENCE PATTERNS

A. Question Words Used as Indefinites

Questions	Positive and Negative Answers
Nĭ măi shémma?	Wo măi yidyăr dūngsyi.
' What are you buying?'	'I'm buying a few articles.'
	Wo bùmăi shemma.
	'I'm not buying anything.'
Tāmen dōu chĭng shéi?	Tāmen chĭng jiwei péngyou.
'Whom are they inviting?'	'They are inviting a few friends.'
	Tāmen bùchĭng shei.
	'They aren't inviting anyone in particular.'
Nĭ yàu dwoshau?	Wŏ jyòu yàu yidyăr.
'How much do you want?'	'I just want a little.'
	Wŏ búyàu dwōshau.
	'I don't want much.'
Nĭmen dōu yŏu shémma tsài?	Wŏmen yŏu jige Jūnggwo tsài.
'What dishes do you have?'	'We have several Chinese dishes.'
	Wŏmen méi shemma tsài.
	'We don't have much in the way of dishes.'
Nĭ yŏu dwōshau chyán?	Wŏ yŏu yidyăr chyán.
'How much money do you have?'	'I have a little money.'
	Wŏ méi dwōshau chyán.
	'I haven't much money.'

When a question word appears after a negative verb, it loses its interrogative effect and acquires an indefinite sense, translating into English as the indefinite adjective 'any' or the still more indefinite form '(not) much in the way of.'

B. Question Words as Inclusives before dōu

1. Standard Pattern:

Shéi dōu syĭhwan ta.   Everybody likes him.

Shémma rén dōu bùjrdàu.   Nobody knows (about it).

Něige dōu syíng.   Either (any) one will do

Dwōshau chyán dou syíng.   Any amount of money will do.

When a question word appears in the subject position, followed by dōu it may be equivalent to a non-interrogative inclusive expression (exclusive with a negative verb) such as English 'everyone' or 'everything' ('no one' or 'nothing'). The pattern is:

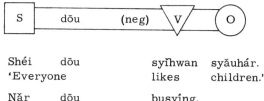

Shéi   dōu   syīhwan   syǎuhár.
'Everyone   likes   children.'

Năr   dōu   busyíng.
'No place   is satisfactory.'

The adverb yě may be substituted for dōu in most cases, but appears more frequently with negative verbs.

2. Patterns with Transposed Object

    a. Transposed to position between subject and verb:

Tā   shéi   dōu   búwèn.
'As for him, he asks no one.'

Tā shémma   dōu   bùjrdàu.
'He doesn't know anything.'

Wǒ nărde tsài   dōu   ài chř.
'I enjoy dishes from everywhere.'

    b. Transposed to topic position, before the subject:

Shémma gēer, wǒ dōu   búhwèi   chàng.
'I can't sing any songs at all.'

Něijāng hwàr, wǒ dōu   búmài.
'I won't sell any of the paintings.'

C. Intense Exclusiveness with yi-M N dōu

    Wǒ yidyǎr dōu búhwèi chàng   I don't know a bit about how to sing.
      gēer.

Wǒ (lyán) yìmáu chyán dōu méiyǒu.	I don't even have a dime.
Wǒ (lyán) yíge dz̀ dōu búhwèi syě.	I don't know how to write even a single character.
Wǒ (lyán) yíjyu Jūnggwo hwà dōu budǔng.	I don't understand even a single sentence of Chinese.

To express an intense degree of exclusiveness, as in the English phrase 'not even a single one' or 'not even a little,' the pattern is a NU-M-(N)-phrase (or some expression which signifies a very small number or amount), followed by dōu and a negative verb.

For additional emphasis, the coverb lyán 'even' may be placed before the object. This coverbial phrase (CV-O) may stand either before or after the subject of the sentence.

Wǒ lyán yíge dz̀ dōu buhwèi syě.	I can't write (even) a single character.
Lyán yíge dz̀, wǒ dōu buhwèi syě.	Not (even) a character can I write.

D. A General Pattern for Coverbial Expressions (CV-N)

gēn Lǐjyā chǐng wǒ gēn tāmen (yikwàr) chī fàn.   The Li family invited me to eat with them.
Tāmen gēn wǒ hěn kèchi.   They are very courteous toward me.
Wǒ tsúngchyán gēn Lǐ Syan-sheng sywé Jūngwén.   I formerly studied Chinese under Mr. Li.
Tā bùgēn wǒ yàu chyán.   He did not ask money of me.

gěi Lǐ Taitai gěi wǒmen dzwò fàn.   Mrs. Li cooked for us.
Tāmende syǎuhár gěi wǒmen shwō gùshr.   The children told stories to us.

tì Lǐ Syansheng tì Lǐ Taitai mǎi tsài.   Mr. Li bought the groceries for Mrs. Li.

yùng Wǒmen dōu yùng kwàidz chī fàn.   We all ate with chopsticks.

dwèi Lǐjyā dwèi wǒ tài hǎu le.   The Li's are just too good to me.
Tā dwèi wo shwō: Byé chīle!   He said to me: Don't eat any more!

It will be seen from the above examples that the pattern introduced in Lesson 8 for dzài may serve as the general pattern for all coverbs. The coverb and its object, forming a coverbial expression, stands before the main verb as an adverbial modifier and is the equivalent of a prepositional phrase in English.

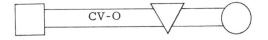

Jūnggwo rén   yùng kwàidz chī   fàn.
'Chinese people eat with chopsticks.'

NOTES

1. Indefinites

   Question words used as indefinites are non-interrogative and are always unstressed; hence tone marks are omitted.

   Note that the QW is not used in the positive answers, since this would cause confusion between question and answer. (Exception: ji-, which is used in both positive and negative answers.)

   QW used as indefinites always <u>follow</u> the verb and may not be transposed.

2. Inclusives

   The simple statement of inclusion uses a QW followed by <u>dōu</u> (or <u>yě</u>). This combination always appears <u>before</u> the verb. The QW is always stressed and the subject may either precede or follow it, thus offering an option in patterns. The sentences may be either positive or negative.

   In the intensified form— with or without the CV <u>lyán</u>— a NU-M expression is substituted for the QW. <u>Lyán</u> is commonly omitted before <u>yī</u>- but not before other numbers or descriptives.

Yíge dōu buyàu.	(I) don't want a single one.
Lyán èrshrge dōu bugòu.	Even 20 isn't enough.
Lyán syānsheng dōu bùjrdàu.	Even the teacher doesn't know.

   Intensified statements are more common in the negative than in the positive but positives are possible:

Wǒ lyán yíge dōu yàu.	I want even one.
Lyán tā dōu hwèi.	Even he knows how.

3. Coverbs

   A coverb cannot stand alone, it must be followed by an object. The coverbial phrase thus formed functions like an adverb, always standing before a verb, most commonly after the subject, but sometimes, for emphasis, before it.

   The most appropriate English translation for a given coverb differs with the main verb of the sentence. In the English sentence 'He bought something <u>for</u> me' the preposition 'for' corresponds to <u>gěi</u> if it means 'for my benefit,' but corresponds to <u>tì</u> if it means 'in my stead.'

4. Descriptive Use of shr

   <u>Shr</u> may stand between the subject and a descriptive phrase or sentence in the sense of 'It is true (of the subject) that . . .'

Jūnggwo rén shr yùng kwàidz chř fàn.	It is characteristic of Chinese that they eat with chopsticks.
Tā búshr dzai jèr nyàn shū, shr dzai nèige sywésyàu nyàn shū.	It is not here that he is studying, it is at the other school.
Tā shr dzai Běijīng jù; ta gēge shr dzai Shànghǎi jù.	He lives in Peking, his brother lives in Shanghai.

Tā syàndzài (shr) dzwò
shémma ne? Tā (shr) syě
syìn ne.

What is he doing now? He is writing
a letter.

5. Distinction between yǒu and shr

Compare these pairs of sentences:

Cháhúli yǒu shémma? Yǒu chá.

What is there in the teapot? There is
tea.

Cháhúli shr shémma? Shr chá.

What is (it that is) in the teapot? It is
tea.

Ménwàitou yǒu rén tán hwà ne.
Ménwàitou shr dàjyē.

Outside the gate are people talking.
Outside the gate (it) is the main street.

Lóushàng yǒu sānjyān wòfáng.
Lóushàng (dōu) shr wòfáng.

Upstairs there are three bedrooms.
Upstairs it's (all) bedrooms.

Yǒu is used to introduce a temporary characteristic or situation while shr
is used to introduce a permanent description.

TRANSLATION OF THE INTRODUCTORY DIALOGUES

1. Going Out to Eat

Chén: I'd like to have some Chinese food. Who will join me?

Syú : I'll eat with you.

Chén: Can you use chopsticks?

Syú : I'm completely inexperienced.

5　Chén: If you'd rather use knife and fork, the restaurant has them. If you
want to learn to use chopsticks, I'll teach you.

Syí : Is there a good Chinese restaurant here?

Chén: There's a little restaurant in town called the New China. I hear the
food there isn't bad.

10　Syú : On what street is the New China?

Chén: It's at 68 Middletown Avenue.

Syú : Oh, I know the place. Is there only one Chinese restaurant here?

Chén: There are two others, but the places are too dirty. I don't care to
eat the food they prepare, because it's not clean.

(In the restaurant)

15　Chén: What dishes do you like?

Syú : I like everything.

Chén: Do you like fish?

Syú : Very much.

Chén: All right, three dishes and a soup. Is that enough?

20 Syú :   Fine.

Chén: Shall we have a drink?

Syú :   Thanks, I don't drink.

Chén: I'll pour you some tea.

Syú :   Let me pour it.

25 Chén: Don't stand on ceremony. This teapot is too big and doesn't pour
well. Here, have a drink of tea!

Syú :   Thank you.

2. Writing Letters

Hé   :   Dù, old boy, I'd like to write home. Do you have any notepaper?
Can you give me a couple of sheets?

Dù   :   Sure, I've both notepaper and envelopes. Help yourself. Do you
have a pen?

5 Hé   :   Yes, I have a pen.

Dù   :   In writing letters, do you use a brush pen or a steel pen?

Hé   :   I can't write Chinese characters or use a Chinese brush pen. I can
only write English and use a pen.

Dù   :   I suppose your family often write to you?

10 Hé   :   My wife does. The older boy is studying now and is very busy; he
doesn't often write to me. The youngest son is too little and can't
write yet. He asks his older brother to write for him.

Dù   :   And you have to answer them all?

Hé   :   Sure. If I don't answer them, they won't write to me. And then I
15   won't know what they are doing.

Dù   :   Right. Here are three envelopes and ten sheets of paper. Do you
think that will be enough?

Hé   :   Plenty. I haven't time to write three letters.

Dù   :   All right, you go ahead and write. I won't talk to you any more. I
20   have things to do too.

Lesson 10

MOVEMENT AND DIRECTION

DIALOGUE

Planning a Trip to the City

Jāng : Nǐmen dau nǎr chyu?

Lǐ : Wǒmen dau Nyǒuywē chyu. (See Note 4 for other city names.)

Jāng : Nǐmen dzwò hwǒchē chyù ma?

Lǐ : Bù, wǒmen dzwò chìchē.

5 Jāng : Wèishémma búdzwò fēijī?

Lǐ : Tsúng jèr dau Nyǒuywē méiyou fēijī.

Jāng : Nǐmen dau nèr chyu dzwò shémma?

Lǐ : Wǒmen chyù kàn lyǎngge péngyou, yě syǎng mǎi yidyǎr dūngsyi.

Jāng : Nǐmende péngyou dzai Nyǒuywē shémma dìfang jù?

10 Lǐ : Dzai chénglǐtou, Yibǎi-yīshr Jyē, lyòushrlyòuhàu.

Jāng : Nǐmen háidz yě dōu chyù ma?

Lǐ : Dzwèi syǎude buchyù. Dàde dōu chyù.

Jāng : Wèishémma buchǐng nǐmende péngyou dau jèr lái?

Lǐ : Tāmen hěn syǐhwan lái, kěshr shr̀ching tài dwō, háidz yě tài syǎu,
15 swóyi syàndzài bunéng lái.

Jāng : Nǐmen dàu Nyǒuywē chyu, jyòu shr kàn péngyou chyu ma?

Lǐ : Búshr, hái syǎng mǎi yidyar dūngsyi ne.

Jāng : Nín syǎngyau mǎi shémma dūngsyi?

Lǐ : Wǒ yau gěi women dà érdz mǎi yilyàng dz̀syíngchē. Tā yǐjing nyàn
20 shū le. Wǒ syǎng tā yǒule dz̀syíngchē, tā jyou kéyi chí chē dau sywésyàu chyu nyàn shū chyu.

Jāng : Nà tài hǎule, kěshr jèr méiyou mài dz̀syíngchē de ma?

Lǐ : Yǒu shr yǒu, kěshr bútài dwō. Chē yě hěn gwèi. Wǒ syǎng hái shr
dzai Nyǒuywē mǎi hǎu.

25 Jāng : Nín shwōde hěn dwèi. Dzài Nyǒuywē mǎi pyányi. Hǎu, wǒ dzǒule.
Nín tsúng Nyǒuywē hwéilai, women dzài tán ba! Dzàijyàn.

Lǐ : Dzàijyàn.

VOCABULARY

Nouns (N)

dzwǒ-	PW: left	
yòu-	PW: right	
chyán-	PW: front	These directional place words
hòu-	PW: back	are bound forms except after
lǐ-	PW: in	the CV wàng (see Lesson 8, Vo-
wài-	PW: out	cabulary, and Lesson 10, Notes
shàng-	PW: up	1 and 2).
syà-	PW: down	

chē   N: vehicle (M:-lyàng)
chìchē   automobile, car (lit. 'gas vehicle')
hwǒchē (M: -tàng)   (railroad) train (lit. 'fire wagon')
fēijī (M: -jyà)   airplane, plane (lit. 'flying-machine')
chwán (M: -jř)   boat, ship
dżsyíngchē   bicycle (lit. 'self-propelled vehicle')

chējàn   PW: station shop (for vehicles)
fēijichǎng   PW: airfield
hwǒchējàn   PW: railroad station

Táiběi   PW: Taipei
Syānggǎng   PW: Hongkong

gūngkè   N: lessons

Adverbs (A)

dzěmma?   in what way? by what means? how? why?
dzěmmale?   what's the matter?
jèmma (dzèmma)   in this way, by this means, like this
nèmma   in that way, by that means, so
němma?   in which direction?

                   Wàng němma dzǒu?
                   'Which way do I go?'

nà   MA: in that case

                   Nà tài hǎule.
                   'That's fine!'

                   Nà dzěmma syíng a?
                   'How can that be acceptable?'

                   Nà busyíng ba?
                   'That won't do, will it?'

yídìng   definitely, certainly
buyídìng   not necessarily

Verbs (V)

lái   FV: come (here)
chyù   FV: go (there) (see Note 3b)

tsúng	CV:	from (a place)
hwéi	FV/A:	return to, go back to; back
hwéilai	FV:	return (here), come back
hwéichyu	FV:	return (there), go back

Wǒ tsúng jyāli lái.
'I came from home.'

Tā budàu fàngwǎr chyu.
'He doesn't go to the restaurant.'

Nín hwéilai buhwéilai? Yídìng hwéilai.
'Are you coming back? Yes, definitely.'

Wǒ bùyidìng hwéichyu.
'I'm not sure I'll return there.'

dzǒu	FV:	walk, go, depart
dàu	FV/CV:	arrive (of vehicles and persons); to (a place); at
wàng	CV:	toward (in a given direction)

Tāmen dōu dzǒule.
'They have all departed.'

Tā hái méidàu jyā ne.
'He hasn't yet reached home.'

Wǒ dǎswan dàu Syānggǎng chyu.
'I plan to go to Hongkong.'

Tsúng nèr, nǐ yàu wàng běi dzǒu.
'From there, you should go north.'

| dzwò | FV/CV: | sit, ride on, ride in; by (a conveyance with seats) |
| dzwòsya | FV: | sit down |

Chǐng nín dzwò jèr.
'Please sit here.'

Chǐng dzwò yidzwò, hē yidyǎr chá.
'Please sit awhile and have some tea.'

Nǐ cháng dzwò fēijī ma?
'Do you often fly?'

Chǐng dzwò, chǐng dzwò!
'Please be seated!'

Tā dzěmma chyù? Dzwò chwán chyù ma?
'How is he going? By boat?'

Nǐmen dōu dzwòsya ba!
'You'd better all sit down!'

| chí | FV/CV: | ride (astraddle); astride |

Nín hwèi chí dz̀syíngchē buhwèi?
'Can you ride a bicycle?'

Wǒ dǎswan chí dz̀syíngchē chyù.
'I'm planning to go by bicycle.'

fēi	FV:	fly
kāi	FV:	drive (a car, engine); (of trains, boats, planes) start, leave

Nín hwèi kāi chìchē ma?
'Can you drive a car?'

Hwǒchē tsúng jèr kāi ma?
'Does the train leave from here?'

pà	AV/FV:	be afraid to, be afraid of
kǔngpà	FV/MA:	(before negative verb) it is to be feared that; (before positive verb) probably, perhaps

Nǐ pà dzwò fēijī ma? Búpà.
'Are you afraid to ride in an airplane?'
'No.'

Byé pà! Wǒ gēn nǐ yíkwàr chyu.
'Don't be afraid. I'll go with you.'

Tā shémma dōu búpà.
'He isn't afraid of anything.'

Kǔngpà tā bunéng lái.
'I'm afraid he can't come.'

Kǔngpà tā láile.
'I guess he's arrived.'

kàn(kan)	FV:	see, visit

Wǒ syǎng chyù kànkan ta chyu.
'I think I'll go to see him.'

yùbei	AV/FV:	prepare, get ready for; prepare to

Gūngkè, búyùbei busyíng.
'It won't do not to prepare the lesson.'

Tā yùbei dàu Fàgwo chyù nyàn shū.
'He's preparing to go to France to study.'

wēnsyi	FV:	review, brush up

Gūngkè yě děi chángchang wēnsyi.
'Lessons have to be frequently reviewed too.'

kǎu	FV:	examine, take or give an examination
kǎushì	VO:	take or give an examination
	N:	examination, test

Wǒ hái děi kǎu jige sywésheng ne.
'I still have several students to examine.'

Syàndzài kǎushì le.
'We're now having exams.'

shàngkè	VO:	go to class; start class
syàkè	VO:	dismiss class; get out of class

Expression

Yǒu shr yǒu, kěshr . . .	That's so, but . . .

Common Sayings

Jyòude búchyù, syīnde bulái.	If the old does not go, the new will not come.
Búpà màn, jyòu pà jàn.	Don't be afraid of slowness, just be afraid of standing still.

SENTENCE PATTERNS

A. Coming and Going (with lái and chyù)

Nǐ fùchin lái bulai?	Is your father coming?
Tā shwō tā yídìng lái.	He says he's certainly coming.
Wǒ mǔchin yě dǎswan lái.	My mother is planning to come too.
Tāmen lyǎngwèi dōu chyù ma?	Are both of them going?
Fùchin chyù, kěshr mǔchin buchyùle.	Father is going, but Mother is not going after all.

In this pattern, lái and chyù are used as main verbs in functive sentences. Lái indicates movement toward the speaker, or his point of reference, while chyù indicates movement away from the speaker.

B. Starting Point and Destination (with Coverbs tsúng 'from' and dàu 'to')

Tā tsúng nǎr lái?	From where does he come?
Wǒ tsúng jyāli lái.	I come from home.
Nǐ dàu shémma dìfang chyù?	Where are you going?
Wǒ budàu sywésyàu chyù.	I'm not going to school.
Wǒ dàu jyēshang chyù.	I'm going (out) on the street.

These two coverbs, tsúng 'from' and dàu 'to,' followed by appropriate PW, indicate the point of departure and the destination of the action of the main verb lái or chyù, which they precede. The question words of place are nǎr? and shémma dìfang?

C. Purpose of Coming and Going

Tāmen dàu jèr lái nyàn shū.	They come here to study.
Wǒmen dàu jyēshang chyù mǎi dūngsyi.	We are going on the street to shop.
Chǐng dàu wǒmen jyā lái wárwar.	Please come to our home to have a good time.
Wǒmen dǎswan dàu jèr lái jù.	We plan to come here to live.

Nǐmen dāu nèr chyù <u>dzwò
shémma</u>?   What are you going there <u>to do</u>?

Nǐmen wèishémma budàu Syāng-   Why don't you go to Hongkong <u>to learn</u>
gǎng chyù <u>sywé Jūnggwo hwà</u>?   <u>Chinese</u>?

In this pattern, the purpose of coming or going is expressed by a verb or
verb and object placed after the main verb <u>lái</u> or <u>chyù</u>. Question expressions
such as <u>wèishémma</u>? 'why?' 'for what reason?' and <u>dzwò shémma</u>? 'to do
what?' are used. The pattern is:

Purpose

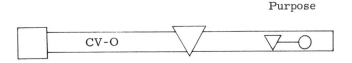

Wǒ   (dàu sywésyàu)   lái   sywé Jūngwén.
'I come (to school) to study Chinese.'

Wǒmen (dàu fàngwǎr)   chyù   chī fàn.
'We go (to the restaurant) to eat.'

D.   <u>Means of Conveyance</u> (with Coverbs dzwò <u>'sitting on'</u> and chí <u>'riding astride'</u>)

Nǐ dzěmma chyù?   How are you going there?

Nǐ dzwò chìchē chyù ma?   Are you going by car?

Dzwò hwǒchē chyù, dzwò fēijī   Which is less expensive, to go by
chyù, něige pyányi?   train or by plane?

Wèishémma budzwò chwán chyù?   Why not go by boat?

Chí dżsyíngchē chyù, syíng   Will riding a bicycle do?
busying?

Wǒmen bunéng chí dżsyíngchē   We can't go (there) by bicycle, can we?
chyù ba?

To indicate the means of conveyance used in coming or going, the coverb
<u>dzwò</u> 'sitting on,' 'going by' followed by its object (the conveyance), stand be-
fore the main verb <u>lái</u> or <u>chyù</u>. When the conveyance is a bicycle or animal,
the coverb <u>chí</u> 'riding' (lit. 'straddling') is used. The questions <u>dzěmma</u>?
'how?' and <u>dzwò shémma</u> 'go by what?' are commonly used.

E.   Direction (with Coverb <u>wàng</u>)

wàng němma dzǒu?   move in which direction?
wàng němma dzǒu   move in that direction (pointing)
wàng dzwǒ dzǒu   move to the left
wàng wài dzǒu   move toward the outside, outside
wàng lǐ dzǒu   move toward the inside, inside
wàng nǎr dzǒu?   go toward what place?
wàng tā ner dzǒu   go over toward him there
wàng wǒ jer dzǒu   move over toward me here
wàng nèige dà fángdz ner dzǒu   go over toward that big house

The pattern for direction follows the standard pattern of a coverbial phrase
standing before the main verb. The coverb <u>wàng</u> 'towards,' followed by a

nominal element indicating direction stands before the main verb of motion. The main verb is commonly dzǒu 'go,' 'move' (lit. 'walk'). The question expression is wàng němma? 'which direction?.'

Wàng may be followed by a place word, such as jèr or nèr, or by a nominal expression followed by jèr or nèr. The question word is nǎr? 'where?,' 'what place?'

NOTES

1. Lái and chyù after the Coverb wàng:

   Lái and chyù may be substituted for dzǒu after wàng:

wàng němma chyù?	go in which direction?
wàng nǎr chyù?	go where? go toward what place?
wàng dzwǒ lái	come to the left
wàng syà lái	come down

2. Particularized Verbs such as chí 'ride astride,' kāi 'drive a motor vehicle,' kàn 'look,' nyàn 'read,' shwō 'speak' may also follow a coverbial phrase with wàng:

Nǐ wàng nǎr kāi?	Which way are you driving?
Wàng chyán kāi.	Drive forward.
Byé wàng němma kāi.	Don't drive that way.
Wàng syà nyàn.	Read on (down the page).
Nǐ kéyi wàng syà shwō.	You may continue (what you are saying.)

3. Sequence of Coverbial Expressions before lái and chyù

   The following sentences show the normal sequence:

tsúng jèr dàu nèr chyu	go from here to there
tsúng jèr dzwò chē chyu	go from here by car
dzwò chē dàu nèr chyu	go there by car
tsúng jèr dzwò chē dàu nèr chyu	go from here to there by car

   a. Note that a 'conveyance' phrase may not follow dàu but may stand either before or after tsúng.

   b. Note that for emphasis or contrast a coverbial phrase may assume the topic position. In such cases, chyù is usually repeated after the main verb.

Dàu nèr chyu, dzwò chwán chyu hǎu.	In going there, it's best to go by boat.

4. Foreign Proper Names are usually transliterated— approximating the native pronunciation, but a few are translated:

Transliterated		Translated	
New York	Nyǒuywē	Salt Lake City	Yánhúchéng
Washington	Hwáshèngdwùn	New Haven	Syīngǎng
Chicago	Jřjyāgē		
Boston	Bwōshrdwùn		

TRANSLATION OF THE INTRODUCTORY DIALOGUE

<u>Planning a Trip to the City</u>

	Jāng:	Where are you going?
	Lǐ :	We're going to New York.
	Jāng:	Are you going by train?
	Lǐ :	No, we're going by car.
5	Jāng:	Why don't you go by plane?
	Lǐ :	There are no planes from here to New York.
	Jāng:	What do you plan to do there?
	Lǐ :	We are going to see a couple of friends, and we want to do a little shopping.
10	Jāng:	Whereabouts in New York do your friends live?
	Lǐ :	In the city, 66 110th Street.
	Jāng:	Are all your children going, too?
	Lǐ :	The smallest is not going. All of the older ones are going.
	Jāng:	Why don't you invite your friends to come here?
15	Lǐ :	They would like very much to come, but they have too much to do, and the children are too small, so they can't come now.
	Jāng:	Are you going to New York just to see some friends?
	Lǐ :	No, we're planning to do a little shopping too.
	Jāng:	What are you planning to buy?
20	Lǐ :	I want to buy a bicycle for our oldest son. He is already in school. I think when he has a bicycle he can ride it to school (to study).
	Jāng:	That's fine! But aren't there any stores here that sell bicycles?
	Lǐ :	Yes, there are, but not too many. And the bicycles are very expensive. I still think it would be better to buy one in New York.
25	Jāng:	What you say is quite right. It's cheaper to buy one in New York. Well, I'm leaving. We'll talk again when you get back from New York. Good-bye.
	Lǐ :	Good-bye.

Lesson 11

COMPLETED ACTION—TIME WHEN

DIALOGUE

Report on the Trip to the City

    Kwéi: Nǐmen jīntyan dzǎushang dau nǎr chyule?

    Lǐ :   Dau Nyǒuywē chyule.

    Kwéi: Dau chénglǐtou chyule meiyou?

    Lǐ :   Chyùle. Wǒmen dau Yibǎi-yīshr Jyē, yige péngyou jyāli chyule.

5 Kwéi: Péngyou jřdau nǐmen yau chyu kàn tamen ma?

    Lǐ :   Bùjrdàu.

    Kwéi: Tāmen dzai jyā budzai jyā?

    Lǐ :   Syānsheng dzai jyā, kěshr tàitai dau jyēshang mǎi dūngsyi chyule.

    Kwéi: Nǐmen dzai tāmen jyāli chřfàn le meiyou?

10 Lǐ :   Méiyou. Yīnwei tàitai búdzai jyā, swóyi wǒmen dau fàngwǎr chyù chř fàn chyule.

    Kwéi: Nǐmen chyùde shr něige fàngwǎr?

    Lǐ :   Shr Shwùn Lì Ywán— yige Jūnggwo fàngwǎr. Dzai Èrshrsān Jyē.

    Kwéi: Où, nǐmen chřde shr Jūnggwo fàn ma?

15 Lǐ :   Shřde! Shwùn Lì Ywán dzwòde Jūnggwo tsài fēicháng hǎuchř. Tāmen shémma tsài dōu néng dzwò.

    Kwéi: Nǐmen jyàude dōu shr shémma tsài?

    Lǐ :   Yígùng jyàule wǔge tsài. Kěshr tsàide míngdz wǒ yǐjing dōu wàngle, jyòu jřdau dōu hěn hǎuchř. Wǒ yíge rén chřde dzwèi dwō.

20 Kwéi: Nín hái dàu byéde dìfang chyùle méiyou?

    Lǐ :   Byéde dìfang dōu méichyù. Chřle fàn, jyou kāi chē hwéilaile.

    Kwéi: Nǐmen hwāle bushǎu chyán ba?

    Lǐ :   Dwèile, wǒmen hwāde chyán bushǎu. Swóyi syàndzài nǎr dōu bunéng chyùle.

VOCABULARY

Nouns (N)

-kè   M: (for lessons)

                    Jèikè shr dìshryīkè.
                    'This lesson is Lesson 11.'

dì-	SP:	(ordinal prefix for numbers)

                dìyī   'the first'
                dìèrge   'the second person/thing'
                dìsānběn 'the third volume'

dzwótyan	MA/N:	yesterday
jīntyan	MA/N:	today
míngtyan	MA/N:	tomorrow
dzǎushang	MA/N:	morning
jūngwǔ	MA/N:	noon
wǎnshang	MA/N:	evening

Wǒ dzwótyan dzài Nyǒuywē.
'Yesterday I was in New York.'

Wǒ dzǎushang dzài sywésyàu, wǎnshang
   dzài jyā.
'I am at school mornings, and evenings I am
   at home.'

Wo jūngwǔ dzài fàngwárli chr̄ fàn.
'Noons I eat at a restaurant.'

dzǎufàn	breakfast (lit. 'early meal')
jūngfàn (wǔfàn)	lunch (lit. 'middle meal')
wǎnfàn	dinner, supper (lit. 'late meal')

Wǒmen dzǎushang chr̄ dzǎufàn, jūngwǔ chr̄
   jūngfàn, wǎnshang chr̄ wǎnfàn.
'We eat breakfast in the morning, lunch at
   noon, and supper in the evening.'

hwāfei	expense
byéde	other (see Note 5)
byéren	other people

Wǒ buywànyi sywé byéde gūngkè.
'I don't want to take any other courses.'

Byéren dōu shwō bùhǎukàn; wǒ shwō hǎukàn.
'Everyone else says it is not good-looking,
   but I say it is.'

lyànsyí	exercise, drill

Nǐmen děi dzwò jèige lyànsyí.
'You must do this exercise.'

Adverbs (A)

méi-	(negates completed action; see Pattern B)

Syānsheng méilái.
'The teacher didn't come.'

Tā hái méilái ne.
'He hasn't yet arrived.'

Wǒ méimǎi nèilyàng chìchē.
'I didn't buy that car.'

bàntyān	MA:	for a long time, for quite a while
jyòu (yau)	A:	immediately, right away

Wǒmen jyòu yau dzǒule.
'We're just about to leave.'

kwài (yau) A: soon, quickly

Wǒ péngyou kwài hǎule.
'My friend will soon be well again.'

yòu A: again (in the past)

Wǒde gāngbǐ yòu hwàile.
'My pen is broken again.'

gāng(gāng) A: just, just this minute, just now (recently)

Tā gānggāng hái dzài jèr ne.
'He was here just a minute ago.'

Wǒ gāng tīngshwō.
'I just heard about it.'

Verbs (V)

dzǎu	SV:	be early
wǎn	SV:	be late, tardy

Yǐjing tài wǎnle.
'It's already too late.'

jyàu FV: call for, order (food in a restaurant)

Nín jyàule jǐge tsài?
'How many dishes did you order?'

hwā	FV:	spend
hwā chyán	VO:	spend money

Tā jeige rén hěn ài hwā chyán.
'This fellow likes to spend money.'

kànjyan	FV:	see (lit. 'look and perceive')
tīngjyan	FV:	hear (lit. 'listen and perceive')

Nǐ kàn neige rén; tā hái méikànjyan nǐ ne.
'Look at that man; he hasn't seen you yet.'

Nǐ dzai nǎr kànjyan ta le?
'Where did you see him?'

Wǒ tīngjyan jige hěn yǒuyìsz de gùshr.
'I heard several very interesting stories.'

lyànsyí FV: practice, drill (see under Nouns)

Wǒmen děi chángchang lyànsyí syě dz̀.
'We must constantly practice writing.'

Shrde!   EX: That's right!

Expression

Wǒ yíge rén . . .   I, myself, . . .

Common Sayings

Hwā chyán rúngyi,   It's easy to spend money,
  jèng chyán nǎn.   but hard to earn it.

Tsǎudìli shwō hwà,   (You may) speak (out) in the field,
  lùshang yǒu rén   (but) on the road there will be people
  tīng.   listening.

Yǎn jyàn shr shŕ;   What the eye sees is true;
  ěr tīng shr syū.   what the ear hears is false.

Yǎn bújyàn,   If the eye doesn't see it,
  syīn bufán.   the heart won't worry about it.

SENTENCE PATTERNS

A. Completed Action with -le

1. Verbs and -le

Jāng Syansheng yǐjing láile.   Mr. Jang has already come.

Jāng Taitai láile, yòu dzǒule.   Mrs. Jang came, and left.

Tā dàu Nyǒuywē chyùle.   She's gone to New York.

Tā gēn Mǎ Taitai yikwàr chyùle.   She went together with Mrs. Ma.

In Lesson 6 it was stated that the particle -le basically indicates a change
of status. When -le is used after verbs that express action (or any phase
of action), this change of status is seen in the achievement or completion
of this action, or any stage along the way toward ultimate completion.
The addition of appropriate adverbs or other elements or context alone
will clarify the particular point of completion referred to. The pattern
is:

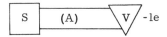

Jāng Syansheng   láile.
'Mr. Jang (came or) has come.'

Jāng Taitai dàu Nyǒuywē chyule.
'Mrs. Jang went (or has gone) to New York.'

2. Verbs with Simple Objects and -le

Wǒmen yǐjing chàngle gwógēer   We have already sung the national
  le.   anthem.

Tā màile tāde chǐchē le.	He's sold his car.
Wǒ gēn ta tánle hwà le.	I have talked with him.
Wǒ gěile tāmen chyán le.	I have given them money (I've paid them).

When a simple unquantified object is present, completion of action is indicated not only by the particle le standing at the end of the sentence (sentence le), but by the presence of a second -le immediately after the verb (verb -le). The pattern is:

Tà   màile   tāde   chǐchē   le.
'He has sold his car.'

3. Verbs with Measured Objects and -le

Tā hwàle sānjāng hwàr.	He painted three pictures.
Tāmen tánle bàntyān hwà.	They talked for quite a while.
Tā mǎile hǎusyē dūngsyi.	He bought a lot of things.
Nǐ syěle dwōshau dž?	How many characters did you write?

When the object is preceded by an expression of quantity, only the verb -le is required.

B.   Negated and Suspended Action with méi- (see Lesson 6, Pattern A-3a)

Chén Syansheng méichyù.	Mr. Chen didn't go.
Chén Syansheng hái méichyù ne.	Mr. Chen hasn't gone yet.
Wǒmen hái méichǐ fàn ne.	We haven't eaten yet.
Tā hái méihǎu ne.	He hasn't recovered yet.

The negative adverb méi-(yǒu), 'has not,' may stand before a verb to negate the completed aspect. Addition of the adverb hái and the final particle ne indicates suspension of the action with the probability that it will eventually be completed. Either hái or ne may be omitted without materially affecting the meaning. The pattern is:

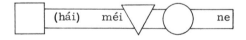

Chén Taitai   (hái)   méisywé kāi chē (ne).
'Mrs. Chen has not yet learned how to drive.'

C.   Time of an Action

The time of an action (or condition) is indicated in Chinese by a time word

(TW) or expression standing before the verb. Most time words being of more than one syllable may stand either before or after the subject of the sentence.

| (TW) | | (TW) | | |

Syàndzài   wǒ   méi   shr̀.
              Wǒ syàndzai   mei   shr̀.
'Right now I have nothing to do.'

Dzwótyan   wǒ   syě   syìn.
              Wǒ dzwótyan   syě   syìn
'Yesterday I wrote letters.'

Mǐngtyan   wǒ   hwà   hwàr.
              Wǒ mǐngtyan   hwà   hwàr.
'Tomorrow I am going to paint.'

NOTES

1. Time Meanings

To distinguish past, present, and future, Chinese may use auxiliary verbs but in general relies on time words or expressions or merely on the time one may infer from the context. This use of time words is illustrated in Pattern C.

We have already noted in Lesson 6 that Chinese uses a number of particles to indicate distinctions of aspect, as shown below:

Aspect

Fact	Tā syě syìn.	He writes letters. (In answer to the question: Does he write letters?)
Custom	Tā syě syìn.	He writes letters. (In answer to the question: What does he do?)
Continuance	Tā syě syìn ne.	He is writing letters. (In answer to the question: What is he doing?)
Change of status	Tā syě syìn le.	He is (now) writing letters. (Implying that he was not previously.)
	Tā busyě syìn le.	He is no longer writing letters.
Completion	Tā syěle syìn le.	He has written the letters. He did write the letters.
Determination	Tā bùsyě syìn.	He won't write the letters.

The translations given are all on the supposition that the point of view is <u>now</u>. To shift to a past or future point of view requires only a change in the time word in Chinese, but requires a tense change in English. Thus:

<u>Dzwótyan</u> tā syě syìn.   Yesterday he wrote letters.
        tā syě syìn ne.   he was writing letters.
        tā syě syìn le.   he wrote letters (for a
                                              change).

Dzwótyan tā (yǐjing) syěle syìn le.	Yesterday he did write the letters. (or: he had already written the letters.)
Mǐngtyan tā (yàu) syě syìn. tā jyou syě syìn le.	Tomorrow he is going to write letters. he'll write the letters (since he did not do so today.)

Note that completed action may be clarified by adding the adverb yǐjing (already), while anticipated action may be clarified by the addition of the auxiliary verb yàu or syǎngyàu, or by the adverb jyou. However, none of these additions are required.

2. Completion of Action and Time

It was noted in Lesson 6 that -le in itself indicates the fact of change but not the tense, and that time words and/or context indicates the time of change in status. This holds true for the use of -le in indicating completion of action, which may take place at any time in the past, present or future. The sentences below show -le indicating completion in a variety of time settings:

Tā dzwótyan (jyou) láile.	He came yesterday.
Wǒ jǐntyan wǎnshang kànjyan ta le.	I saw him this evening.
Tāmen mǐngtyan (jyou) dzǒule.	They are leaving tomorrow.
Sywésheng gāngtsái dàule.	The student just arrived.
Tāmen dàule, jyou dzǒule.	They arrived and (then) departed.
Tā tàitai kwài yau láile.	His wife will be coming soon.

3. Question Forms with -le

Questions inquiring whether the action is completed or not appear below. Sentences under (b) involve objects, but the pattern is the same as those under (a).

a. Lǐ Syansheng láile meiyou?	Has Mr. Li come?
Lǐ Taitai yě láile ma?	Did Mrs. Li come too?
Tāmende háidz láile méilái?	Did their children come?
Lǐ Syaujye méilái ma?	Didn't Miss Li come?
Lǐ Syaujye hái méilái ne ma?	Hasn't Miss Li come yet?
Dzwèi syǎude háidz méilái ba?	The smallest child didn't come, did he?

b. Nǐn chr̄(le) fàn le meiyou?	Have you eaten?
Jǐntyande bàu nín kànle meiyou?	Have you read today's paper?
Nǐ wèn(le) ta syìng shémma le meiyou?	Have you asked him what his name is?

4. Purpose

The basic pattern for expressing purpose was introduced in Lesson 10. The purpose verb follows the verb of the main action. Common variants of this pattern are these:

a. Action Incomplete

Tā dàu Syānggǎng chyu jyāu shū.
Tā dàu Syānggǎng chyu jyāu shū chyu.
Tā dàu Syānggǎng jyāu shū chyu.

He is going to Hongkong to teach.

b. Action Completed

Tā dàu Syānggǎng chyu jyāu shū chyule.
Tà dàu Syānggǎng jyāu shū chyule.

He has gone to Hongkong to teach.

5. 'Other'

a. In the general sense of 'different,' 'other' may be expressed by byéde or byéren:

Wǒ buyàu byéde.   I don't want anything else.
Méiyou byéren.   There's no one else.

b. In the specific sense of 'the other,' it is expressed by the specifier nèi- with appropriate measure:

Búshr tā, shr nèiwei.   It isn't he, it's the other man.
Nèiběn shū hǎu.   The other book is better. (That book is better.)

6. Distinguishing jyòu 'only,' jyòu 'immediately,' and jyou 'then'

In the sense of 'only' or 'immediately,' jyòu is stressed and should retain its tone. In the sense of 'then' it is not stressed and the tone is not marked.

Wǒ jyòu yǒu sānge.   I have only three.
Wǒ jyòu chyù.   I'll go immediately.
Tā jyou hwéi jyā le.   So he returned home.
Tā chrle fàn jyou dzǒule. When he had eaten, he left.

7. Introduction of a first clause by yì, followed by jyou and a second clause, adds an element of immediacy expressed in English by 'as soon as' or 'once':

Tā yì tīngshwō Wáng Syansheng láile, jyou chyu kàn ta.   'As soon as he heard of Mr. Wang's arrival, he went to see him.'

8. Méi-

The adverb méi- is used as the negative for completed aspect of the verb. Since it is usually possible to substitute méiyou for méi- in such situations, we may regard méi- as a contraction for the negated verb méiyou, which corresponds to the negative form of the perfect tense in English— 'have not.'

Méi- occurs also as a contraction for méiyou when the latter is the main verb, as in: Tā méi(you) chyán 'He hasn't any money.'

TRANSLATION OF THE INTRODUCTORY DIALOGUE

Report on the Trip to the City

       Kwéi: Where did you go this morning?

       Lǐ :   We went to New York.

       Kwéi: Did you go into the city?

       Lǐ :   Yes, we went to a friend's home on 110th Street.

 5   Kwéi: Did the friends know you were coming to see them?

       Lǐ :   No, they didn't.

       Kwéi: Were they at home?

       Lǐ :   The husband was home, but the wife had gone out to shop.

       Kwéi: Did you eat at their house?

10   Lǐ :   No, since the wife was not at home, we went to a restaurant to eat.

       Kwéi: Which restaurant did you go to?

       Lǐ :   It was the Shwùn Lǐ Ywán— a Chinese restaurant. It's on 23rd Street.

       Kwéi: Oh, you ate Chinese food, did you?

       Lǐ :   Yes. The Chinese dishes Shwùn Lǐ Ywán makes are uncommonly
15   tasty. They can make all kinds of dishes.

       Kwéi: What dishes did you order?

       Lǐ :   We ordered five dishes in all. But I've forgotten the names of the
               dishes; I only know everything was delicious, and I ate the most.

       Kwéi: Did you go anywhere else?

20   Lǐ :   Nowhere else. After dinner we drove back home.

       Kwéi: I suppose you spent a lot of money?

       Lǐ :   Right, we did spend a lot. So now we can't go anywhere else.

Lesson 12

TIME EXPRESSIONS BEFORE AND AFTER THE VERB

DIALOGUE AND NARRATIVE

1. The Calendar

Syānsheng :   Jyāu nǐmen Jūngwén de Lyóu Syansheng jīntyan bìngle. Jèilǐ-
bài bunéng lái jyāu shū. Syàsyīngchī tsái néng lái, swóyi wǒ
tì ta.

Sywésheng: Lyóu Syansheng bìngle! Shémma bìng? Tā shr shémma shrhou
bìngde?

Syānsheng :   Tā shr dzwótyan yèli bìngde. Tā jèijityan tài lèile, yòu shēngle
yidyǎr chì, swóyi jyou bushūfule.

Sywésheng: Tāde bìng lìhai ma?

Syānsheng :   Búyaujǐn, tāde bìng bùhen lìhai. Tā shwō, tā syīwang nǐmen
dōu dwō nyàn, dwō lyànsyi. Tā bìng hǎule, hwéilai de shrhou,
nǐmende Jūnggwo hwa dōu hěn hǎule, tā jyou bùshēng chìle.

Sywésheng: Hǎu, wǒmen yídìng jèmma dzwò. Báityan, wǎnshang dōu
lyànsyi. Nà Lyóu Ss. yídìng jyou gāusyìng le.

Syānsheng :   Nà hěn hǎu! Wǒ tīngshwō nǐmen kànle yige Jūnggwo dyànyǐngr.
Shr něityan? Dǔng budung?

Sywésheng: Shr chyántyan yèli. Dǔng yidyǎr. Nèi shr yige dǎjàngde dyànyǐngr. Shr 1937nyán syàtyan Jūnggwo gēn Řběn dǎjàngde shr̀-
ching.

Syānsheng :   Jūnggwo gēn Řběn dǎle dwōjyǒude jàng?

Sywésheng: Dǎle hěnjyǒu, dǎle bānyán.

Syānsheng :   Dwèile. Yìnyán jyòu yǒu 365tyān ne! Yìnyán yǒu jǐge ywè ne?
Jūnggwo hwà dzěmma shwō, nǐ jřdau ma?

Sywésheng: Yìnyán yǒu shŕèrge ywè.

Syānsheng :   Yíge ywè yǒu jǐge syīngchī?

Sywésheng: Yíge ywè yǒu sżge-dwō syīngchī.

Syānsheng :   Měige syīngchī yǒu chītyān. Měige ywè yě dōu yǒu sānshrtyān
ma?

Sywésheng: Bùyídìng! Yǒujige ywè shr sānshrtyan, yǒujige ywè shr sān-
shryītyan. Kěshr, měinyande dièrge ywè jyǒu yǒu èrshrba-
tyān.

Syānsheng :   Dièrge ywè Jūnggwo hwà jyàu Èrywè. Dìsānge ywè jyàu Sānywè.
Dìyíge ywè jyàu shémma, nǐ jrdau ma?

Sywésheng: Wǒ syǎng nèi jyàu Yīywè. Měige lǐbaide dìyītyān jyàu Lǐbaiyī,
dièrtyan jyàu Lǐbaièr, dìsāntyan jyàu Lǐbaisān, dwèi ma?

35   Syānsheng :   Dwèile. Kěshr <u>Sunday</u> bújyàu Lǐbaichī, jyàu Lǐbaityān, yě
                     kéyi jyàu Syīngchītyān. Nèityan rénrén dōu budzwò shr̀.
                     Yǒude chyu wár, yǒude chyu dzwò lǐbài.

      Sywésheng: <u>Sunday</u> jyàu Syīngchityān. Nà bùnán!

      Syānsheng :   Swóyi wǒ shwō, Jūnggwo hwà hěn rúngyi sywé.

2. A Friend's Trip Abroad

Wǒ yǒu yige péngyou syìng Sž. Yǒu yityān Sž Syansheng dau Yìdalì chyule.
Tā búshr yíge rén chyùde, shr gēn lyǎngge péngyou yíkwàr chyùde. Tāmen
dzwò chwán dzwòle wǔtyān jyou dàule Fàgwo.

Tāmende hwǒchē shr Lǐbaisān kāide; dièrtyān dzǎushang jyou dàule

5 Lwómǎ le. Dàule Lwómǎ, tāmen jyou dau yige péngyou jyā chyu jù chyule.
Sž Syansheng gēn tade péngyou dzai neige rénde jyāli jùle bànnyán; hòulái
jyou hwéi Měigwó le.

Míngnyán wǒ yě děi dau Yìdalì chyu kànkan. Yǒu rén shwō búbì chyù; hái
yǒu rén shwō byé chyù. Kěshr wǒ shwō wǒmen dōu yīngdāng dau Yìdalì chyu

10 kànkan.

VOCABULARY

Nouns (N)

měi, měi-	SP:	each
		Měi yíge rén yǒu lyǎngjř bǐ. 'Each one has two pens.'
		Wǒ měisāntyān chyù kànkan ta. 'I go every three days to see him.'
-tyān	M:	(for days)
-yè	M:	(for nights)
		Tā dzǒule sāntyān sānyè le. 'He's been gone three days and three nights.'
-nyán	M:	(for years)
		Yìnyán yǒu sānbǎi-lyòushr-wǔtyān. 'There are 365 days in a year.'
-swèi	M:	(for number of years old)
		Lǐ Syansheng sānshr-wǔswèi le. 'Mr. Li is 35 years old.'
		Syǎuhár jǐswèi le? 'How old is the child?'
chyùnyán	MA/N:	last year

jīnnyán	MA/N:	this year
míngnyán	MA/N:	next year

Wǒ chyùnyan hěn máng, jīnnyan yě máng,
kěshr míngnyán jyou búnèmma mángle.
'I was very busy last year and this year too,
but I won't be so busy next year.'

chwūntyān	MA/N:	spring (season)
syàtyān	MA/N:	summer
chyōutyān	MA/N:	autumn, fall
dūngtyān	MA/N:	winter

ywè	month
Yīywè	January
Èrywè	February
shàngywè	last month
syàywè	next month

lǐbài	week
Lǐbaityān	Sunday
Lǐbaisān	Wednesday
shànglǐbài	last week
syàlǐbài	next week

syīngchī	week
Syīngchi-r̀	Sunday
Syīngchisz̀	Thursday
Syīngchilyòu	Saturday
shàngsyīngchī	last week
syàsyīngchī	next week

Jèige ywè shr jǐywè?
'What month is this?'

Yìnyánde dìyíge ywè jyàu Yīywè.
'The first month of a year is called January.'

Yìnyán yígùng yǒu wǔshrèrge syīngchī.
'A year has 52 weeks altogether.'

chyántyān	MA/N:	day before yesterday
hòutyān	MA/N:	day after tomorrow
báityān	MA/N:	daytime, during the day
yèli	MA/N:	nighttime, at night
bànyè	MA/N:	midnight

Tā chyántyān méilái, shwō hòutyān yě bulái.
'He didn't come day before yesterday and
says he's not coming day after tomorrow
either.'

Yǒurén báityān dzwò shr̀, yèli nyàn shū.
'Some people work in the daytime and study
at night.'

Tāmen bànyè tsái hwéi jyā.
'They didn't get home until midnight.'

shŕhou   N: time

                          Shémma shŕhou le?
                          'What time is it?'

                          Shémma shŕhou chŕ fàn?
                          'What time do we eat?'

                          Tā láide shŕhou hěn dzău.
                          'It was very early when he arrived.'

bìng   N: illness, disease
bìngrén   N: sick person, patient

                          Nèige bìngrénde bìng burúngyi hǎu.
                          'That patient's ailment is not easily cured.'

dyànyǐng(r)   N: moving picture, movies (M: -chǎng, a show)
dyànyǐngywàn   PW: movie house, cinema

                          Wǒmen dàu dyànyǐngywàn chyu kàn dyàn-
                          yǐngr, hǎu bubǎu?
                          'How about going to the movie house to see
                          a movie?'

syīwang   N: hope, expectation (see under Verbs)

                          Měiyíge fùchin dwèi ta érdz yǒu hěn dàde
                          syīwang.
                          'Every father has high hopes for his son.'

                          Jèijyàn shŕ jēn méi syīwang le.
                          'This matter has become hopeless.'

Řběn   PW: Japan

                          Adverbs (A)

tyāntyān   A: day by day, daily
nyánnyán   A: year by year, yearly
ywèywè   A: month by month

                          Nèige rén tyāntyān hē chǐshwěi.
                          'That man drinks pop every day.'

                          Tā nyánnyán hwéi Syānggǎng chyù.
                          'He returns to Hongkong every year.'

tsái   A: then and only then, not until

                          Tāmen míngtyan tsái lái (ne).
                          'They're not coming till tomorrow.'

                          Tāmen chyántyan tsái dàude.
                          'They came only day before yesterday.'

-jyǒu   BF: for a long time; long since
hǎujyǒu   A: for a long time
hěnjyǒu   A: for a long time
bùjyǒu   A: before long
dwōjyǒu?   A: how long?

Tā dzǒule hěnjyǒu le.
'He's been gone a long time.'

Verbs (V)

bìng(le)   FV: be ill, be sick (see under Nouns)

Wǒ péngyou dzwótyan bìngle, kěshr jīntyan
   hǎule.
'My friend became ill yesterday, but today
   he has recovered.'

dzwòlǐbài   VO: engage in worship, attend church

Nín jīntyan yàu dzài nǎr dzwòlǐbài?
'Where are you going to church today?'

shēngchì   VO: get angry, be angry

Byé gēn ta shēngchì!
'Don't get angry at him!'

Jèige háidz ài shēngchì.
'This child gets angry easily.'

dǎjàng   VO: make war, fight

Jèigwó gēn nèigwó budǎjàng jyou hǎule.
'When this country and that country no longer
   make war, things will be better.'

syīwang   N/AV: hope; hope that, hope for, expect that

Wǒmen dōu syīwang nǐmen cháng lái.
'We hope you will come often.'

hēi   SV: be black (opposite bái); be dark (opposite
                        lyàng)
bái   SV: be white
lyàng   SV: be light, bright

Chìchē, yǒurén shwō hēide hǎukàn, yǒurén
   shwō báide hǎukàn.
'Some say black cars are better looking,
   some say white.'

Jèijyan wūdz bugòu lyàng.
'This room is not light enough.'

yàujǐn   SV: be important

búyaujǐn   SV: be unimportant; never mind! don't worry!

Jèijyan shr̀ching hěn yàujǐn.
'This affair is quite important.'

Búyaujǐn, wǒmen hòutyan chyù ba!
'Never mind, we'll go day after tomorrow!'

lìhai   SV: be fierce, severe, serious

Tā gēge jēn lìhai, wŏmen dōu pà ta.
'His elder brother is quite violent, we're all afraid of him.'

Tāde bìng hěn lìhai, burúngyi hǎule.
'His malady is very serious; it isn't something from which one recovers easily.'

gāusyìng   SV: be happy, pleased

Wŏ yí kànjyan ta, wŏ jyou bùgāusyìngle.
'As soon as I set eyes on him, I'm unhappy.'

yùnggūng   SV: be studious, work hard (at studies)

Yíge sywésheng hěn yùnggūng, yíge sywésheng búyùnggūng.
'One student is studious, another isn't.'

Expression

rénrén dōu   everyone

Rénrén dōu syīhwan kàn dyànyĭngr.
'Everybody likes to watch the movies.'

Common Sayings

Pàngdz búshr yìkŏu chīde.
A fat man doesn't get that way by one mouthful (applied figuratively to official affluence).

Yì rén nán chèn bǎi rén yì.
One person has a hard time suiting the tastes of a hundred. (You can't please everyone.)

Sāntyān dǎ yú; lyǎngtyān shài wǎng.
Three days of fishing; two days of drying nets.

SENTENCE PATTERNS

A. Time When (with Time Expressions before the Verb)

Wŏmen jīntyan hěn máng.
We are very busy today.

Lǐbailyòu wŏmen budàu sywésyàu lái.
We don't come to school Saturday.

Nèilyǎngge ywè sywésheng hěn gāusyìng.
The students were very happy during those two months.

Nín něityan dzŏu? Wŏ míngtyan dzŏu.
Which day are you leaving? I'm leaving tomorrow.

Wŏmen lyòuge ywè méikàn dyànyĭngrle.
We haven't seen a movie for six months.

The time when or period in which an action or situation occurs or does not occur is indicated by a time expression which stands before the main verb of the sentence (the reverse of the normal English word order). This time

expression functions like a movable adverb, and forms a 'time setting' for
the action or conditions of the verb. The pattern is:

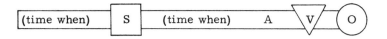

Wǒmen   jīntyan   nyàn Dîshŕèrkè.
'We study Lesson 12 today.'

Jèilyǎngge ywè sywésheng   hěn yùnggūng.
'These last two months the students have worked hard.'

Wǒ   yíge ywè   méikàn dyànyǐngr.
'I didn't see a movie for a month.'

B. Time as Measure of Action

1. Without -le

Wǒ hěn syǎng sywé yidyǎr   I want very much to study a little
Jūnggwo hwà.   Chinese.

Wǒ dǎswan sywé yinyánde   I plan to study a year of Chinese.
Jūngwén.
or Wǒ sywé Jūngwén, dǎswan sywé yinyán.

2. With Verb -le Only

Wǒmen dzai jèr jùle báge ywè.   We lived here for eight months (at one
                                  time).

Wǒ sywéle jige ywède Ȓwén.   I studied a few months of Japanese.
or Wǒ sywé Ȓwén sywéle jige ywè.

3. With Both Verb -le and Sentence le

Tāmen mángle lyòuge ywè le.   They've been busy for six months (up
                                  till now).

Wǒ sywéle lyòuge ywède Jūng-   I've studied six months of Chinese (to
wén le.   date).
or Wǒ sywé Jūngwén, sywéle lyòuge ywè le.

A time expression which measures how long an action or state goes on,
stands after the main verb. It may serve as a modifying element before
the object, or as the object itself. With verb -le only, the statement indicates completion at some time in the past. The use of both verb le and
sentence le indicates only partial completion of the action— up to the time of
the report— but ultimate completion still lies in the future. The patterns are:

Wǒ   sywéle   lyòuge ywède   Jūngwén
'I studied six months of Chinese.' 'I studied Chinese for six months.'

Wǒ   sywéle   lyòuge ywède   Jūngwén le.
'I have studied six months of Chinese so far.'

Wǒ   sywé   Jūngwén,   sywéle   lyòuge ywè le.
'I have studied Chinese for six months, to date.'

C. The shr . . . de Construction

    1. Clauses without Objects:

Tā shr <u>shémma shŕhou</u> láide?	<u>When</u> was it that he came?
Tā shr <u>dzwótyan</u> láide.	He came <u>yesterday</u>.
Tā shr <u>tsúng năr</u> láide?	<u>From where</u> did he come?
Tā shr <u>tsúng Syānggăng</u> láide, búshr <u>tsúng Táiwān</u> láide.	<u>From Hongkong</u>, not <u>from Taiwan</u>.
Tā shr <u>dzěmma</u> láide?	<u>How</u> did he come?
Tā shr <u>dzwò chwán</u> láide ma? Shŕ.	Did he come <u>by boat</u>? Yes.
Tā búshr <u>dzwò fēijī</u> láide ba? Búshr.	He didn't come <u>by plane</u>, did he? No.
Tā shr <u>gēn shéi</u> láide?	<u>With whom</u> did he come?
Tā shr <u>gēn ta fùchin</u> (yikwàr) láide.	He came (together) <u>with his father</u>.

The shr . . . de clausal construction is used to stress various circumstances connected with the action of the verb (such as time, means, purpose, etc.), rather than the action itself. It asks and answers the questions as to when, how, why, from where, with whom, etc. The shr stands
before the particular circumstance to be stressed, and the -de follows
the main verb. Shr is sometimes omitted in a positive sentence.

    2. Clauses with Objects:

Nǐ shr dzài něige fàngwăr chŕde Jūnggwo fàn?	In which restaurant did you eat Chinese food?
Nǐ shr dzài năr sywéde Jūnggwo hwà.	Where was it that you studied Chinese?
Nǐ shr něityan dàude jèr?	On which day did you arrive here?
Nǐ shr něinyán măide chìchē?	In which year did you buy a car?
Chìchē shr něinyán măide?	In which year was the car bought?
Shū shr yī-jyǒu-sż-bānyán syěde.	The book was written in 1948.

When an object is involved, the de normally stands between the verb and its object. A common variant is to transpose the object to a position before shr. (Some native speakers place the de after the object—V-O-de—but this form is not recommended.) The preferred variants are:

a.

        Tā   shr   dzwótyan   láide.
        'He came yesterday.'

        Tā   shr   chyùnyan   mǎide   chìchē.
        'He bought a car last year.'

b.

        Nèige chìchē, tā   shr chyùnyán   mǎide.
        'It was last year that he bought that car.'

3. Incomplete and Completed Action

Tā shr míngtyan chǐng kè, búshr jīntyan.	It is tomorrow that he is inviting guests, not today.
Tā shr shànglibǎi bìngde.	It was last week that he got sick.

The shr . . . de construction is applied only in cases where the action may be regarded as having been completed, while in cases of anticipated or current action, shr is used without de.

NOTES

1. Time Words

Time words have two main functions:

a. As Adverbs (MA) they stand before a verb or other adverb to form a time background for the verb:

Wǒ jīntyan búchyù.	I'm not going today.
Shànglǐbài tā méidzwò shr̀.	He didn't work last week.

b. As Nouns (N) they may function as subject or object of a verb or modify another noun (with -de):

Jīntyan shr Lǐbaisz̀.	Today is Thursday.
Dzwótyande bàu, nín kànle meiyou?	Did you see yesterday's paper?

2. Types of Time-When Expressions (standing before the verb)

a. Time Words and Phrases, such as:

tsúngchyán	formerly	dzwótyan wǎnshang yesterday evening

jīntyan	today	tyāntyān jūngwu	at noon every day
yèli	in the night	Chíywè Sżhàu	July 4th
nèityan	that day	dièrtyan	the second or next day
jèijige ywè	these few months	měilǐbaityān	each Sunday

b. Time Clauses, such as:

syǎude shŕhou	when one is young
sywé Jūnggwo hwà de shŕhou	when one is learning Chinese
tsúng Lǐbaiyī dàu Lǐbaiwǔ	from Monday till Friday
tā láide nèityan	the day that he came

c. Lapse of Time before Negated Verbs

Wǒ sāntyan méichŕ dūngsyi.	I didn't eat a thing for three days.
Sāntyan bùchŕ fàn busyíng.	It won't do not to eat for three days.
Wǒ nèilyǎngnyán méikànjyan tā.	I didn't see him those two years.
Wǒ hěnjyǒu méidau sywésyàu láile.	I haven't come to school for a long time.

3. Types of Time Expressions which Measure Action (standing after the verb)

    a. NU-M(de) and NU-M N(de)

| wǔtyān | five days | sānge lǐbài | three weeks |
| shŕnyánde Jūngwén | ten years of Chinese | yígebàn ywède Řwén | a month and a half of Japanese |

    b. Indefinite Quantities of Time Elements

| Tāmen dzǒule hěnjyǒu le. | They've been gone for a long time. |
| Tā yùbei gūngkè, yùbei hěnjyǒu le. | He spent a lot of time in preparing his lessons. |

4. Quantified Objects and -le

A sentence in which the object is quantified may take verb -le only, or both verb -le and sentence le. Either constitutes a finished statement, but there is a difference in aspect. With verb -le only simple completion at some time in the past is indicated ('once upon a time,' 'once'). With the presence of sentence le, the action of the verb is brought up to the present, marking the completion of a stage in the process ('so far,' 'up till now,' 'to date'), with the prospect that there is another stage ahead. Observe the following sentences:

Wō chŕle wǔwǎn fàn.	I ate five bowls of rice (at that time).
Wǒ chŕ(le) wǔwǎn fàn le.	I have eaten five bowls of rice (so far).
Wǒ dzwòle shŕtyānde hwǒchē.	I rode a train for ten days.
Wǒmen dzài jèr jù(le) lyòuge ywè le.	We've been living here for six months (now).

5. Alternative Position of Object in shr . . . de Pattern

The preferred pattern for the shr . . . de construction involving objects is that introduced in Pattern C2 above. An alternative position for the object is between the verb and -de (V-O de). Compare the two positions in the following sentences:

V<u>de</u> O Nín shr dzai něige   'In which Chinese restaurant did you
             Jūnggwo fàngwárli   eat?'
             chřde fàn?

V-O<u>de</u> Nín shr dzai něige   'In which Chinese restaurant did you
             Jūnggwo fàngwárli   eat?'
             chř fàn de?

6. <u>Previous and Succeeding Time Units</u>

Note in the following table the irregularities in the common terms for the
unit 'before' the present one, and the unit 'after' the present one.

		<u>Year</u>	<u>Week</u>	<u>Month</u>
2nd before	chyántyān	chyánnyán	shàngshanglǐbài	shàngshangywè
1st before	dzwótyān	chyùnyán	shànglǐbài	shàngywè
<u>Current</u>	<u>jīntyān</u>	<u>jīnnyán</u>	<u>jèige lǐbài*</u>	<u>jèige ywè*</u>
1st after	míngtyān	míngnyán	syàlibài	syàywè
2nd after	hòutyān	hòunyán	syàsyalǐbài	syàsyaywè

7. <u>Reduplication of Nouns</u>

This lesson introduces the measures -<u>tyān</u> 'day' and -<u>nyán</u> 'year,' and also
the reduplicated forms <u>tyāntyān</u> 'daily' and <u>nyánnyán</u> 'annually.' Similarly
the noun <u>ywè</u> 'month' may be reduplicated to form <u>ywèywè</u> 'monthly.'

This principle of reduplication is extended to nouns, but limited to monosyllables, e.g.:

    rén 'man'   rénren 'everyone'
    jyā 'family'   jyājya 'every family'

The totalizing adverb <u>dōu</u> follows these reduplicated nouns:

Lǎu Hwáng shr (yi)ge hǎu sywé-   'Hwang is a good student; everyone
sheng; sywésyàuli rénren dōu   in the school likes him.'
syǐhwan ta.

Wǒmen jùde neige dìfang, jyājya   'Where we live every family has a
dōu yǒu chìchē.   car.'

8. <u>Shr</u> . . . de <u>Construction Compared with Nominal Clause</u>

In the <u>shr</u> . . . de construction <u>shr</u> stands immediately before an adverbial
expression which is to be stressed. When it is a nominal rather than an adverbial expression which is to be stressed, <u>shr</u> likewise stands before the
noun, but the resultant pattern is a nominal clause. The two patterns are
illustrated below:

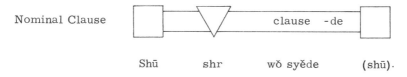

Nominal Clause

        Shū   shr   wǒ syěde   (shū).

_____

* The prefix <u>běn</u>- is also common before <u>lǐbài</u> and <u>ywè</u>.

Adverb

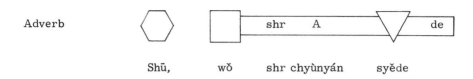

Shū,   wǒ   shr chyùnyán   syěde

9. Use of tsái in Incomplete and Completed Action

Note that the particle ne (optional) ends an expression of incomplete or anticipated action, while -de is required after an expression of completed action:

Incomplete: Tā míngtyan tsái lái ne.   'He isn't coming until tomorrow.'

             Tā chřle fàn tsái dzǒu   'He won't leave until he has eaten.'
             ne.

Completed: Wǒ dzwótyan tsái   'I arrived only yesterday.'
             dàude.

             Tā chřle fàn tsái   'He didn't leave until he had eaten.'
             dzǒude.

10. The seven-day week and names for the days were introduced by Christian
     missionaries. Lǐbaityān or Lǐbai-ř means 'worship day.' Reaction against
     the spreading use of Christian terminology around the turn of the century
     produced a new set of labels in keeping with existing words for month
     (ywè 'moon') and day (ř 'sun'). Syīngchī means 'star period.' Both systems
     were in common use until the Communist regime banned the use of the
     Christian names.

     TRANSLATION OF THE INTRODUCTORY DIALOGUE AND NARRATIVE

     1. The Calendar

     Teacher: Mr. Lyóu, who teaches you Chinese, is sick today. He won't be
               able to come to teach this week. Since he can't come until next
               week, I have come to teach in his place.

     Student : Mr. Lyóu is sick! What's his ailment? When was he taken sick?

   5 Teacher: He fell sick last night. He got too tired the last few days, and he
               lost his temper again, so now he doesn't feel well.

     Student : Is he seriously ill?

     Teacher: It's all right, he isn't seriously ill. He says he hopes you will
               all study harder and practice more. If when he gets better and
  10   comes back, your Chinese has improved, he won't be upset any-
               more.

     Student : Good, we'll certainly do so. We'll practice day and night. Mr.
               Lyóu will certainly be pleased.

     Teacher: Fine! I hear you watched a Chinese movie. What day was it?
  15   Did you understand it?

Student : It was night before last. We understood a little of it. It's a war movie about the fighting between China and Japan in the summer of 1937.

Teacher: How long did China and Japan fight?

20 Student : A long time— eight years!

Teacher: Right. A year has only 365 days. How many months in a year? How do you say it in Chinese?

Student : A year has twelve months.

Teacher: How many weeks in a month?

25 Student : A month has something over four weeks.

Teacher: Each week has seven days. Does each month have thirty days?

Student : Not necessarily. Several of the months have thirty days, others have thirty-one days. But the second month of each year has only twenty-eight days.

30 Teacher: In Chinese the second month is called Èrywè, and the third month is Sānywè. Do you know what the first month is called?

Student : I think it is called Yīywè. The first day of each week is called Lǐbaiyī, the second Lǐbaièr, and the third Lǐbaisān. Right?

Teacher: Correct. But Sunday is not called Lǐbaichī, it is called Lǐbaityān,
35 or Syīngchityān. On that day nobody works. Some go out and play, some go to church.

Student : So Sunday is Syīngchityān. That's not hard!

Teacher: That's why I say that Chinese is quite easy to learn.

2. A Friend's Trip Abroad

I have a friend named Smith. One day Mr. Smith went to Italy. He didn't go alone, he went with a couple of friends. They traveled by boat and in five days reached France. Upon arriving in France, they disembarked and boarded a train.

5 Their train left on Wednesday, and the next morning they arrived in Rome. When they got to Rome they went to live at a friend's home. Mr. Smith and his two friends stayed in that man's home for half a year, and then returned to America.

Next year I must also go to Italy to have a look around. Some say there
10 is no need to go. Others say don't go. But I say everyone ought to visit Italy.

Lesson 13

RELATIVE TIME—CLOCK TIME

DIALOGUE

Work Time, Play Time

Lyóu: Nǐ měityan dzǎushang shémma shrhou chǐlai?

Bái : Wǒ měityan chàbudwō lyòudyǎn jūng chǐlai.

Lyóu: Nǐ jǐdyǎn jūng chr̄ dzǎufàn?

Bái : Lyòudyǎn-sānkè.

5 Lyóu: Shémma shrhou dau chénglǐtou chyu dzwò shr?

Bái : Chǐdyǎn-yíkè dau chìchējàn chyù. Chē chǐdyǎn-sz̀shrwǔ kāi.

Lyóu: Nǐ měityan dzwò shr̀ dzwò jǐge jūngtóu?

Bái : Chíge jūngtóu. Shàngwǔ tsúng bādyǎnbàn dau shŕèrdyǎn; syàwǔ
tsúng yìdyǎn-yíkè dau sz̀dyǎn-sānkè. Yàushr shŕching máng, yǒude
10 shrhou wǔdyǎn jūng tsái hwéi jyā ne.

Lyóu: Wǎnshang búdzwò shr̀ ba?

Bái : Wǎnshang búdzwò shr̀ le. Tsúngchyán wǒ wǎnshang chángchang hái
dzwò lyǎngge jūngtóude shr̀, kěshr syàndzài lǎule, wǎnshang búdzwò
shr̀ le.

15 Lyóu: Nǐ méi shr̀ de shrhou dzwò shémma?

Bái : Yǒude shrhou dzai jyāli kàn shū, yǒude shrhou dau wàitou chyu kàn
péngyou, yě yǒude shrhou dau dyànyǐngrywàn chyu kàn dyànyingr.

Lyóu: Jinyán yǐchyán nǐ búshr yǒu yige Yìndu péngyou ma? Tā hái dzai jer
jù ma?

20 Bái : Tā syàndzài búdzai jer jùle, hwéi Yìndu chyule. Jèige rén hěn yǒuyìsz. Wǒ rènshr ta hǎujinyán le. Yǒu yinyán tā dǎswan dau Jūnggwo
chyu. Tā syě syìn gàusung wo shwō tā yǐchyán méichyùgwo Jūnggwo,
syǎngyau chyu kànkan. Tā dzai chwánshang de shrhou sywéle jijyù
Jūnggwo rén cháng yùngde hwà. Tā yǐjing hwèi shwō sānjyu hwà le:
25 Nín hǎu a? Syèsye. Dzàijyàn. Hòulái tā gēn wǒmen jùle yíge-dwō
lǐbài, yòu sywéle bushǎu Jūnggwo hwà.

Lyóu: Tā méidau Jūnggwo byéde dìfang chyu ma?

Bái : Tā syān dzai Shànghǎi jùle yíge lǐbài, hòulái jyou dzwò hwǒchē dau
Běijīng chyule. Wǒ péngyou chǐng wo gěi ta jyèshau jiwèi Jūnggwo
30 péngyou, yīnwei ta lyán yíwèi dōu burènshr. Wǒ jyou gěi ta jyèshaule
jiwèi.

Lyóu: Tā hwéi Yìndu chyu yǐhòu, gěi nín syě syìn le meiyou?

Bái : Tā cháng gěi wo syě syìn; wǒ yě cháng gěi tā syě syìn. Tā gàusung
wo hěn dwō Yìndude shr̀ching; wǒ yě gàusung tā hěn dwō Jūnggwode

118

35   shr̀ching. Tā hwéi jyā de shrhou, wǒ gēn ta dau chējàn chyu. Tā
         dwèi wo shwō: Wǒ hěn syīhwan Jūnggwo. Wǒ yǐhòu hái yàu hwéi-
         lai.

VOCABULARY

Nouns (N)

tóu, tóu-	SP:	first (in a series)

        Tóu yíge ywè wǒ shémma dōu budǔng.
        'The first month I didn't understand any-
           thing.'

-dyǎn	M:	(for hours on the clock)
-kè	M:	(for quarter-hours)
-fēn	M:	(for minutes)
-tsż	M:	times (occurences, repetitions)
-hwéi	M:	times (occurences, repetitions)
jūng	N:	o'clock

        Sāndyǎn jūng le.
        'It's three o'clock.'

jūngtóu	N:	hour (60 minutes of time)

        Jīntyān wǒ nyánle lyòuge jūngtóude shū.
        'Today I studied for six hours.'

yìhwěr	NU-M:	a little while

        Tā dzai jer dzwòle yìhwěr jyou dzǒule.
        'He sat here a while and then left.'

shàngwǔ	MA/N:	forenoon, morning, A.M.
syàwǔ	MA/N:	afternoon, P.M.

        Shàngwǔ ta dzai sywésyàu nyàn shū, syàwǔ
           dzai jyāli yùbei gūngkè.
        'In the mornings he is at school studying, in
           the afternoon at home preparing his les-
           sons.'

dàjyā	N:	everyone

        Wǒ yàu gěi dàjyā shwō yige gùshr.
        'I want to tell you all a story.'

dżjǐ	N:	self, oneself

        Wǒ shr dżjǐ dzwò fàn.
        'I get my own meals.'

Běijīng	PW:	Peking
Shànghǎi	PW:	Shanghai
Yìndù	PW:	India

Adverbs (A)

dzài   A: then (in the future), not until then

                             Nín míngtyān dzài dzǒu ba.
                             'Don't leave until tomorrow.'

tsái   A: only, just, merely

                             Jèmmasyē ròu tsái sānmáu chyàn!
                             'All this meat for only 30 cents!'

                             Syàndzài tsái shŕdyǎn jūng.
                             'It's now only ten o'clock.'

syān . . .   A . . . A: first . . . and then
   dzài
                             Wǒmen syān chŕ fàn dzài dzǒu ba!
                             'Let's have dinner first and then go.'
                             'Let's have dinner before we go.'

yī . . .   A . . . A: as soon as . . . (then)
  (jyou)

lìkè (jyou)   MA: immediately
yìhwěr (jyou)   MA: shortly, in a moment, in a little while

                             Tā lìkè jyou rènshr le.
                             'He recognized it immediately.'

                             Tāmen yìhwěr jyou lái.
                             'They will be here in a moment.'

yàu(shr)   A/MA: if, in case

                             Yàushr nǐ búyàu, wǒ jyou yàu.
                             'If you don't want it, I do.'

                             Rén yàu méiyou chyán, dzěmma chŕ fàn?
                             'If one has no money, how can one eat?'

yǐchyán   MA: previously, formerly (like tsúngchyán)
yǐhòu   MA: afterward (like hòulái), later

                             Yǐchyán wǒ dzai Jūnggwo, yǐhòu wǒ yàu dau
                                Řběn chyu.
                             'Previously I was in China, later I am going
                                to Japan.'

. . . yǐchyán   MA: before . . . ; . . . ago
. . . de shŕhou MA: while . . . ; at the time when . . .
. . . yǐhòu   MA: after . . .

                             Wǒ hwéi jyā yǐchyan děi kàn yige péngyou.
                             'Before I go home, I must see a friend.'

                             Wǒ dzai Syānggǎng de shrhou, mǎile yìjāng
                                jwōdz.
                             'When I was in Hongkong, I bought a table.'

                             Wǒ kànle ta yǐhòu jyou dzwò fēijī hwéilai.
                             'After I've seen him, I'll come back by plane.'

tsúnglái	MA:	heretofore, in the past (with negative verb)
jyānglái	MA:	in the future, later on, someday

Wǒ tsúnglái búhwèi dzwò fàn, jyānglái děi
gēn tàitai sywéyisywé.
'I have never learned to cook; someday I
must learn how from my wife.'

Verbs (V)

chà	FV:	differ by, lack; (with clock time) be before
chàbudwō	MA:	almost, it doesn't lack much of . . .
chàyidyǎr	MA:	almost, it lacks a little of . . .
chàyidyǎr méi-V	EX:	barely escape V-ing

Hái chà yíkwài chyán.
'It still lacks a dollar.'

Sāndyǎn chà yíkè.
'It's a quarter before three.'

Nèige fángdz, wǒ chàyidyǎr méimàigei ta.
'I just missed selling him the house.'

gwò	FV:	pass, exceed; cross over

Wǒ gwò lyǎngtyān dzài chyù.
'I'll go again after a couple of days.'

Wǔdyǎn gwò shŕfēn le.
'It's ten past five.'

chǐlai	FV:	arise, get up
rènshr	FV:	know, recognize, be acquainted with

Wǒ tsúngchyán búrènshr ta, syàndzài rènshr
le.
'Formerly I wasn't acquainted with him,
now I have come to know him.'

kàn	FV:	consider, regard, think

Nín kàn jeige gāngbǐ syíng busying?
'Do you think this pen will do?'

jyàn	FV:	meet, see, interview (more formal than kàn)
(gěi) . . . jyèshau	FV:	introduce . . . (to)

Tā gěi wo jyèshau yige péngyou.
'He introduced me to a friend.'

Wǒ gěi dàjyā jyèshau yìběn shū.
'Let me show you a book.'

syōusyi	FV:	rest

Wǒmen syōusyi yìhwěr dzài kàn shū.
'We'll rest a while before studying.'

kěnéng	AV/SV:	may, be possible, maybe

Tā kěnéng méijyàngwo nǐ.
'Maybe he hasn't met you.'

Nà hěn kěnéng!
'That's quite possible!'

Particle (P)

-gwò   BF: (verb ending indicating experience; see Note 3)

Nǐ chígwo dżsyíngchē méiyou? Méichígwo.
'Have you ever ridden a bicycle?' 'No!'

Nín chřgwo fàn le ma? Hái méi ne.
'Have you eaten?' 'Not yet.'

Wǒ tsúnglái méiyùnggwo kwàidz.
'I have never used chopsticks before.'

Common Sayings

Note the Chinese pattern, especially common in short proverbial sayings, for expressing two alternatives and implying that if the first alternative is (not) true, then the second will (not) be true.

Bùjīng yíshř, bujǎng yíjř.	If you don't have experience, you don't grow in knowledge.
Yìjř búdùng, bǎijř buyáu.	If one branch doesn't move, the many branches won't stir. (If someone doesn't take a lead, no one will do anything.)

Other sayings bring to mind English counterparts:

Gwò ěr jř yán bukětīng.	Rumors (words which pass the ear) shouldn't be listened to.
Gwò hé chāi chyáu.	To tear up the bridge after crossing the stream.
Yìhwéi shēng; èrhwéi shú.	The first time he is 'green'; the second time he is 'ripe.' (He learns by experience.)

SENTENCE PATTERNS

A. Time When by the Clock

Questions: Shémma shŕhou (le)?   What time is it?
Jǐdyan jūng (le)?

Answers : yìdyǎn jūng   1:00 o'clock
yìdyǎn (gwò) shŕfēn   10 minutes past 1:00
yìdyǎn-shŕwǔfēn   15 minutes past 1:00
(yìdyǎn-yíkè)   (a quarter past 1:00)
yìdyǎn-èrshrfēn   1:20
yìdyǎn-sānshrfēn   1:30
(yìdyǎnbàn)   (half past 1:00)

yìdyǎn-sźshrfēn	1:40
yìdyǎn-sźshr-wǔfen	1:45
(yìdyǎn-sānkè)	(three quarters past 1:00)
(lyǎngdyǎn chà yíkè)	(a quarter to 2:00)
(chà yíkè lyǎngdyǎn)	(a quarter to 2:00)
lyǎngdyǎn-dwō jūng	after 2:00 o'clock
sźwǔdyǎn jūng	4 or 5 o'clock
shŕyī-èrdyǎn jūng	11 or 12 o'clock

The three commonest units for designating and measuring time by the clock are: -dyǎn 'hour,' -kè 'quarter-hour,' and -fēn 'minute.' These measures are preceded by appropriate numbers, and followed by the noun jūng (except where context permits its omission).

B. Amounts of Clock Time

Questions:	Shū, kànle dwōshau shŕhou (le)?	How long have (you) been reading?
	Shū, kànle jǐge jūngtóu (le)?	How many hours have (you) been reading?
Answers :	bànge jūngtóu	half an hour
	yíge jūngtóu	one hour
	yígedwō jūngtóu	an hour and more
	yígebàn jūngtóu	an hour and a half
	lyǎngge jūngtóu	two hours
	sźwǔge jūngtóu	four or five hours
	shŕjige jūngtóu	from 11 to 19 hours
	wǔfen jūng	five minutes
	shŕwǔfen jūng	15 minutes
	(yíkè jūng)	(a quarter of an hour)
	sźshrwǔfen jūng	45 minutes
	(sānke jūng)	(three quarters of an hour)
	yíge jūngtóu líng yíkè	an hour and a quarter
	sānge jūngtóu líng wǔfēn	three hours and 5 minutes
	chà shŕfen jūng yíge jūngtóu	an hour lacking 10 minutes

The noun jūng 'hour,' preceded by the M -dyǎn, may denote quantity of time as well as a point in time; the noun jūngtóu 'hour,' preceded by the M -gè, is often substituted when a quantity of time is referred to.

C. Expressions of Relative Time

1. General Expressions of Relative Time

Wǒ yǐchyán méichŕgwo Jūnggwo fàn. Yǐhòu wǒ yàu cháng chŕ.
'I have never eaten Chinese food before. I'm going to eat it often after this.'

Tā tsúngchyán jyāu shū. Tā gàusung wǒ tā jyānglái bujyāu shū le.
'In the past he's taught school. He tells me he is not going to teach in the future.'

When yǐchyán and yǐhòu are used as movable adverbs they indicate general 'time when.' In this use they are often interchangeable with tsúng-

chyán and hòulái introduced in Lesson 6 and behave like other movable
adverbs.

2. Specific Expressions of Relative Time

Wǒ shàngkè yǐchyán děi yùbei gūngkè.
'I must prepare the lesson before I go to class.'

Wǒ shàngkè de shŕhou bunéng shwō Yīngwén.
'I cannot use English while I'm in class.'

Wǒ syàkè yǐhòu děi syōusyi jifen jūng.
'I have to rest a few minutes after class.'

Wǒ sānnyán yǐchyán budzài jèr.
'I wasn't here three years ago.'

The terms yǐchyán 'before,' yǐhòu 'after,' and -de shŕhou 'while,' may be
placed immediately after a word, phrase, or clause to form a specific
time-when expression. The entire expression functions as a movable adverb.

D. Compound Sentences and jyou 'then'

1. Yàushr nǐ chyù, wǒ jyou búbì chyùle.
'If you go, then I won't need to go.'

Nǐ (yàushr) búchyù, wǒ jyou děi chyùle.
'If you don't go, then I'll have to go.'

Wǒ (yàushr) dzài chŕ, jyou bushūfule.
'If I eat more, I'll feel uncomfortable.'

2. Wǒmen chŕle fàn, jyou dzǒu.
'After we've eaten we'll leave.'

Gwòle syīnnyán, wǒmen jyou búshàngkè le.
'After the New Year, we'll no longer be going to class.'

Wǒmen dzai jyēshang dzǒule yìhwěr jyou hwéi jyā le.
'Having taken a stroll up the street we returned home.'

3. Yì gěi syǎuhár táng chŕ, tā jyou gāusyìngle.
'As soon as you give a child candy to eat, he's happy.'

Hǎidz yí dàle, jyou busyīhwan nyàn shū le.
'As soon as a child grows up, he doesn't like to study.'

Wǒ yì gēn ta shwō, tā jyou shēng chì le.
'As soon as I spoke to him, he got angry.'

Tā gāng yì hwéilai, jyou yàu kàn ta fùchin.
'Just as soon as he returns, he wants to see his father.'

Three types of conditioning phrases and clauses appear in the compound
sentences given above. Unlike English, these conditioning elements precede the main statements, with the unstressed jyou 'then' standing between
the two clauses.

1. Supposition ('if,' 'in case . . . ,' 'then') is expressed by the pattern: yàushr . . . jyou. Unlike English, jyou is usually expressed, whereas yàushr

is more often omitted. The pattern is:

Yàushr nǐ   chyǔ,   wǒ   jyou   búchyùle.

2. Another type of conditioning clause is formed by a verb with verb le only (with or without an object). The pattern is:

$$S \quad V \quad le \quad O, \quad jyou \ldots$$

Wǒmen chřle fàn,   jyou dzǒu.
'When we have eaten, we'll leave.'

3. The Chinese equivalent for the more definite expression 'as soon as' is formed by placing yì immediately before the verb of the dependent clause. The pattern is:

$$S \quad yì \quad V \quad O, \quad jyou \ldots$$

Syǎuhár yì chř táng jyou gāusyìng le.
'Children are happy, as soon as they eat candy.'

NOTES

1. Inquiring the Year, Month, Week, Day and Hour

In asking and giving this information, as in asking and giving prices (see Lesson 5), no verb is necessary, although shř is sometimes used. The particle of completion (le) is sometimes attached to both question and re-ply:

Shémma shŕhou(le)?   What time is it?
  Wǔdyǎnbàn(le).   5:30.
Syàndzài jǐdyǎn jūng(le)?   What time is it now? A quarter past
  Sāndyǎn-yikè (le).   three.
Jīntyan(shr) lǐbaijǐ(le)?   What day of the week is today?
  Lǐbaièr(le).   Tuesday.
(Shr) jǐhàu(le)? Èrshrbá-   What day of the month? The 28th.
  hàu(le).
Jīnnyán shr Yī-jyǒu-lyòu-   This year is 1965.
  wǔnyán(le).

2. Sequence of Time Units

In a series of time units such as years, months, weeks, days, divisions of the day, and time by the clock, the large units precede the smaller ones.

jīntyan syàwǔ sżdyǎn jūng   4 o'clock this afternoon
měi Lǐbaityān shàngwǔ   11 o'clock every Sunday morning
  shŕyīdyǎn jūng

chyùnyán Chíywè sżhàu   8:30 P.M. the 4th of July last year
wǎnshang bādyǎnbàn

3. Experiential Verb Ending -gwò

When it is desired to indicate that an action or condition has or has not ever been experienced, the verb ending -gwò (lit. 'cross over') is attached to either positive or negated verbs:

Nín dzwògwo fēijī meiyou? Méidzwògwo.
'Have you ever been on a plane?' 'No, I never have.'

Nín kàngwo Jūnggwo bàu ma? Méikàngwo, wǒde Jūngwén busyíng.
'Have you ever read a Chinese newspaper?' 'No, I haven't, my Chinese is insufficient.'

This ending often indicates little more than what is indicated by -le. In this use it may be considered as an integral part of the verb, and the resulting combination behaves with respect to -le like any other verb. Or it may take the place of -le in some situations:

Nǐ dàu sywésyàu chyùle meiyou? Chyùgwole.
'Have you been to the school?' 'Yes, I have.'

Nín chrgwo fàn le ma? Chrgwole, syèsye.
'Have you eaten?' 'Yes, I have, thank you.'

4. The Ordinal Specifiers dì- and tóu- Contrasted

The ordinal specifier dì- indicates any simple unit of a series (as dìyī 'number one,' dìyīkè 'the first lesson,' dìchītyān 'the seventh day,' etc.). The ordinal specifier tóu-, on the other hand, indicates the first unit or group of a series (as tóuyíge 'the first one,' tóulyǎngběn 'the first two books,' tóuwǔnyán 'the first five years,' etc.).

5. The Measures -tsż and -hwéi

a. Specific occurrence follows the time-when pattern, with the measures -tsż or -hwéi preceded by the appropriate SP-NU:

Wǒ tóuyítsż kànjyan nín shr dzài wǒmen sywésyàu.
'The first time I saw you was in our school.'

Tā jèi jihwéi lái shr kāi chìchē láide.
'These few times that he came, it was by car.'

Wǒ lyǎngtsż chyù kàn ta, tā dōu méidzài jyā.
'The two times I went to see him, he wasn't home.'

b. Repeated occurrence follows the pattern for amount of time. The measures -hwéi and -tsż may be preceded by an actual number or by an expression of indefinite number:

Wǒ chyùle hǎujǐhwéi.
'I went a good many times.'

Wǒ chrle bushǎutsżde Jūnggwo fàn.
'I ate Chinese food quite a few times.'

When the object is a person or place, the frequency expression stands after the object:

Wǒ gàusung ta hěndwōtsż le.
'I have told him a great many times already.'

Řběn, tā chyùgwo háujǐhwéi le.
'He has already been to Japan many times.'

6. Negated Verbs before yǐchyán

The expression chř fàn yǐchyán is interchangeable with méichr fàn yǐchyán. Both should be translated in the positive sense as 'before dinner.' This holds true for many clauses used as time referents.

Tā dàu wàigwo chyù yǐchyán . . .⎫
Tā méidàu wàigwo chyù yǐ- ⎬ Before he went abroad . . .
  chyán . . .   ⎭

Wǒ hwéi jyā yǐchyán . . . ⎫
Wǒ méihwéi jyā yǐchyán . . .⎬ Before he returned home . . .

Sywésheng shàngkè yǐchyán . . .⎫
Sywésheng méishàngkè yǐ-   ⎬ Before the students went to class . . .
  chyán . . .   ⎭

7. What Time?

In inquiring about time, two situations need to be distinguished:

a. 'What time is it (now, by the clock)?' The Chinese recognize the fact that clock time changes from moment to moment, a situation which calls for the use of the particle le. Hence the correct inquiry is: (Syàndzài) shémma shŕhou le?

b. 'What time is set for the occurrence?' (meeting, dinner, etc.) is concerned with a fixed time, so does not call for the particle le. E.g.: Shémma shŕhou chř fàn?

8. Jyou, tsái, and dzài after Time Expressions

All three are used after a time expression in the sense of 'then,' 'at that time.' In this use all three are unstressed. But the following distinctions are maintained:

a. Tā míngtyan jyou dzǒu implies that he is leaving sooner than expected—in fact, as early as tomorrow. In English this is often indicated by stressing 'tomorrow.'

b. Tā míngtyan tsái dzǒu implies that he is going later than expected, 'not until tomorrow.'

c. Nǐ míngtyan dzài dzǒu ba! has the same implication as in the case of tsái, but with the difference that tsái is used only in declarative sentences, while dzài is used only in imperative sentences. ('Don't go before tomorrow.')

Note that all three also have stressed forms with slightly different meanings:

jyòu   immediately (see Lesson 11)
dzài   again (see Lesson 5)
tsái   just, only

9. Chàyidyăr is used adverbially to indicate that an act in prospect lacks little
    of actually occurring. However, whether it is followed by a positive verb
    or a negative verb, the resultant meaning is the same— the act did not occur.

> Nèijyan shr̀, wǒ chàyidyăr
> gàusung ta le.
>
> Nèijyan shr̀, wǒ chàyidyăr
> méigàusung ta.

I almost told him about it.

10. Chàbudwō is likewise used adverbially to indicate that an act in process
    lacks little of accomplishment. It is used only with positive verbs.

Tā chàbudwō hăule.	He is almost well.
Tā hwāle chàbudwō shŕkwai chyán le.	He has spent almost ten dollars.
Chàbudwō lyănggdyăn jūng le.	It's almost two o'clock.

11. Chà followed by a time measure may stand either before or after the hour:

Yìdyăn chà yíkè le.	It's a quarter to one.
Chà wŭfen jūng sāndyăn le.	It lacks five minutes of three o'clock.

TRANSLATION OF THE INTRODUCTORY DIALOGUE

Work Time, Play Time

Lyóu : What time do you get up every morning?

Bái : I get up about six o'clock every day.

Lyóu : At what time do you eat breakfast?

Bái : Six forty-five.

5 Lyóu : What time do you go to town?

Bái : I go to the station at seven fifteen. The train leaves at seven forty-
         five.

Lyóu : How many hours a day do you work?

Bái : Seven hours. In the forenoon, from 8:30 to 12:00; in the afternoon,
10   from 1:15 to 4:45. If business is heavy, sometimes I don't go home
         until after five o'clock.

Lyóu : You don't work evenings, do you?

Bái : I no longer work evenings. I often used to put in a couple of hours
         in the evening, but I'm getting old and can't work evenings anymore.

15 Lyóu : What do you do in your free time?

Bái : Sometimes I read at home, sometimes I go out and visit with friends,
         and sometimes I even go to a movie house and watch a film.

Lyóu: Didn't you have an Indian friend several years ago? Is he still living here?

20 Bái : He's no longer living here. He's gone back to India. That man is very interesting. I've known him for many years. One year he was thinking of going to China. He wrote me saying he had never been to China (before) and was thinking of visiting here. While on shipboard, he learned a few phrases commonly used by Chinese. He could already say three phrases: 'How do you do?' 'Thank you,' and 'Goodbye.' After landing, he stayed with us for over a week and learned quite a lot of Chinese.

25

Lyóu: Didn't he go anywhere else in China?

Bái : First he stayed a week in Shanghai, and then went by rail to Peking. My friend asked me to introduce him to a few Chinese friends because he didn't know a soul. So I introduced him to a few people.

30

Lyóu: Did he write to you after he got back to India?

Bái : He writes to me often, and I write to him frequently. He tells me a lot about Indian affairs, and I tell him a lot about happenings in China. When he left for home, I saw him to the railway station. He said to me: I like China very much. I'm coming back again.

35

Lesson 14

EXPRESSION OF MANNER

DIALOGUE

<u>A Good Story</u>

Yáng : (pǎuje) Eī, Lǎu Wú, nǐ dzǒu lù dzěmma dzǒude jèmma kwài a?
Gāngtsái wǒ dzai lùshang dzǒuje kànjyan nǐ hái dzai ménwàitou
jànje ne, yòu wàng dzwǒ kàn, yòu wàng yòu kàn, bùjrdàu wàng
němma dzǒu. Hòulái nǐ wàng jèmma dzǒu, dzǒude fēichàng kwài.
5 Wǒ jyàu ni, nǐ yě méitīngjyàn. Wǒ jyou kwàikwāide wàng chyán pǎu,
syǎng gēn ni yíkwàr dàu chénglǐtou chyu. Nǐ chyu dzwò shémma
chyu?

Wú : Méi shemma shr̀. Nǐ láile, wǒmen jyou dau chágwǎr chyu hē bēi
chá, hǎu buhǎu?

10 Yáng : Hǎujíle! Wǒ ye méi shr̀. Chyántou yǒu yige syīnkāide syǎu
chágwǎr. Tyāntyān yǒu rén dau ner chyu shwō syàuhwar. Jēn
yǒuyìsz! Nǐ kàn dau nèr chyu, hǎu buhau?

(Tāmen lyǎngge rén dzǒuje dzǒuje jyou dàule neige syǎu chágwǎr
le. Ménwàitou yǒu sz̀-wǔjāng jwōdz, yǒu sye rén dzai ner dzwòje
15 tán hwà ne. Tāmen lyǎngge rén dàude shrhou, dàjyā dōu jèngdzai
syàuje ne. Bùjrdàu wèishemma. Lǎu Yáng jyou wèn:)

Yáng : Nǐmen dàjyā dōu syàu shémma ne? Shr Hwáng Sān shwō syàuhwar
ne ba.

(Dzai jwōdz ner dzwòje de yíge rén shwō:)

20 Rén : Kěbushr̀ ma! Nǐmen tīngting jèige syàuhwar. Lǎu Hwáng, nǐ dzài
shwō yitsz̀ gěi tāmen lyǎngge rén tīngting.

Hwáng: Shr jèmma hwéi shr̀: Wǒmen sywésyàude syānsheng chángchang
dzai wǎnshang kāi hwèi; yǒude shrhou kāidau bànyè. Kāi hwèi yǐhòu
hái děi hē yidyǎr chá, chr̄ yidyǎr dyǎnsyin; yèli yìdyǎn-bàn tsái
25 hwéi jyā. Yǒu yiwèi Tsáu Syansheng chàbudwō měilǐbài dōu yàu yǒu
jemma jitsz̀ hwéi jyā hwéide hěn wǎn. Sānge lǐbài yǐchyán kāile
sāntsz̀ hwèi, dōu sànde hěn wǎn. Tsáu Taitai dà bugāusyìng.
Lyǎngge lǐbài yǐchyán yòu yǒu sz̀ge wǎnshang kāi hwèi dōu sànde
hěn wǎn; tàitai gèng bugāusyìng le. Shànglǐbài kāile wǔtsz̀ hwèi,
30 dōu gwòle bànyè tsái sàn hwèi. Jèihwéi Tsáu Syansheng hwéi jyā,
yì kāi mén jyou kànjyan jwōdzshang yǒu yifēng syìn. Tā kànle
yikàn, syān bumíngbai shr dzěmma hwéi shr̀, syìnshangde hwà yě
búdà dǔng. Yòu kànle yikàn, mànmārde jyou míngbai le: shr ta
tàitai syěde. Syìnshang shwō:

35 Chyántyan yèli nǐ shr dzwótyan hwéilaide. Dzwótyan yèli nǐ shr
jīntyan hwéilaide. Yàushr jīntyan wǎnshang nǐ hái shr míngtyan

hwéi jyā, nǐ yàu jīdau nǐ tàitai yǐjing hwéi ta mǔchinde jyā chyule . . .

(Tā shwō dau jèr, dàjyā you dōu syàule.)

VOCABULARY

Nouns (N)

mén	door
chwānghu	window
lù	road, path; way, route (M:-tyáu)

Nèityáu lù dzwèi hǎudzǒu.
'That road is the easiest to travel by.'

dēng — lamp, light

Nǐ neige dēng gòu lyàng ma?
'Is your lamp bright enough?'

yánsè, yánsher — color

Nǐnde chìchē shr shémma yánsè? Shr hēide.
'What color is your car?' 'It's black.'

jyātíng — family, home

Tāmende jyātíng shr hěn kwàilède yige jyātíng.
'Their home is a very happy home.'

syàuhwar — joke, humorous story

Tā hěn hwèi shwō syàuhwar.
'He's good at telling jokes.'

syǎushwōr — novel

Yǒuren ài kàn syǎushwōr.
'Some people love to read novels.'

hwèi — meeting, gathering (of people)

Adverbs (A)

gèng — A: more, still more, even SV-er

Tā gēge gèng gāu.
'His elder brother is even taller.'

fēicháng — A: unusually, extraordinarily

Nèijang hwàr fēicháng hǎu.
'That painting is extraordinarily good.'

jèng(dzai) — MA: just in the midst of

Tāmen jèngdzai chī fàn ne.
'They are right in the midst of eating.'

Tāmen jèng tán hwà ne.
'They're just in the midst of talking together.'

dāngrán   MA: of course, naturally

Dāngrán Jūnggwo fàn hǎuchř.
'Of course, Chinese food is delicious.'

yòu . . . yòu   both . . . and; (with negative) neither . . . nor
méi . . . méi   neither . . . nor

Jèige gāngbǐ yòu hǎuyùng yòu pyányi.
'This pen is both easy to use and inexpensive.'

Nèijyān wūdz yòu méi mén, yòu méi chwānghu.
'That room has neither door nor windows.'

kwàikwārde   A: quickly, hurry up and . . .
mànmārde   A: slowly
hǎuhāurde   A: properly, nicely

Kwàikwārde shwō!
'Hurry up and say it!'

Mànmārde dzwò!
'Do it slowly!'

Byé chǎule! Hǎuhāurde nyàn shū ba!
'Stop your noise and tend to your studying!'

shr . . . (hái)shr   (see Sentence Pattern C)

Verbs (V)

kāi   FV: open
kāikai   FV: open (up)
dǎkai   FV: open (containers, boxes, etc.)
kāi hwèi   VO: open a meeting, hold a meeting

gwān   FV: close (doors, windows)
gwānshang   FV: close (up)
sàn hwèi   VO: close a meeting, dismiss

Chǐng gwānshang mén, kāikai chwānghu.
'Please close the door and open the window.'

Chǐng nǐmen dōu héshang shū.
'Please all close your books.'

Wǒmen dǎswan bādyǎn jūng kāi hwèi, shř-
dyǎn sàn hwèi.
'We plan to open the meeting at eight and
close at ten.'

Byé kāi dēng!
'Don't turn on the light.'

jàn(je)   FV: stand

                          Chǐng nǐ dzai jèr jàn yìhwěr.
                          'Please stand here a few minutes.'

                          Byé dzai wàitou jànje!
                          'Don't stand outside!'

děng(je)   FV: wait, wait for

                          Wǒmen dzai pùdzli děng ta ba!
                          'Let's wait for him in the store!'

                          Búbì děngje!
                          'It isn't necessary to wait!'

                          Chǐng děng yìděng, wǒ yìhwěr jyou hwéilai.
                          'Please wait a minute; I'll be right back!'

pǎu   FV: run
kū   FV: cry, cry about
syàu   FV: laugh, smile; laugh at

                          Syǎuhár dōu ài pǎu.
                          'Children like to run.'

                          Syǎuhár kūle bàntyān.
                          'The child cried for a long time.'

                          Tā kū shémma ne?
                          'What's he crying about?'

                          Tāmen lìkè jyou syàule.
                          'They immediately started to laugh.'

syàuhwa   FV: joke, humorous anecdote; laugh at

                          Byé syàuhwa ta!
                          'Don't laugh at him!'

kwài   SV: be quick, fast
màn   SV: be slow

                          Chìchē kāide hěn kwài.
                          'The car was driven rapidly.'

                          Fēijī kwài; chwán màn.
                          'Planes are fast, ships are slow.'

píngcháng   SV/A: be ordinary, common; ordinarily
tèbyé   SV/A: be special; distinctive; specially

                          Tā píngcháng bùhē jyǒu.
                          'Ordinarily he doesn't drink.'

                          Nèiwei syānsheng hěn tèbyé.
                          'That gentleman is quite different.'

kwàilè   N/SV: happiness; be happy, joyful

                          Tāde jyātíng tèbyé kwàilè.
                          'His home is an especially happy one.'

héshr̀	SV: be suitable, fitting; fit (as clothes)

Tā chwānde yīshang butài héshr̀.
'The clothes he wears do not quite fit.'

Tā dzwòde jèige shŕching dzwèi héshr̀.
'The work he is doing is well suited to him.'

chīngchu	SV: be clear, distinct

Tā syě dz̀, syěde buchīngchu.
'He doesn't write clearly.'

húng	SV: be red
hwáng	SV: be yellow
lán	SV: be blue
lyù	SV: be green

Tā syǐhwan húngde chìchē, wǒ syǐhwan
  lyùde. Nǐ syǐhwan shémma yánsede?
'He likes a red car, I like a green one.
  What color car do you like?'

kěsyàu	SV: be laughable, amusing

Jèijyan shr̀ching jēn kěsyàu.
'The incident was most amusing.'

Particles (P)

-je	(verb ending, indicating continuance; see Note 4)
-jíle	(SV ending, indicating an exaggerated degree)

Jèige tsài hǎuchr̄jíle!
'This dish is extremely delicious.'

Tāmende péngyou dwōjíle.
'They have a very very large number of
  friends.'

-de	(verb ending, indicating manner; see Note 1)

Expressions

Kěbushr̀ ma!	Why, of course! Now isn't that the truth!
Dzěmma hwéi shr̀?	How come? How did this happen?
(Shr̄) jèmma hwéi shr̀:	It happened this way:
(Shr̄) nèmma hwéi shr̀.	That's the way it was.
Méi nèmma hwéi shr̀!	There's no such thing!
Yílù píngān!	A pleasant journey (to you)! (Peace all the way!)

<u>Common Sayings</u>

Jèi shān wàngje, nèi shān gāu.	Looking from this mountain, that mountain seems higher.
Gwàje yángtóu, mài gǒu ròu.	Hanging out a sheep's head, he sells dog meat. (He is deceptive.)

SENTENCE PATTERNS

A. <u>Manner and Degree of an Action or Condition</u>

1. When no object is expressed:

Syānsheng jyāude hǎu.	The teacher teaches well.
Nèige sywésheng sywéde dzwèi kwài.	That student learns the fastest.
Nín láide hěn dzǎu.	You have come very early.
Tā syěde jēn bútswo.	He writes quite well.
Tā chàngde hǎujíle.	He sings extremely well.
Tā érdzde bìng hǎude hěn màn.	His son is recovering very slowly.

To describe the manner or degree of an action or condition, the verb is followed by the particle -de, forming a noun clause, which then stands as subject to a stative verb or other descriptive expression, thus:

Tā   shwōde   hěn chīngchu.
'He speaks very clearly.'

2. When the verb of action has an object, either (a) the object alone, or (b) the entire action (S-V-O) may be pre-stated as a topic:

Jèige dz̀,   tā syěde   hěn chīngchu.
'This character, he has written very clearly.'

Chìchē,   tā kāide   tài kwài.
'He drives too fast.'

b.

Tā syě Jūnggwo dz̀,   syěde   hěn chīngchu.
'He writes Chinese characters very clearly.'

Tā kāi chìchē,   kāide   tài hwài.
'In driving, he drives too fast.'

B. <u>Commands and Requests</u> (with kwài and SV-yidyǎr)

    1. Kwài shwō!   Hurry up and say it!

       Kwài lái!   Come here quickly!

       Kwài gàusung wo!   Tell me quickly!

       Kwài shàngkè chyu!   Hurry to class!

       Kwài lái chr̄ fàn!   Come quickly to dinner!

The adverb <u>kwài</u> may stand before a verb (object) to express an urgent command. In this situation <u>kwài</u> tends to mean 'hurry up and do' something. In the examples which follow, the meaning of SV-<u>yidyǎr</u> is to do something in a certain manner.

    2. a. Màn yidyǎr shwō!   Speak a little slower!

         Dzǎu yidyǎr lái!   Come earlier!

         Kwài yidyǎr kāi!   Drive a little faster!

         Wǎn yidyǎr syàkè ba!   Let's end class a little later!

The expression SV-<u>yidyǎr</u> (with <u>kwài</u> and certain other SV) may stand before the main verb as an adverbial modifier to indicate request or milder command.

       b. Shwō kwài yidyǎr!   Say it a little faster!

         Dzǒu màn yidyǎr!   Walk a bit slower!

         Syě dà yidyǎr!   Write it a little bigger!

         Shwō chǐngchu yidyǎr!   Speak a little clearer!

         Lái dzǎu yidyǎr.   Come a bit earlier!

The expression SV-<u>yidyǎr</u> may also stand after the main verb, without change in the meaning of the SV. But some main verbs will not permit both positions.

C. <u>Alternative Choice Questions</u> with shr

    1. Nǐ shr chyù, shr búchyù?   Are you going or not?
       Tā shr jyāu Fàwén, shr jyāu   Does he teach French or German?
         Déwén?

    2. Shr nǐ chyù, shr wǒ chyù?   Are you going, or am I?
       Shr jīntyan chyù, shr   Is it today or tomorrow that (you)
         míngtyan chyù?   are going?
       Shr tā gěi nǐ de, shr nǐ gěi   Did he give it to you, or did you give
         tā de?   it to him?

    3. Shr báityan chyù, háishr yèli   (Are you) going in the daytime or at
        chyù (ne)?   night?
       Shr dzwò hwǒchē kwài, háishr   Is it faster to go by train or to drive
         kāi chìchē kwài (ne)?   (a car)?
       Nǐ shr dzwò chwán chyùde,   Did you go by boat or by plane?
         háishr dzwò fēiji chyùde.

This is an elaboration of the choice-type question introduced in Lesson 1, where the choice was between the positive and negative forms of the same verb. Other alternatives introduced above are: a choice between different subjects, different verbs and different objects; also between adverbial modifiers, and between modifying clauses. Variations in the pattern include:

shr . . . shr
shr . . . háishr
háishr . . . háishr
(but not háishr . . . shr).

D. Interrogative Uses of Sentence Particle ne?

1. In Question-Word Questions:

Nín wèishémma buchyù ne?   And why aren't you going?

Wǒ dzěmma néng chyù ne?   But, how can I go?

Wàng němma dzǒu ne?   Well, which way do we go?

Shéi jyèshau tā ne?   And who will introduce him?

Tā shwō shémma ne?   Well, what did he say?

The final particle ne at the end of a question-type question gives an effect similar to that made in English by introducing the question with 'and,' 'but,' or 'well.'

2. In Abbreviated Questions:

Tā hwèi chàng gēer.   Nín ne?
'He knows how to sing.'   'Well, how about you?'

Tsúngchyán wǒ dzài Jūnggwo.   Syàndzài ne?
'Formerly I was in China.'   'And now?'

Nèijang jwōdz tài syǎu?   Jèijang ne?
'That table is too small.'   'Then, how's this one?'

Tā yǒu tàitai le.   Nǐ ne?
'He has a wife now.'   'And have you?'

Tāmen dōu láile.   Nǐde péngyou ne?
'They've all come.'   'But, where's your friend?'

The final particle ne is used at the end of an abbreviated question which usually follows a statement just made. Only enough of the question is given to make clear what is asked, and the rest omitted.

NOTES

1. Two Distinct Uses of the Particle -de

The use of the particle de introduced in Pattern A is the descriptive use, to be distinguished from the use to indicate modification, treated in Lesson 7. Contrast the following:

Description : Nín láide jēn dzǎu.   You came quite early.

	Tā pǎude dzwèi kwài.	He runs the fastest.
Modification:	Wǒ dzwòde tsài bù-hauchř.	The dishes I cook are no good.
	Tā syěde dōu hěn yǒuyìsz.	Everything he writes is interesting.

2. Note that the negative bu- stands before the descriptive element, not before the verb of action. (Contrast the English: 'I don't run very fast.')

3. Commands and Requests Involving Manner

The particle ba (see Lesson 7) may be added to commands (see Pattern B above) to soften them into suggestions or requests: Chǐng, chǐng nǐ, or chǐng nín standing before a command similarly turns it into an invitation:

Syě dà (yi)dyar!	Write it larger!
Syě dà dyar ba!	Better write larger.
Chǐng nín syě dà (yi)dyar!	Please write it larger.

4. Uses of the Particle -je

a. The addition of the particle -je to certain verbs prolongs the action or state of the verb:

Chǐng nín dzai jèr děngje wo, wǒ jyòu hwéilai.	Please wait for me here, I'll be right back.
Nín dzwòje, wǒ jànje.	You sit and I'll stand.

b. A sentence may have both verb je and sentence ne:

Mén kāije ne.	The door is standing open.
Tāmen jèngdzai chřje fàn ne.	They're just in the midst of eating.

c. Verbs with -je may also serve as adverbial modifiers of the main verb which follows. Such verbs may or may not be followed by objects:

Wǒmen kéyi dzwòje tán hwà.	Let's sit down and talk. (lit. 'chat sitting')
Tāmen shr dzǒuje chyùde.	They walked there. (lit. 'went there walking')

5. Yě . . . yě and yòu . . . yòu

Each of these pairs of linking adverbs translate readily as 'both . . . and.' There is however a difference in connotation when the verbs so linked are stative verbs. Thus:

Jèiwei syáujye yòu hǎukàn yòu tsūngming.	The girl is both good-looking and intelligent.

This is a flattering remark, but the same stative verbs may be linked by yě . . . yě to carry a sense of reluctant admission and are usually followed by kěshr introducing a reservation:

Jèiwei syáujye yě hǎukàn yě tsūngming, kěshr tā búhwèi dzwò fàn.	True the girl is both good-looking and intelligent, but she can't cook.

This distinction does not hold true when the verbs are other than stative verbs.

TRANSLATION OF THE INTRODUCTORY DIALOGUE

Yáng : (running) Hey, Wú, why do you walk so fast? Just now I was walking along and saw you standing outside the door, looking to right and left. You didn't know which way to go. Then you walked in this direction very rapidly. I called to you, but you didn't hear, so

5 I quickly ran ahead hoping to go to town with you. What are you going for?

Wú : Nothing. Now you have come, let's go to a teahouse and have a cup of tea. O.K.?

Yáng : Good! I haven't anything to do either. Up ahead there's a small

10 teahouse recently opened. Every day people go in there to tell jokes. It's a lot of fun. How about going there?

(So the two of them, walking along, arrived at the little teahouse. Outside the door were four or five tables, and a number of men were sitting there talking. Just as the two arrived, some people

15 were laughing. They didn't know why. Lǎu Yáng asked:)

Yáng : What are you all laughing about? I'll bet it's Hwáng Sān telling jokes.

(One of those sitting at the tables remarked:)

You couldn't be more right. Listen to this story. Hwáng, tell it

20 again for these two fellows.

Hwáng: Well, it was this way. The teachers in our school frequently hold meetings in the evening, sometimes lasting until midnight. After each meeting they have to have tea and refreshments, so it's one-thirty before they get home. A certain Mr. Tsáu got home late a

25 few times almost every week. Three weeks ago there were three gatherings, all of which broke up very late. Mrs. Tsáu didn't like it. Again two weeks ago there were four evenings when the meeting lasted very late. His wife was still more upset. Last week they held five meetings which did not break up till after midnight.

30 This time Mr. Tsáu went home, opened the door, and saw a letter lying on the table. He read it this way and that and at first didn't comprehend what it was all about and couldn't grasp the meaning of the words. After another look, he began slowly to understand. His wife had written it and it said:

35 Day before yesterday you got home yesterday. Yesterday you got home today. If tonight you get home tomorrow, you may understand that your wife has already gone home to her mother.

When he got this far, the crowd all had another big laugh.

Lesson 15

COMPOUND VERBS

NARRATIVE

Planning a New House

Dzwótyan wǒ gēn Lǎu Wáng tsúng chágwǎr dzǒuhwei jyā de shrhou, tā gàusu wo shwō: Wǒmen jùde neige fángdz tài syǎule. Wǒ mǎide shrhou, wǒmen jyòu yǒu yíge syǎuhár; syàndzài yǒu lyòuge le. Fángdz bugòu jù le.

Wǒ jyou wèn tā syǎng bāndau nǎr chyu jù, dǎswan mǎi dwóma dàde fángdz.
5 Tā shwō: Wǒmen syǎngyau bāndau chéngwàitou chyu. Syāngsya ānjing yidyǎr. Lùshangde chìchē shǎu. Háidz yǒu dìfang wár. Chénglǐtou wǒmen syàndzài jùde shr lyòujyān fáng; chéngwàitou wǒmen dǎswan mǎide shr shŕèrjyān.

Wǒ kàn, shŕèrjyān wūdz tài dwō; tāmen búbì mǎi nèmma dàde fángdz. Wǒ jyou yòu shwō: Nǐmen yìjyā báge rén dzěmma néng yùng shŕèrjyān wūdz ne?
10 Yíge rén yìjyān wūdz bugòu ma? Dàgài nǐmen dǎswan cháng chǐng ke ba?

Tā shwō: Nǐ buyàu syǎng yíge rén yìjyān wūdz jyou gòule. Hái děi yǒu kètīng, fàntīng, chúfáng ne! Wǒ yě chángchang syǎng syě yidyǎr dūngsyi, méi dìfang syě. Háidz cháng chǎu. Swóyi wǒ yě děi yǒu (yi)ge shūfáng.

Wǒ hái wèn ta jeige syīn fángdz yǒu jǐtséng lóu. Tā shwō sāntséng; měi
15 yitséng yǒu szjyān wūdz. Wǒ syǎng wèishemma yàu sāntséng lóu ne? Tyāntyan shànglóu syàlóu hěn lèi. Kěshr jei búshr wǒ mǎi fángdz, shr tā mǎi. Wǒ jyou shwō: Wǒ busyǐhwan cháng shàng syà lóutī. Nǐde syīn fángdz yǒu dyàntī ba?

Tā shwō: Sāntséng lóu de fángdz dōu méiyou dyàntī. Nǐ kàn, jyòushr wǎn
20 shang shànglóu, dzǎushang syàlóu; měityān dōu shr dzai yīlóu dzwò shř. Wǒde shūfáng yěshr dzai yīlóu.

Wǒ shwō: Jèi shr nǐde shŕching. Nǐ syǐhwan jù shemma fángdz, nǐ kéyi mǎi shemma fángdz. Wǒ ke busyǐhwan jù sāntséng lóu de fángdz. Nǐ dzài syǎngsyang, bānjyāde jeijyān shŕching búshr syǎu shř. Nǐmen syàndzài yǒude
25 jyājyu— jwōdz, yǐdz, chwáng, shemmade— dōu děi tsúng jyòu fángdzli chyu bānchulai, dzài bāndau syīn fángdzli chyu. Dzài shwō, bāndau syīn fángdz yǐhòu, jyājyu yídìng bugòu, jyou děi mǎi syīnde le. Syàndzài jyājyu hěn gwèi a! Jèisye hwā chyán de shŕching, nǐ dōu syǎnggwole ma?

Tā shwō: Nǐ shwōde dōu hěn dwèi, kěshr wǒmen bunéng bùbānjyā. Nǐ syàn
30 dzài méiyou háidz, nǐ jyou bunéng míngbai wǒmen jyālide wèntí.

Kǔngpà tā shwōde hěn dwèi. Dzài wǒ kàn, háidz shǎu, wèntí yě shǎu, jyāli yě jyou ānjingle.

VOCABULARY

Nouns (N)

-fáng   BF: combining form indicating a house, building or room (M: -jyān, room)

shūfáng	PW:	study, den
wòfáng	PW:	bedroom
chúfáng	PW:	kitchen

Wǒ mǎile sānjyān fáng.
'I bought a three-room house.'

kètīng	PW:	living room
fàntīng	PW:	dining room

jyājyù	furniture
chwáng	bed
ťánjwǒ(r)	dining table

lóutī	stairs, stairway
dyàntī	elevator (lit. 'electric ladder')
ménkǒu(r)	doorway, gateway, entrance

hēibǎn	blackboard

pyàu	ticket (M: -jāng)
ménpyàu	admission ticket

shān	mountain, hill
fēng	wind
yǔ	rain
sywě	snow

Adverbs (A)

yěsyǔ	MA:	perhaps, maybe, possibly

Tā yěsyǔ lái, yěsyǔ bulái.
'Maybe he'll come, maybe he won't.'

dàgài	MA:	probably, most likely

Dàgài tā buláile.
'Probably he isn't coming after all.'

dwó(ma)	MA:	to what extent? how? how (big, small, etc.)!

Tā syǎng mǎi dwó dàde fángdz?
'How large a house is he thinking of buying?'

Nǐmende háidz dwóma dàle?
'How old is your child now?'

Jèige háidz dwóma dàle!
'How your child has grown!'

Verbs (V)

gwā	FV:	(of wind) blow
gwāfēng	VO:	blow (wind)

Dzwótyan gwāfēng, gwāde hěn lìhai.
'The wind blew hard yesterday.'

gǎn	AV:	dare to, venture to

Wǒ bugǎn chyù wèn ta.
'I don't dare go ask him.'

-lái	BF: (verb ending indicating movement toward the speaker, or toward some point related to him)
-chyù	BF: (verb ending indicating movement away from the speaker and toward some definite point)
jìn	FV: enter
jìnlai	FV: come in
jìnchyu	FV: go in
jìnchéng	VO: go into town

Chǐng jìnlai dzwòdzwo.
'Please come in and sit a while.'

Mén hái kāije ne, jìnchyu kànkan ba!
'The door is still open, go in and have a look.'

chū	FV: exit
chūlai	FV: come out
chūchyu	FV: go out
chūmén(r)	VO: go out, leave the house

Lǐ Syansheng búdzai jyā, tā chūchyule.
'Mr. Lǐ is not at home, he's gone out.'

Wǒ jīntyān yìtyān méichūmén.
'I haven't been out of the house all day today.'

shàng	FV: ascend, mount
shànglai	FV: come up
shàngchyu	FV: go up
shàngjyē	VO: go shopping
shàngchē	VO: board a car or train
shànglóu	VO: go upstairs
shàngsywé	VO: go to school, attend school
shàngbān	VO: go to work
shàngshān	VO: climb a mountain

Wǒmen dōu dzai lóushang děng nín ne. Chǐng shànglai ba!
'We're all upstairs waiting for you. Please come up!'

syà	FV: descend
syàlai	FV: come down
syàchyu	FV: go down
syàsyāng	VO: go to the countryside
syàyǔ	VO: rain (lit. 'precipitate rain')
syàsywě	VO: snow (lit. 'precipitate snow')

Tāmen dōu tsúng shānshang syàlaile.
'They have all come down from the mountain.'

Méiyou lóutī, dzěmma néng syàchyu?
'Since there are no stairs, how can one get down?'

-dzài   BF: (verb ending) at, on, in

Nǐ jàndzai jèr, wǒ jàndzai ménkǒur.
'You stand here, I'll stand at the door.'

Tā syàndzài jùdzai chéngwàitou.
'He now lives outside the city.'

-dàu   BF: (verb ending) to, as far as

Wǒmen sywédau dìshŕwǔkè le.
'We have studied as far as Lesson 15.'

-gěi   BF: (verb ending) for, for the benefit of, to

Tā neige jyòu chē sùnggěi byéren le.
'That old car of his has been given to someone else.'

bān   FV: move (something), transport (goods); move (one's residence)
bānjyā   VO: move (one's residence)
bāndau   FV: move to
bāngwolai   FV: move (something) across (in this direction)
bānchuchyu   FV: move (things) out

Chǐng bāndau lóushang chyu.
'Please move it upstairs.'

Nǐmen něityān bānjyā?
'Which day are you moving?'

Jèisye dūngsyi dōu búyàule, děi bānchuchyu.
'This stuff is no longer wanted and will have to be moved out.'

sùng   FV: send, deliver (goods); escort, see (persons) off
sùngdau   FV: send to, escort to
sùnggei   FV: present (gifts)
sùngsyìn   VO: deliver a letter, send word

Nǐ mǎide syīn chìchē, shémma shrhou sùnglai?
'When is the new car you bought to be delivered?'

Tāmen dōu sùng wo shàng chwán le.
'They all saw me off at the boat.'

Wǒmen syǎng sùng nín yìdyǎr Jūnggwo
cháyè.
'We'd like to present you with some Chinese tea.'

dài	FV: lead, accompany; take, bring, bring along
dàidau	FV: take (something) to (somewhere)
dàihwéi	FV: take (something) back to (somewhere)

Jèibén shū, nǐ kéyi dàihwei jyā chyu.
'You can take this book back home.'

Wǒ dài ni chyu, hǎu buhau?
'How about my accompanying you there?'

tǎng	FV: lie, recline
tǎngsya	FV: lie down
tǎngje	FV: lie down

Nǐ bushūfu, tǎngsya ba!
'If you are unwell, lie down.'

Tā tǎngje kàn shū ne.
'He is lying down reading.'

Expressions

dzài shwō	furthermore, what's more, moreover
dzài wǒ kàn	in my opinion, as I see it
shémmade	and so forth, etc.
bùgǎndāng	You flatter me! (I dare not assume the honor.)

Common Sayings

Jyòu rén, jyòudau lyǎur; sùng rén, sùngdau jyā.	When you save a man, save him completely; when you escort a man, see him all the way home.
Shwōdau nǎr, bàndau nǎr.	However far you commit yourself, carry it out.
Shwōdau Tsáutsau, Tsáutsau jyou dàu.	Speak of Tsáutsau and Tsáutsau appears. (Speak of the devil and he appears.)

SENTENCE PATTERNS

A. Verbs of Movement Compounded with lái and chyù

Chǐng jìnlai! Wǒ bunéng jìnchyu, mén gwānje ne.
'Please come in.' 'I can't go in, the door is closed.'

Kwài shàngchyu ba! Tāmen dōu dzai lóushang děngje nǐ ne.
'Better hurry and go up. They're all upstairs waiting for you.'

Nín búsyàlai ma? Wǒ dzěmma néng syàchyu? Méiyou dyàntī.
'Aren't you coming down?' 'How can I go down? There's no elevator.'

Nǐmen shr shémma shŕhou bānlaide?
'When was it that you folks moved here?'

The verbs lái 'come here' and chyù 'go there' may serve as endings to verbs of movement, such as jìn 'enter,' chū 'exit,' shàng 'ascend,' syà 'descend,' bān 'move,' etc., to form compound verbs. When an object is indicated, it is usually transposed to the topic position. The pattern is:

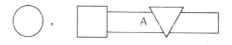

Shū,   wǒ   dōu dàilaile.
'I have brought   along the books.'

B.   Verbs of Movement Compounded with V-lái and V-chyù

Neige gāu shān, wǒmen shr dzǒushangchyude.
'We walked to the top of that high mountain.'

Dūngsyi dōu dàihweilaile ma?
'Did you bring everything back?'

Shūjwōr kéyi bāndàu shūfángli chyu.
'You may move the desk into the study there.'

Tāmen kāihwéi Nyǒuywē chyule.
'They have driven back to New York.'

Certain verbs of movement ending in -lai and -chyu function not only as main verbs (as shown in Pattern A) but in turn may serve as endings to certain other verbs (such as sùng 'deliver,' dài 'bring or take along,' dzǒu 'walk,' pǎu 'run,' etc.). When an object is indicated, this compound is split up, and the appropriate place word inserted just before the final ending -lai or -chyu. The object may also be prestated. The pattern is:

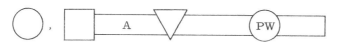

Yǐdz,   tā   dōu bāndau   lóushang chyule.
'They have taken all the chairs upstairs.'

C.   Verbs Compounded with -dzài, -dàu, and -gěi

1.   Verbs of Position Compounded with -dzài 'at a place'

Nǐ jùdzai něityau jyē?   Which street do you live on?

Nǐ ywànyi dzwòdzai nǎr?   Where do you wish to sit?

Wǒ méidzwòdzai nèige yǐdz-   I did not sit on that chair.
   shang.

Wǒ méisyědzai shūshang.   I didn't write in my book.

Jàndzai ménkǒurde neiwei   What is the name of the gentleman
   syānsheng syìng shémma?   standing in the doorway?

The verb dzài 'be located at' has been present as a main verb and as a
coverb 'at.' Dzai may also serve as an unstressed ending to verbs such
as jàn 'stand,' dzwò 'sit,' jù 'live,' syě 'write,' etc. Verbs compounded
with -dzai require a place word as object (see Note 1).

2. Verbs of Movement Compounded with -dàu 'to a place'

Wǒmen míngtyan bāndau chéng-   We are moving into the city tomorrow.
  lǐtou lai.

Nǐmen nyàndau dìjǐkè le?   To what lesson have you studied?

Chǐng nǐ kāidau dà mén chyán-   Please drive to the front of the main
  tou chyu.   gate.

Tā shwō gùshr, shwōdau nǎr le?   What point has he reached in telling
                                        the story?

The verb dàu 'reach' has appeared in two of its functions of main verb
and coverb 'to.' Dàu may also function as an unstressed ending to verbs
of movement like dzǒu 'walk,' kāi 'drive,' hwéi 'return,' ná 'take,' bān
'move,' nyàn 'read' or 'study,' etc. Compounds with -dau require place
words for objects, and lái 'to here' or chyù 'to there' often appears after
the place word.

3. Certain Verbs Which End in -gěi 'to' or 'for'

Wǒmen neige chìchē buyùng le, yǐjing sùnggei péngyou le.
'We don't use our car anymore, we've already given it to a friend.'

Nǐ syěde nèisyē syìn nǐ dōu shr syěgei shéi de?
'To whom did you write all those letters?'

Néng buneng nyàngei wǒ tīngting?
'Can you read it for me to hear?'

Nèige gùshr wèishémma méishwōgei wǒmen tīngting?
'Why haven't you told us that story?'

The verb gěi has appeared as a main verb 'give' and a coverb 'to' or 'for.'
Gěi is also used as an unstressed ending to verbs like sùng 'present,' syě
'write,' shwō 'speak,' nyàn 'read' or 'study,' etc. Compounds with -gěi
(like the verbs gěi and gàusung) take both direct and indirect objects. The
direct object is usually transposed to the front of the sentence:

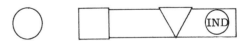

Jèibèn shū,   wǒ   sùnggei nín.
'I'm presenting you with this book.'

NOTES

1. Two ways of expressing location are illustrated by these pairs of sentences:

Wǒ dzai jèr jù.   Wǒ jùdzai jèr.

Wǒ dzai yǐdzshang dzwòje.   Wǒ dzwòdzai yǐdzshang.
Wǒ dzai ménkǒur jànje.   Wǒ jàndzai ménkǒur.
Wǒ dzai wàitou děngje.

In the first instance of each pair, the pattern is that of the coverbial phrase used as an adverbial modifier of the main verb; in the second, a compound verb is used, followed by a place word as object. The coverbial pattern tends to stress the action, while the compound verb pattern tends to stress the place, but this is not a hard and fast rule and is frequently modified by voice emphasis.

2. Compounds with -dzài. So far, we have met the following verbs indicating position, which may be compounded with -dzài: jàn 'stand,' dzwò 'sit,' jù 'live,' děng 'wait.'

3. Compounds with -gěi. The ending -gěi indicates that something is done for the benefit of someone, hence 'giving' a service. So far we have the following verbs which may be compounded with -gěi: mài 'sell,' syě 'write,' nyàn 'read aloud,' shwō 'speak,' 'narrate,' sùng 'make a present of,' 'deliver to.'

4. Compounds with -dàu. Since -dau indicates a goal or point of attainment it will combine with any verb indicating movement or progress. So far we have met the following: bān 'lift and move,' sùng 'deliver,' 'escort,' kàn 'read,' syě 'write,' sywé 'study,' syǎng 'think,' pǎu 'run,' dzǒu 'walk,' gwò 'pass over,' hwéi 'return,' kāi 'drive a car,' fēi 'fly,' yùbei 'prepare,' dzwò 'do,' 'make,' wēnsyi 'review,' kǎu 'be examined.' There will be many more verbs in this category than in items 2 and 3 above.)

TRANSLATION OF THE INTRODUCTORY NARRATIVE

Planning a New House

Yesterday when Lǎu Yáng and I were walking home from the teahouse he said to me: The house we are living in has become too small. When I bought it we had only one child; now we have six. The house is no longer big enough to live in.

5   So I asked him where he thought of moving, and how big a house he thought of buying. He said: We are thinking of moving out of the city. It's a little quieter in the country; there are fewer cars on the road. The children will have a place to play. In town, the place in which we now live has six rooms; in the suburbs, we plan to have twelve rooms.

10 Twelve rooms seemed to me too many; they didn't need a place as large as that. So I said: There are eight in your family; how can you use twelve rooms? Isn't a room apiece enough? I suppose you're planning to have a lot of company, right?

He said: Don't think that a room apiece is enough. We still have to have a
15 living room, a dining room and a kitchen. And I often want to do a little writing, but there's no place to write. The kids are often noisy. I need a study.

I went on to ask him how many stories the new house would have, and he
said three stories with four rooms to a floor. I wondered why he wanted
20 three floors; going up and down stairs every day would be very tiring. But
then, it wasn't I who was buying the house, it was his purchase. So I said:
I wouldn't like to be constantly going upstairs and down. I suppose your new
house has an elevator?

He replied: A three-story house doesn't have an elevator. Look, you just
25 go upstairs in the evening and downstairs in the morning. All day long your
activities are all on the first floor. And my study is on the first floor.

I said: It's your business. Buy any kind of house you'd like to live in. I
wouldn't care to live in a three-story house. Think it over again; this business of moving is no small matter. The furniture you now have— tables,
30 chairs, beds, etc.— all have to be moved out of the old house and into the
new. What's more, after you get moved into the new house, you're likely to
find that your furniture is inadequate and you'll have to buy new. Furniture
is very expensive right now. Have you taken into account all these things
which require money?

35 He said: All you say is quite true, but we just have to move (can't not move).
You have no children at present, so you can't appreciate the problems of our
family.

Of course what he said is right. In my opinion, the fewer the children, the
fewer the problems, and the more peaceful the home.

Lesson 16

THE BǍ CONSTRUCTION

DIALOGUE

Starting on a Trip

Lù :   Lǎu Wú, tīngshwō nǐmen yàu chyù lyǔsyíng. Dǎswan dàu nǎr chyù ne?

Wú :   Wǒmen syǎng dàu hǎibyār chyu wár jityān. Gēn wǒmen yíkwàr chyù, hǎu buhǎu? Rén dwō yǒuyìsz.

Lù :   Nǐ shwōde budwèi ba? Yǒuren shwō: Rén dwō, hǎu dzwò shr̀; rén
5   shǎu hǎu chř fàn. Wǒmen yàushr gēn nimen yíkwàr chyù, nǐ dàide dūngsyi kǔngpa bugòu lyǎngjyā chřde ba?

Wú :   Nǐmen yě kéyi dài yidyǎr chřde lai. Nǐmen chř nǐmende, wǒmen chř wǒmende. Shéi yě búbì dwō hwā chyán le.

Lù :   Nínde yìsz hěn hǎu, syèsye nín, kěshr jèitsz kǔngpa wǒmen bunéng
10   chyù, yīnwei míngtyan lái lyǎngge kèren yàu dzai wǒmen jyāli jù jityān. Kěshr nǐmen dzǒude shrhou, wǒ kéyi kāi chē sùng nǐmen dàu chējan chyu, hǎu buhǎu?

Wú :   Dwō syè, dwō syè! Jèitsz wǒmen búshr dzwò hwǒchē chyù, shr kāi chìchē chyù. Wǒmen chyùde neige hǎibyār búdàu yìbǎi-wǔshr-yīnglǐ.
15   Sz̀ge jūngtóu jyou kéyi kāidàule. Kāi chē fāngbyan. Syíngli dōu kéyi fàngdzai chēshang, jyou búbì shǒuli náje le.

Lù :   Nǐmen shr shémma shrhou dzǒu ne?

Wú :   Yìhwěr jyou dzǒu, yīnwei 'dzǎu dzǒu, dzǎu dàu.' Yàushr dàude tài wǎnle, kǔngpa bufāngbyan.

20 Lù :   Nèmma wǒ syàndzài jyou bāng nǐ bān dūngsyi ba! Jèi syāngdz busyǎu a! Kéyi fàngdzai chēshang shémma dìfang?

Wú :   Hǎu, chǐng nín syān bāngju wo bǎ nèige syāngdz fàngdzai chēhòutou. Nèr yǒu dìfang.

Lù :   Jèijyan yīshang ne? Kéyi bǎ yīshang gwàdzai chēlǐtou ba?

25 Wú :   Hǎu. Kéyi bǎ byéde syíngli dōu fàngdzai chìchēlǐtou— sānge syǎu syāngdz, lyǎngge dà syāngdz, hái yǒu nèige hédz shr lùshang chřde dūngsyi. Jèige píbāu wǒ dz̀jǐ náje.

Lù :   Rén dōu dzwòdzai nǎr? Méi dìfang dzwò rén le ba?

Wú :   Syān bǎ dūngsyi dōu fàngshang, wǒmen dzài syǎng rén dzěmma dzwò
30   ba!

Lù :   Syíngli jēn bushǎu! Nǐmen lyán jyājyù yě dōu dàidau hǎibyār chyu ma?

Wú :   Nǎrde hwà! Wǔge rén dài jèmmasye dūngsyi budwō. Yàushr lyǎngge dàren chūchyu wár jityān, syíngli jyou shǎule. Kěshr dàije sānge háidz, syíngli jyou dwōle.

35 Lù :   Nǐmen dǎswan dzài hǎibyār jù jǐtyān ne?

Wú :   Jù yíge lǐbài. Syàlibaisz̀ hwéilai.

Lù :   Yíge lǐbài děi hwā bushǎu chyán ba?

Wú :   Yě budwō. Aīyā, wǒ kǒudàrli méi chyán! Wǒ wàngle dài chyán le!

Lù :   Búyàujǐn, wǒmen jyāli yǒu chyán syān jyègei nin yùng.

40   Wú :   Dwō syè, dwō syè! Nǐ néng jyègei wo yìbǎikwai chyán ma? Bufāngbyan ba?

Lù :   Méishemma bùfāngbyan. Nín děng wo hwéi jyā gēn wo tàitai yàu chyu.
Nín dàgài bùjrdàu women jyāli shr chyán dōu fàngdzai tàitai shǒuli.
Wǒ yùng chyán de shrhou děi gēn ta yàu. Nín děngdeng, wǒ jǐfen jūng
45   jyou hwéilaile.

Lù :   Chyán nálaile. Wǒ tàitai syān buwányi gěi nemma dwō chyán, pà wǒ
hwāle, kěshr wǒ yǐ gàusung ta shr yàu jyègei nǐmen de, tā jyou gěile.
Tā hěn syǐhwan nín tàitai.

Wú :   Chǐng nín tì wo syèsye nín tàitai. Nǐmen jēn bāngle wo bushǎude máng.
50   Wǒ yǐ hwéilai lìkè jyou hwángei nǐmen.

Lù :   Bùmáng, bùmáng. Nǐmen děi dzǒule ba?

Wú :   Shr̀, wǒmen yàu dzǒule. Gwò jityān jyàn.

Lù :   Dzàijyàn.

VOCABULARY

Nouns (N)

shǒu	hand

Nǐ shóuli yǒu shémma?
'What's in your hand?'

Nǐ yùng něige shǒu syě dz̀? Wǒ yùng dzwǒ
shǒu.
'With which hand do you write?' 'I use my
left hand.'

tóu	head

Màudz dàidzai tóushang.
'Hats are worn on the head.'

lyǎn	face (lit. or fig.)

Chr̄ fàn yǐchyán yàu syǐ shǒu syǐ lyǎn.
'One should wash one's face and hands before eating.'

píbāu	leather case, briefcase, billfold
písyé	leather shoes
syāngdz	suitcase, trunk, box, case
syíngli	baggage
kǒudàr	pocket, (soft) bag

hédz	box (smaller than <u>syāngdz</u>)
shēngdż	new word, vocabulary (lit. 'unfamiliar word')

Měikède shēngdż butài dwō ba?
'There are not too many new words in each lesson, are there?'

| chyáng | wall |
| chéngchyáng | city wall |

Chéngchyángshang yǒu rén.
'There are people on the city wall.'

Chyángshang gwàje jijāng hwàr.
'There are a few pictures hanging on the wall.'

dì	ground, land
dìsya	floor
hǎibyār	seashore

| swǒyǒude | all, every, all there are |

Swǒyǒude rén dōu dzǒule.
'Everyone has gone.'

Tā swǒyǒude dìfang dōu dàugwo.
'He's been everywhere.'

Adverbs (A)

| lǎu | A: always, ever; (followed by negative) never |

Nǐ wèishémma lǎu buchyu kàn ta?
'Why don't you ever go to see him?'

Verbs (V)

bǎ	CV: (see Sentence Patterns)
ná	FV: take, grasp, hold, carry in one's hand
náchilai	FV: pick up (with the hand)
náje	FV: hold, be holding (in the hand)
náhwéi	FV: take back

Tāmen buhwèi ná kwàidz.
'They do not know how to handle chopsticks.'

Nǐ shóuli náje shémma ne?
'What are you holding in your hand?'

Náchi shū lai!
'Take up your book!'

fàng	FV: put (something somewhere) (lit. 'let go of')
fàngdzai	FV: put (something) in a place
fàngje	FV: lie, be lying (of inanimate objects)
fàngsya	FV: put (something) down

Nín hē kāfēi fàng táng bufàng?
'Do you put sugar in your coffee?'

Jèisye shū dōu fàngdzai nǎr?
'Where shall we put all these books?'

Dzài dìsya fàngje busyíng ma?
'Can't they rest on the floor?'

Byé fàngsya!
'Don't set it down!'

bāng(ju)	FV :	help, assist (someone)
bāngmáng	VO :	render assistance

Wǒ bāng nín dzwò hǎu buhǎu?
'How about my helping you do it?'

Chǐng nín bāngju wo bān jèige syāngdz.
'Kindly help me move this case.'

Jèijyan shr̀ching burúngyi dzwò, děi chǐng
   nín bāng wo yidyǎr máng.
'This is not easy to do, I must ask you to
   give me a little assistance.'

jì(de)   FV : remember, keep in mind

Tā syìng shémma nǐ hái jìde ma?
'What is his name, do you still remember?'

Wǒ bujìdele. Wǒ wàngle.
'I don't remember.' 'I have forgotten.'

gwà	FV :	hang (an article); hang from (a position)
gwàje	FV :	be hanging
gwàdzai	FV :	hang in (a position)

Màudz gwàdzai nǎr?
'Where does one hang one's hat?'

Wǒ gěi nín gwàshang.
'Let me hang it up for you.'

Dzai ménshang gwàje ne.
'It's hanging on the door.'

jyè		FV : borrow, lend
jyègei		FV : lend to
gēn . . . jyè	CV . . . V :	borrow from

Wǒ gāng jyèle lyǎngběn shū.
'I just borrowed a couple of books.'

Shr̀ gēn shéi jyède?
'Who did you borrow them from?'

Shr̀ yíge péngyou jyègei wo de.
'They were loaned to me by a friend.'

> Jyè rénde shū, kéyi; jyè rénde chyán, buhǎu.
> 'It's all right to borrow someone's books,
>   but it's bad to borrow a person's money.'

| hwán | FV : return (a loan), pay back |
| hwángei | FV : return (something) to, give back to |

> Wǒ jyègei ta de chyán, tā hái méihwángei
>   wo ne.
> 'The money I loaned him, he has not yet re-
>   paid.'

| yàu | FV : demand, request |
| gēn . . . yàu | CV . . . V : ask (someone) for (something) |

> Nǐ gēn ta yàu yijāng jř, hǎu buhau?
> 'How about asking him for a sheet of paper?'

rēng	FV : throw
rēngdzai	FV : throw into
rēngle	FV : throw away

> Nèiběn shū ta rēngdzai dìsya le.
> 'He threw the book on the ground.'

> Nèijāng jř hái néng yùng; byé rēngle!
> 'That sheet of paper is still usable; don't
>   throw it away!'

| lyǔsyíng | N/FV : travel; take a trip |

> Lyǔsyíng hěn yǒuyìsz.
> 'Travel is very interesting.'

> Tāmen dōu syǎng dau Táiwān chyu lyǔsyíng.
> 'They are all planning to travel to Taiwan.'

| fāngbyàn | SV : be convenient |

> Kǔngpà nín yùng kwàidz bufāngbyan ba?
> 'I'm afraid it won't be convenient for you to
>   use chopsticks.'

| búdàu | SV : be less than, be not as much as |

Expression

| Nǎrde hwà! | Where did you get such an idea? |

Common Sayings

| Hǎu jyè, hǎu hwán; dzài jyè bunán. | If you are good about borrowing and repay-ment, it won't be hard to borrow again. |
| Méiyou gāu shān, bùsyǎn píng dì. | If there are no high mountains, the flatness of the land is not noticeable. |

SENTENCE PATTERNS

A. The bǎ Construction

Tā bǎ tāde chìchē màile.	He has sold his car.
Nǐmen bǎ jīntyande gūngkè yùbeile meiyou?	Have you prepared today's lesson?
Nǐmen něityan bǎ dūngsyi bānchyu?	What day are you moving the things?
Kwài bǎ chyán nálai.	Hurry and bring the money.
Bǎ jèisye jyòu shū dōu nádzǒu.	Take all these used books away.
Dzài bǎ nǐde yìsz shwōchulai.	Give us your idea again.
Tā méibǎ gāngbǐ náhweichyu.	He didn't return the pen.
Nǐ kéyi bǎ neiběn dzájr̀, dàihwéi sywésyàu lai.	You may bring that magazine back to school.
Bǎ jèisye shū gēn nèisye fàngdzai yikwàr.	Put these books and those together (in one place).
Byē bǎ shǒu fàngdzai kǒudàrli.	Don't put your hands in your pockets.
Wǒ ywànyi bǎ jeige pǐbāu sùnggei nǐ.	I want to give you this leather case.
Wǒ budǎswan bǎ nei wǔkwai chyán hwángei tā.	I don't plan to pay him back that five dollars.
Wǒ bǎ neiběn bàu kànle yítsz̀.	I looked that newspaper over.
Nimen yīngdāng bǎ měikède shēngdz dwō lyànsyi jitsz̀.	You should practice the new words several times over.
Chǐng bǎ chwānghu kāikai.	Please open the window.
Wǒ syān bǎ jèijyan shr̀ching syǎngyisyang.	I'll first think this matter over.

The coverb bǎ serves to transpose the object of the main verb to a position between the subject and the main verb. A similar effect would be produced in English by the pattern 'take the car and sell it' instead of 'sell the car.' The main verb of a sentence in which the bǎ construction is used must have a verb-ending or other completive element following it.

1. The particle -le, or some other final particle.

2. The verb-endings -lái, -chyù, -dàu, hwéi, or -dzǒu.

3. The verb-ending -dzai followed by a place word.

4. The verbs gěi and gàusung, and the verb-ending -gěi followed by an indirect object (as gàusung nǐ, hwángei tā).

5. A quantified expression (such as yìhwéi, hǎujǐtsz).

6. Or the verb may be reduplicated (as kāikai, syǎngyisyang).

NOTES

1. Three Types of Sentence Structure

   a. Normal word order, as was noted in Lesson 1, is: subject—verb—object:

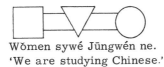

Wǒmen sywé Jūngwén ne.
'We are studying Chinese.'

b. Transposed order, introduced in Lesson 3, permits prestatement of the object for emphasis, contrast, to serve as a topic, or to allow a plural object to be totalized with dōu:

R̀bět chìchē wǒ (dōu) méikāigwo.
'I've never driven a Japanese car.'

c. The bǎ construction, by means of the coverb bǎ, brings the object forward to a position between the subject and the verb:

Wǒmen   bǎ tóushŕwŭkè   dōu wēnsyile.
'We have reviewed the first fifteen lessons.'

2. The Coverb bǎ and Its Object

a. The coverb bǎ differs from other coverbs in that its object is also the object of the main verb.

b. The object of bǎ always denotes a specific person or thing; it cannot refer to people or things in general. This is true even when no specification is expressed. E.g., the sentence Tā bǎ dūngsyi dōu nádzǒule should be translated 'He took the things away.' (See the examples under Sentence Patterns.)

c. The negatives bù- and méi-, auxiliary verbs, and most adverbs stand before the coverb. The adverb dōu stands immediately before the main verb when it totalizes the object.

3. Translating a bǎ Sentence

No attempt should be made to render the coverb bǎ into English. For practical purposes, the three types of sentence described in Note 1 may be translated identically:

Tā màile tade chìchē le. ⎫
Tāde chìchē, tā màile.   ⎬   He has sold his car.
Tā bǎ tade chìchē màile. ⎭

However, the following differences in emphasis may be distinguished by asking what question is answered by each:

What <u>happened</u>?   He has <u>sold his car</u>.
What happened to <u>his property</u>?   As to the <u>car</u>, he sold it.
What did he do with <u>his car</u>?   He has <u>sold</u> the car.

4. <u>Some Uses of the bǎ Construction</u>

   a. For verbs of movement with verb-endings -<u>lai</u> or -<u>chyu</u>, the <u>bǎ</u> pattern
      is preferred:

   Bǎ nǐmende shū dàilai.   Bring your books with you.
   Wǒmen bǎ jwōdz bānsyalaile.   We've moved the table down here.

   b. When both an object and a place word are involved, the <u>bǎ</u> pattern is pre-
      ferred:

   Bǎ kèren chǐngdau kétǐngli lai.   Invite the guests into the parlor.
   Chǐng nín bǎ wǒde píbāu dàihwéi   Please take my briefcase back to the
   sywésyàu chyu.   school with you.

   c. With verbs (like <u>gěi</u> and <u>gàusung</u>) which take both direct and indirect ob-
      jects, <u>bǎ</u> moves the direct object forward, leaving the indirect object at
      the end:

   Tā bǎ neige chyán hwángei wǒ   He's paid back the money.
   le.
   Wǒ bǎ nèijyan shr̀ gàusung   I have told them about that affair.
   tāmen le.

   d. When a plural object is totalized with <u>dōu</u>, either the transposed object
      pattern or the <u>bǎ</u> pattern is required:

   Shēngdz̀ wǒmen dōu lyànsyile.   (ambiguous)
   Wǒmen bǎ shēngdz̀ dōu lyànsyile.   We have practiced all of the new words.
   Wǒmen dōu bǎ shēngdz̀ lyànsyile.   All of us have practiced the new words.

   In the first of these three sentences, it is not clear whether <u>dōu</u> refers
   back to <u>wǒmen</u> or to <u>shēngdz̀</u>. With the <u>bǎ</u> construction in the second and
   third sentences the confusion is cleared up.

                TRANSLATION OF THE INTRODUCTORY DIALOGUE

   <u>Starting on a Trip</u>

   Lù : Lǎu Wú, I hear you are taking a trip. Where do you plan to go?

   Wú: We are thinking of going to the shore to play around for a few days.
         How about going along. The more people, the more fun.

   Lù : Didn't you say that wrong? Some people say, 'The more people, the
5   more work done; the fewer people, the more to eat.' If we should go
         with you, I fear there wouldn't be enough to feed two families.

   Wú: You might bring some food too. You eat yours and we'll eat ours.
         Then nobody need be out anything extra.

   Lù : Thanks for your kind thought, but I'm afraid we can't go this time,
10   because a couple of guests are arriving tomorrow to spend a few days

with us. But when you leave, may I take you to the station in my car?

Wú :   Many thanks! This time we aren't going by train, we're going to drive. This seashore place we're going to is less than 150 miles.

15   We can drive there in four hours, and driving is more convenient. All the baggage can be put in the car, and you don't have to carry anything by hand.

Lù :   What time are you leaving?

Wú :   Very shortly, for the earlier we leave the earlier we'll get there. If

20   we arrive too late, I'm afraid it will be inconvenient.

Lù :   Well, I'll help you bring things out. This suitcase is no small item. Where shall I put it in the car?

Wú :   All right, first please help me put that suitcase in the back of the car. There's room there.

25   Lù :   How about this clothing. We can hang it inside the car, can't we?

Wú :   Yes. You can put the rest of the stuff in the car—three handbags, two suitcases; and there's that little box which is food to eat on the way. I'll carry this briefcase myself.

Lù :   Where are all the people to sit? There's no room to seat them, is

30   there?

Wú :   First put all the stuff in, and then we can think about seating people.

Lù :   What a lot of stuff! Are you even taking all your furniture to the shore?

Wú :   What do you mean? This amount of stuff for five people isn't much. If two adults were going off for a couple of days' fun, there would be

35   less baggage. But when you take three kids along, the baggage increases.

Lù :   How many days are you planning to stay at the shore?

Wú :   One week. We return next Thursday.

Lù :   The costs for a week are rather high, aren't they?

40   Wú :   Not too much. Gosh, my pocket book is empty; I forgot to bring any money.

Lù :   Never mind. We have some we can lend you for the present.

Wú :   Thanks a lot! Can you lend me a hundred dollars? Would it be inconvenient?

45   Lù :   There's no inconvenience about it. Wait till I go back to the house and ask my wife for it. You may not know that in our household the money is all in the hands of the lady of the house. When I need money, I have to ask her for it. Wait for me, I'll be back in a few minutes.

I've brought the money. At first my wife didn't want to let me have

50   that much. She was afraid I'd spend it. But as soon as I told her it was to lend you, she handed it over. She's very fond of your wife.

Wú :   Please thank your wife for me. You've certainly helped me out. I'll pay it back as soon as we get home.

Lù :   No hurry, no hurry! I guess you'll have to be leaving now, won't you?

55 Wú :   Yes, we'll be going. See you in a few days.

Lù :   Good-bye!

Lesson 17

RESULTATIVE COMPOUND VERBS

DIALOGUE

About the Chinese Language

(J) Jyāu Jūnggwo hwà de syānsheng.
(S) Sywé Jūnggwo hwà de sywésheng.

S: Wǒ kàn sywé Jūnggwo hwà hěn yǒuyìsz.

J: Nǐ kàn Jūnggwo hwà gēn nǐmen shwōde Yīngwén dōu yǒu shémma butúngde dìfang?

S: Wǒ bǎ Yīngwén jyùdz fāncheng Jūngwén de shrhou, jyou jřdau Yīngwén
5   yùngde dž dwō, Jūngwén yùngde dž shǎu. Shř bushř?

J: Nǐ shwōde hěn dwèi. Jūnggwo yǒu yíjyù súyǔ shwō:

    Dzǒutswòle lù hwéidelái;
    shwōtswòle hwà, hwéibulái.

    Nǐ míngbai bumíngbai?

10 S: Wǒ bumíngbai 'hwéidelái' gēn 'hwéibulái' jeilyǎngge dž. Shr shémma
    yìsz?

J: Wǒ gěi ni jyǎngyijyang ba! Rén dzǒu lù de shrhou yàushr dzǒude lù
    budwèi, tā hái kéyi hwéichyu dzài dzǒu yityáu byéde lù. Kěshr shwō hwà
    de shrhou jyou bùtúngle. Nǐ bǎ hwà shwōchuchyu yǐhòu, jyou méiyou
15   fádz bǎ jèijyu hwà dzài shōuhweilai le.

S: Où, wǒ míngbaile! Jèige súyǔ shwōde butswò. Nín yě jyǎngde hěn
    chīngchu. Yàushr bǎ jèijyù hwà fāncheng Yīngwén, kě jyou dž dwōle.
    Yīngwén shr dzèmma shwō:

    If you take the wrong road, it is possible to return;
20   if you say the wrong word, it is impossible to recover it.

J: Nǐ fānde butswò. Jūngwén yùngde shr lyòuge words; yàushr yùng Jūnggwo
    dž syěchulai, yě jyòu shr shŕsžge dž. Yīngwén ne? Nǐ yùngde shr èr-
    shrsange words.

S: Wèishemma nín shwō 'hwéidelái' gēn 'hwéibulái?' Wǒ háishr bumíngbai
25   jèilyǎngge dž de yìsz. Kéyi bukéyi shwō 'néng hwéilai' gēn 'bùnéng
    hwéilai?'

J: Yě kéyi nèmma shwō; yìsz chàbudwō. Wǒ dzài gěi ni shwō yige lìdz ba!
    Syàndzài shr dūngtyān. Yǒu yityān nǐ tàitai syǎng chř syīgwa, chǐng ni
    shàngjyē gěi ta mǎi yidyar. Nǐ náje chyán jyou shàngjyē le, jǎulái jǎu-
30   chyù, kěshr jǎubujáu, yīnwei méiyou mài syīgwa de. Nǐ hwéi jyā de shr-
    hou yàu gēn ni táitai dzěmma shwō ne?

S: Wǒ kéyi gàusung ta shwō: 'Wǒ méimǎi,' yě kéyi shwō: 'Wǒ bunéng mǎi.'

J: Kǔngpà tā hái yau wèn ni: 'Wèishemma nǐ bunéng mǎi ne?' Nǐ yàu ta
    shēngchī ma?

35 S: Dāngrán búyàu. Nèmma wǒ jyou jèmma shwō: 'Wo méigěi ni mǎi shr
        yīnwei dūngtyān búmài syīgwa.'

    J: Jèmma shwō yě hǎu, kěshr ni búbì yùng nèmmasye hwà. Tā yí wèn de
        shrhou, nǐ kéyi shwō 'mǎibujáu' jyou gòule. Tā jyou míngbai le.
        Dzèmma shwō dwóma jyǎndān a!

40 S: Jēn shr jyǎndān! Nèmma, yàushr pùdzli yǒu syīgwa kěshr tài gwèi,
        yīngdāng dzèmma shwō ne? Jèi yě yǒu jyǎndānde shwōfar ma?

    J: Yǒu. Nǐ kéyi shwō 'Wǒmen mǎibuchǐ.' Nǐ tàitai jyou jřdau shr yīnwei
        jyàchyan tài gwèi, swóyi nǐ méigei ta mǎi syīgwa. Tā jyou bugēn ni
        shēngchìle.

45 S: Jèmma shwō hěn hǎu. Wǒ yīngdāng cháng yùng, yīngdāng dwō sywé.

    J: Dzai jèiběn shūli dìshŕchǐkè jyou yǒu hěn dwō. Yǒu gūngfu, nǐ kéyi dwō
        kànyikàn.

VOCABULARY

Nouns (N)

fádz	way, method, plan
fāngfǎ	way, method, plan
bànfǎ(r)	way to handle a problem, solution
shwōfǎ(r)	way to say a thing
méifádz	no way out, no way to manage

Nǐ jeige fāngfǎ hái bútswò.
'This method of yours isn't bad after all.'

Dwèibuchǐ, wǒ méifádz chyù.
'Sorry, but I can't manage to go.'

Nǐde yìsz hǎu, kěshr bànfǎr búdwèi.
'Your idea is good, but the procedure is
    wrong.'

Chǐng nín tì wǒmen syǎngchu yíge bànfǎ lai.
'Please think out a course of action for us.'

píchi	temperament, disposition
tàidu	attitude, manner

Nǐ péngyoude píchi tài hǎule!
'Your friend has a wonderful disposition!'

Nǐ dwèi tā de tàidu búdwèi.
'Your attitude toward him isn't right.'

gwānsyi	relation, connection, relevance (see under Verbs)
syígwàn	habit, custom

Shǎu chř fàn shǎu shwō hwà dōu shr hǎu
    syígwàn.
'To eat little and say little are good habits.'

syǎusywé(syàu)	elementary school
jūngsywé(syàu)	secondary school, high school
dàsywé(syàu)	college, university

Nǐ shr dzai nǎr shàngde jūngsywé?
'Where did you attend high school?'

yǎnjing	eye
ěrdwo	ear
dzwěi	mouth
jyàchyán	price, cost
lìdz	example
syīgwa	watermelon

Verbs (V)

dyōu	FV: lose, misplace
jǎu	FV: look for, hunt for
jǎujáu	RV: find
jǎulái jǎuchyu	RV: hunt here and there, hunt everywhere

Wǒ dzai lùshang dyōule shŕkwài chyán.
'On the way I lost ten dollars.'

Wǒ jǎule bàntyān, méijǎujáu.
'I hunted a long time but didn't find it.'

jyǎng	FV: talk, explain, discourse
jyǎngyijyang	VO: explain

Nǐ děng wǒ gěi jyǎngyijyang.
'Wait and I'll explain it to you.'

Nèiwei syānsheng jyǎngde hěn yǒuyìsz.
'That gentleman's discussion was very interesting.'

bàn	FV: manage, carry out
bànshr̀	VO: handle a matter of business

Tā hěn hwèi bànshr̀.
'He knows how to manage things.'

Jèige shr̀ching, wǒ tì nín bàn ba.
'Let me handle this matter for you.'

fāpíchi	VO: get angry, lose one's temper

Nèige rén chángchang fāpíchi.
'That man is always getting angry.'

gǎi	FV: change, revise, correct

Wǒ nǎr shwōtswòle, chǐng nín gěi wo gǎigai.
'Please correct me whenever I speak incorrectly.'

Tā neige píchi hái méigǎi ne.
'He hasn't changed that disposition of his yet.'

fān   FV: translate
fānyi   N/FV: translation; translate
fānchéng   FV: translate into

    Kŭngpà nín fānde búdwèi ba.
    'I'm afraid you didn't translate it correctly.'

    Nǐ budŭng, tā kéyi gěi fānyi.
    'If you don't understand, he'll translate it
    for you.'

    Tā bǎ neige Jŭnggwo gùshr fānchéng Yīngwén
    le.
    'He has translated the story into English.'

shōu   FV: receive, collect; put away
shōuchilai   RV: store away
shōuhweilai   RV: get back, recover

    Chē màile, kěshr hái méishōu chyán ne.
    'The car is sold, but he hasn't received pay-
    ment yet.'

    Tā bǎ dūngsyi shōuchilaile, yàu dzǒule.
    'He's put his stuff away and is about to
    leave.'

shwèi   FV: go to sleep, sleep
shwèijyàu   VO: sleep for a period

    Syān shwèi yihwěr dzài dzǒu.
    'Take a nap and then leave.'

    Byé chǎu, wūli yǒuren shwèijyàu ne.
    'Don't make a noise, there's someone sleep-
    ing in the room.'

    Hái shwèije ne ma?
    'Is he still sleeping?'

syǐng   FV: wake up (from sleep)

    Nǐ mŭchin syǐngle meiyou?
    'Has your mother waked up yet?'

jì   FV: transmit mail
jìsyìn   VO: mail letters

    Nǐ gěi ta syěde syìn jìdau nǎr chyu le?
    'To what place did you mail the letter you
    wrote him?'

swǒ(shang)   FV: lock up, secure
swǒ   N: lock

    Tyāntyān wǎnshang yàu swǒ mén.
    'One should lock one's door every evening.'

    Swǒ hwàile, swǒbushàng mén le.
    'The lock is broken and I can't lock the
    door.'

| kĕn | AV: be willing to |

Nǐ kĕn bukĕn chyù jyàn ta.
'Are you willing to go see him?'

Wèishémma bukĕn gàusung wŏ?
'Why won't you tell me?'

| è | SV: be hungry |
| kĕ | SV: be thirsty |

Wŏmen èlc hăujigo jūngtóu le.
'We've been hungry for a good many hours.'

Nín kĕ bukĕ? Yidyăr dōu bukĕ, syèsye.
'Are you thirsty?' 'Not a bit, thank you.'

| jyăndān | SV: be simple, concise |

Méiyou dzài jyăndānde shwōfăr le.
'There is no simpler way of saying it.'

Wŏmen jyāli dzwò fàn dōu shr hĕn jyăndānde.
'Our home cooking is the simplest.'

| bău | SV: be satisfied (after eating) |
| chřbău | RV: eat to satiety, get enough to eat |

Nín chřde tài shău, méichřbău ba?
'You've eaten too little; you haven't had
   enough, have you?'

| wán(le) | SV/RVE: be finished, finish (doing something) |

Nín neijāng shūjwōdz kwài dzwòwánle.
'That desk of yours is nearly finished.'

Wánle!
'It's finished!'

| yŏugwānsyi | SV: be relevant, important |
| méigwānsyi | SV: be irrelevant, unimportant |

Jèijyan shřching dwèi tā méigwānsyi.
'This matter is no concern of his.'

Méigwānsyi!
'It's of no importance!'

| bùtúng | SV: be unlike, different (positive form not used) |

Jèilyàngge bànfă bùtúng.
'These two ways of handling it are different.'

(For a list of common resultative compound verbs see Notes.)

Particles (P)

| -de- | (verbal infix indicating positive potential result) |
| -bu- | (verbal infix indicating negative potential result) See Pattern A. |

<u>Expressions</u>

Dzĕmma bàn?   What's to be done about it?
Jyòu jemma bàn!   Do it this way! So be it!

<u>Common Sayings</u>

Dzŏutswòle lù, hwéidelái;   Go the wrong road—you can return;
  shwōtswòle hwà, hwéi-   say the wrong words—they can't be re-
  bulái.   called.

Hwódau lău, sywédau lău,   Live to old age and learn to old age;
  hái yŏu sānfēn sywébu-   there will still be three-tenths that you
  dàu.   cannot attain to.

Yìjř shŏu pāibuchū bā-   You can't clap with one hand.
  jang.

Jřli bāubujù hwŏ.   You can't wrap fire in paper.

SENTENCE PATTERNS

A. <u>Resultative Compound Verbs</u>

1. Yàushr wŏ yùng Yīngwen shwō nǐmen <u>tīngdedŭng tīngbudŭng</u>?
   'Can you understand if I say it in English?'

2. Nǐde gùshr wèishémma lău <u>shwōbuwán</u> ne?
   'How come your stories are so interminable?'

3. Mĕikède shēngdz yíge jūngtóu <u>sywédehwèi</u> ma? Chàbudwō.
   'Can you learn the new words of each lesson in an hour?' 'Just about.'

4. Jūnggwo fàn nín <u>chřbubău</u> ba? <u>Chřdebău</u>.
   'Can you eat your fill of Chinese food?' 'Yes, I can.'

5. Shānshang yŏu rén, nǐ <u>kàndejyàn</u> ma? <u>Kànbujyàn</u>, ,e yănjing buhău.
   'There are people on the hill. Can you see them?' 'No, I can't, my eyes
   are bad.'

6. Tài wănle, kŭngpà jīntyan <u>sùngbudàule</u>.
   'It's too late. I fear the things can't be delivered today.'

7. Yīnggwo dzsyíngchē dzai Mĕigwo <u>măidejáu</u> ma? Yídìng <u>măidejáu</u>.
   'Can you buy English bicycles in America?' 'Sure, you can!'

8. Nèijyan shřching <u>bànhăule</u> meiyou? Hái <u>méibànhău</u> ne. Lyăngtyān <u>bànbu-
   hău</u>.
   'Has that matter been satisfactorily taken care of?' 'Not yet. You can't
   complete it in two days.'

9. Nèmmasyē dūngsyi nín <u>nábulyău</u> ba?
   'You can't carry all those things, can you?'

10. Nín dwèi wŏ shwōde hwà, wŏ <u>wàngbulyău</u>.
    'I cannot forget what you have said to me.'

11. Wŏmen <u>măibuchǐ</u> syīn chìchē.
    'We can't afford a new car.'

12. Yàushr wǒ <u>kànbuchǐ</u> ta, wǒ jyou <u>dwèibuchǐ</u> ta le.
    'If I look down on him, then I've offended him.'

13. Jèige tsài <u>chřbude</u>, méidzwòhǎu.
    'This dish is not fit to eat, it wasn't properly cooked.'

14. Wǒ syǎng chūchyu, kěshr wǒ <u>kāibukāi</u> mén.
    'I want to go out, but I can't open the door.'

15. Nèige chwānghu <u>gwānbushàng</u>.
    'That window won't close.'

16. Màudz tài syǎu; dàishangle yǐhòu jyou <u>jāibusyàlái</u> le.
    'The hat is too small; once you put it on, you can't get it off.'

17. Shūfánglide shū dōu <u>bāndzǒule</u>.
    'All the books in the study have been moved away.'

18. Nèige shān nǐ <u>shàngdechyù</u> ma? <u>Shàngbuchyù</u>.
    'Can you climb that mountain?' 'No, I can't.'

19. Jwōdz <u>bānjinchyule</u> meiyou? <u>Bānbujìnchyù</u>, jwōdz tài dà.
    'Has the table been moved in (there)?' 'No, the table is too large.'

20. Tā syìng shémma? Wǒ dzěmma yě <u>syǎngbuchilái</u>! Ou, wǒ syàndzài
    <u>syǎngchǐlaile</u>, tā syìng Chén.
    'What is his name?' 'I can't recollect it, try as I may. Oh, now I recollect it. His name is Chen.'

The underscored verbs in the above sentences are potential resultative compounds. Several of these have been introduced in earlier lessons, but without analysis. Most of the component elements are familiar to the student.

The first verb in such a compound designates the action, the second verb indicates the result— actual or potential. <u>Actual</u> result is expressed by a simple combination of the two verbs. <u>Potential</u> result is indicated by the insertion of -<u>de</u>- for the positive form and -<u>bu</u>- for the negative form between the verb of action and the resultative ending.

Actual		Potential	
Positive	Negative	Positive	Negative
kànjyan(le)	méikanjyàn	kàndejyàn	kànbujyàn
mǎijáule	méimǎijáu	mǎidejáu	mǎibujáu
dzwòwán(le)	méidzwowán	dzwòdewán	dzwòbuwán
bānshangchyu	méibanshangchyù	bāndeshangchyù	bānbushangchyù

NOTES

1. Resultative Verb Endings

   a. Functional Endings

Ending	Type of Result	Used with	Limitations
-bǎu -chǐ	satisfaction of appetite afford to respect for, self respect	chř mǎi, chř, jù dwèi	Potential only Potential only

Ending	Type of Result	Used with	Limitations
-dàu	arrival, attainment	dzŏu, pău, bàn, sùng, syăng	
-de	fitness	chř, hē, shwō, jù, kàn	Positive: Vde
-dŭng	understanding, comprehension	tīng, kàn	
-dùng	movement	ná, bān	Potential only
-gānjing	cleanness	syĭ	
-hău	satisfaction, completion	dzwò, bàn, yùbei	
-hwèi	learning mastery	sywé	
-jáu	attainment	jău, măi, shwèi	
-jù	fixity, security	jàn, dzwò, ná	
-jyàn	perception (sensory)	kàn, tīng	
-kāi	separation, having room for	kāi, lí, dzwò	
-lyău	possibility	dzwò, ná, măi, mài, chř	Actual form: le
-tswò	error	dzwò, shwō, syĕ	
-wán	completion	dzwò, shwō, syĕ	

b. Directional Endings

Ending	Type of Result	Used with	Limitations
-chyù	in that direction (away)	Verbs of motion: shàng, syà, jìn, chū, hwéi Transportation: sùng, dài, ná, bān, jì	Actual only
-chūchyu	out		
-jìnchyu	in	sùng, dài, ná, bān, jì	
-hwéichyu	back		
-shàngchyu	up		
-syàchyu	down		
-dzŏu	away	ná, dài, bān	Actual only
-lái	in this direction (toward)	Verbs of motion: shàng, syà, jìn, chū, hwéi Transportation: ná, sùng, dài, bān, jì	Actual only
-chĭlai	up	jàn, swŏ { chàng, syăng, swàn } { ná, dzŏu, pău, bān }	
-chūlai	out		
-hwéilai	back		
-jìnlai	in		
-shànglai	up		
-syàlai	down		

Ending	Type of Result	Used with	Limitations
-shàng	up, on attainment	chwān, dài, gwà gwān, swǒ, kǎu	
-syà	down having room for	dzwò, tǎng dzwò	Actual only

Note: The sample verbs listed under 'Used with' are far from an exhaustive list. Some endings, such as -bǎu and -jyàn are limited by their essential meaning.

2. Resultative Compound Verbs

   a. Not all compound verbs are resultative. (For example, tīngshwō, míngbai, yùbei, lyànsyi, rènshr, jyèshàu are not.) The test for a resultative verb compound is whether or not it can be converted into the potential type by the insertion of -de- and -bu-.

   b. Just because a compound is resultative, it does not follow that both actual and potential types are commonly used. For example, the endings -lyǎu and -chǐ are commonly used in the potential type, but seldom in the actual. (It should be noted, however, that in the case of -lyǎu the actual type has its counterpart in the particle -le, of which it is the 'literary' pronunciation.) And again, the compounds ending in -dzǒu appear commonly in the actual type, and not often in the potential.

   c. Only the actual type of resultative verb is used with the bǎ construction.

   Wǒmen bǎ dūngsyi dōu bāndzǒule.   We have moved everything away.
   Chǐng nǐ bǎ hwà shwōchīngchule.   Please speak clearly.

   d. The object of a resultative verb may be transposed:

   Nǐ tīngdǔng tāde hwà le ma?   Did you understand what he said?
   Tāde hwà, nǐ tīngdǔngle ma?

   Nǐ chǐdelyǎu jèisye fàn ma?   Can you eat all this rice?
   Jèisye fàn, nǐ chǐdelyǎu ma?

   e. Potential type verbs use all of the question forms introduced thus far:

   Nǐ kàndejyàn ma?
   Nǐ kàndejyàn kànbujyàn?
   Nǐ shr kàndejyàn, háishr kànbujyàn ne?
   Shéi kàndejyàn shānshang neilyǎngge rén?

   f. The negative particle méi- may stand before actual type resultatives but not before potential types:

   Nèiben shū wǒ tóuyihwéi kàn méikàndǔng.
   'I didn't understand the book when I first read it.'

   Dièrhwéi kàn háishr kànbudǔng.
   'I still couldn't understand it the second time.'

   g. The following resultative verb compounds were introduced (without analysis) in previous lessons: hwéilai, hwéichyu, kànjyan, tīngjyan, kāikai,

gwānshang, jànchilai, dzwòsya, náchilai, fàngsya, and some other compounds ending in -lai and -chyu.

TRANSLATION OF THE INTRODUCTORY DIALOGUE

About the Chinese Language

(J) A gentleman who teaches Chinese.
(S) A student who is studying Chinese.

S: I think the study of Chinese is very interesting.

J: What differences do you see between Chinese and the English you speak?

S: When I translate Chinese sentences into English I realize that English
uses more words and Chinese fewer. Isn't that so?

5 J: What you say is quite right. There is a Chinese proverb which says:

Dzǒutswòle lù, hwéidelái;
shwōtswòle hwà, hwéibulái.

Do you understand that?

S: I don't understand the words hwéidelái and hwéibulái. What do they
10 mean?

J: I'll explain it to you. When a person is out walking and takes a wrong
road, he can go back and take a different road. But it isn't the same
when you speak. When you have said something, there is no way to re-
tract it.

15 S: Oh, I get you! What the proverb says is right. And your explanation
was very clear. If I should translate this sentence into English, it would
be longer. It would run like this in English:

If you take the wrong road, it is possible to return;
if you say the wrong word, it is impossible to recover it.

20 J: You translated it very well. The Chinese used six words; if it were
written in characters it would take only fourteen characters. But in
English? You used twenty-three words!

S: Why did you say hwéidelái and hwéibulái? I still don't understand those
two expressions. Couldn't you say néng hwéilai and bunéng hwéilai?

25 J: Yes, you can say it that way; the sense is almost the same. Let me give
you another example. It is now winter. One day your wife has a desire
for some watermelon and asks you to go downtown and buy her some.
You take your money, go up the street hunting this way and that, but you
can't find any because nobody's selling watermelons. When you go back
30 home what are you going to say to your wife?

S: I can tell her 'I didn't buy any,' or I can say, 'I couldn't buy any.'

J: I'm afraid she'd ask you, 'Why couldn't you buy me any?' Do you want
her to get mad?

S: Of course not. So I'd say: 'I didn't buy you any because in winter no
35 one sells watermelons.'

J: That's all right too, but you don't need to use so many words. As soon as she asks you, you can say, <u>Măibujáu</u> and that's enough. She'll understand. See how concise it is to say it that way!

40 S: It sure is concise! Well now, if the store does have watermelon but they are too high-priced, what should I say? Does this (situation) also have a concise way of putting it?

J: Yes. You can say, <u>Wŏmen măibuchĭ</u> and your wife will know that the reason you didn't buy her any was that the price was too high. So she wouldn't get sore at you!

45 S: Such expressions are fine. I should use them often; I should learn more of them.

J: Lesson 17 in this book has lots. When you have time you can look at some more.

SIMILARITY AND COMPARISON

A DIALOGUE AND SOME COMPARISONS

1. Having a Table Made

    Chyántyan wǒ gēn wo tàitai shwō wǒmen yīngdāng dwō mǎi yíge shū-
jyàdz, yīnwei wǒ chángchang mǎi syīn shū, kěshr jǐnyán yǐchyán mǎide
neige shūjyàdz yǐjing fàngmǎnle, dōu fàngbusyàle. Swóyi wǒ shàngjyē
jǎu mùjyang dìngdzwò yige dà yidyǎrde shūjyàdz; jǎule bàntyān tsái
5   jǎujáu.

Wǒ: Nǐmen jer néng dzwò shūjyàdz ba?

Mù: Cháng dzwò. Dzwótyan jyou yǒu yige rén lái dìngdzwòle lyǎngge hěn
dàde. Shr syīshr̀de. Nín dàgài yě yàu syīshr̀de ba?

Wǒ: Nǐ dzěmma jr̀dau wǒ yàu syīshr̀de ne?

10 Mù: Wǒ yí kàn nín chwānde yīshang shr syīshr̀de, jyou jr̀dau nín yě syīhwan
syīshr̀de jyājyù.

Wǒ: Nǐ syǎngde bútswò; wǒ shr̀ yàu syīshr̀de, yīnwei wǒmende jyājyu dōu
shr syīshr̀de. Yàushr fàng yige Jūngshr̀de shūjyàdz bútài héshr̀.

Mù: Nèmma, nín syǎngyau dwó dàde shūjyàdz ne?

15 Wǒ: Wǒ hái méijywédìng yàu dwó dàde ne. Nǐmen jer yǒu meiyǒu dzwo-
hǎulede? Wǒ kéyi kànkan ma?

Mù: Yǒu. Nín kàn jèige shūjyàdz, yàushr dzai nínde wūdzli fàngje, dàsyǎu
héshr̀ buhéshr̀?

Wǒ: Jèige bǐ wǒ syǎngde dàdwōle. Kǔngpà wǒ neige syǎu shūfáng fàngbusyà.
20   Jèige shūjyàdz yǒu dwó gāu?

Mù: Jèige yǒu chīchr̀-wǔtswùn gāu, bāchr̀-èrtswùn cháng. Nín kàn tài dà
ma?

Wǒ: Kǔngpà děi ǎi yidyǎr. Wǒmen fángdzde chyáng tsái chīchr̀ gāu. Cháng-
dwǎn yǒu jèigede yíbàn nemma cháng jyou gòule.

25 Mù: Jèmmayàng ba! Wǒ gěi nín hwà yijāng syǎu tú, bǎ nín shwōde chr̀-
tswun yě dōu syěshang. Chǐng nín syān dàihwei jyā chyu lyángyilyáng
nínde shūfáng yǒu dwó dà, fàng shūjyàdz de dìfang dwó dà, kànkan wǒ
jeijāng túshangde chr̀tswun héshr̀ buhéshr̀. Yàushr héshr̀, wǒ jyou
lìkè gěi nín dzwò; yě yùngbulyǎu jǐtyānde gūngfu.

30 Wǒ: Hǎu, wǒ syān hwéi jyā lyáng wūdz chyu. Kěshr, yàushr dìngdzwò ne,
jyàchyán dzěmmayàng?

Mù: Nà děi kàn yùng shémmayàngde mùtou dzwò. Mùtou yǒu pyányide yǒu
gwèide. Nín yàushr syǎng fàngdzai kètīngli, yīngdāng yùng hǎudyǎrde
mùtou. Yàushr fàngdzai shūfángli, búbi yùng nemma gwèide. Dzwèi
35   pyányide sānshrwǔkwai chyán; dzài hǎu yidyǎrde sz̀shrbákwài.

Wǒ: Hǎu, wǒ syān hwéi jyā syǎngsyang ba! Míngtyan dzài shwō ba.

Mù: Nín búdzwò (yi)hwěr?

Wǒ: Wǒ dzǒule.

2. <u>China and America Compared</u>

Jūnggwo bǐ Měigwo dà; Jūnggwo rén yě bǐ Měigwo rén dwō.

Měigwode shān hěn gāu, kěshr Jūnggwode shān gèng gāu.

Jūnggwode hé méiyou Měigwode hé nemma cháng.

Shwōdàu syígwàn, yǒude chàbudwō yíyàng, yǒude chàde hěn dwō.

5 Jūnggwo yǒu bushǎu dà chéng, kěshr méiyou Měigwode dà chéng nemma dwō.

Shànghǎide lóu buǎi, kěshr méiyou Nyǒuywēde nemma gāu. Sh` jyèshang
dzwèi gāude lóu dzai Nyǒuywē.

Jūnggwo rén gēn Měigwo rén chǐde dūngsyi bùyiyàng; chǐ fàn de fāngfǎ yě
bùyiyàng, kěshr chǐ fàn de shǐ´hou chàbudwō.

10 Jūnggwo rén gēn Měigwo rén hēde yě bùyiyàng. Jūnggwo rén píngchang
syǐhwan hē chá; Měigwo rén dzwèi ài hē de shr kāfēi.

Jūnggwo hwà fēicháng rúngyi shwō, bǐ něigwóde hwà dōu rúngyi shwō, kěshr
Jūnggwo dž tèbyé nánsyě.

Jūnggwode gwógēer jēn hǎutīng, gēn Měigwode gwógēer yíyàng hǎutīng;
15   kěshr Měigwo gwógēer bǐ Jūnggwode nánchàng.

VOCABULARY

Nouns (N)

-yàng(r)	M: kind, sort, type
yàngdz	N: pattern, style
shémmayàng(de)?	QW: what sort of?
dzěmmayàng?	QW: how? in what manner?
	EX: How about it? What do you think?
jèmmayàng	MA: in this manner, in this case
nèmmayàng	MA: in that way, in that case

Nín mǎi něiyàngr? Jèiyangr hǎu buhǎu?
'Which kind are you buying? How about this
kind?'

Nèmmayàng shwō búdwèi.
'It's not right to say it that way.'

-bèi	M: (for number of times)
-chǐ	M: foot (measure)
-tswùn	M: inch (measure)
-fēn	M: part, tenth (used in fractions; see Note 4-b)
-shr̀	BF: style, fashion
syīshr̀	N: Occidental style

Syīshr̀de yīshang dōu hěn gwèi.
'Occidental style clothing is quite expensive.'

Syīnshr̀de jwōdz tài dà; wǒ syǐhwan jyòushr̀-
de.
'The new style tables are too big; I prefer
the old style.'

mùjyang	N:	carpenter, woodworker, cabinetmaker
mùtou		wood, lumber
swèishu(r)		age (lit. 'age-count,' used only for adults)

Tāde syānsheng (yǒu) dwodà swèishur le?
'How old is her husband?'

jīngshen   spirit, vivacity

Jīntyān wǒ méi jīngshen.
'I'm feeling low today.'

lǎunyán rén	elderly person
jūngnyán rén	middle-aged person
nyánchīng rén	youth, young person

tú	map, diagram
chř	ruler, footrule
chŕtswùn	measurement
chángdwǎn	size (in length)
dàsyǎu	size (in mass)
shūjyà(dz)	bookcase, bookshelves

hé   river (M: -tyáu)

Adverbs (A)

yíyàng	similarly, equally (see under Verbs)
syāngdāng	fairly, rather
bǐjyǎu	comparatively, relatively
wánchywán	completely, entirely

Jèilyǎngběn shū yíyàng dà.
'These two books are the same size.'

Nèige lóu syāngdāng gāu.
'That building is rather tall.'

Nèijyān wūdz bǐjyǎu gānjing de dwō.
'The other room is in comparison a lot
cleaner.'

Dzwótyan wǒ bushūfu; jīntyan wánchywán
hǎule.
'Yesterday I was under the weather; today
I'm completely recovered.'

ywè lái ywè	more and more
ywè . . . ywè	the more . . . the more

Lǎu Jàu ywè lái ywè pàng.
'Old Jàu gets stouter and stouter.'

Jūnggwo gēer, ywè chàng ywè syǐhwan chàng.
'The more you sing Chinese songs, the more
you enjoy singing them.'

Verbs (V)

kàn   CV/FV: depending on; it depends on (followed by a
                                     sentence)

                             Kàn shr shéi chǐngde nǐ.
                             'It depends on who invites you.'

syàng   FV: resemble, be like
syàng . . . shrde   FV: seem like, seem as though
hǎusyàng . . . (shrde)   MA/FV: seemingly; seem like, look like

                             Tā hěn syàng ta fùchin.
                             'He strongly resembles his father.'

                             Jèikwai dyǎnsyin chřje jēn syàng Jūnggwo
                                 dyǎnsyin shrde.
                             'This piece of cake really tastes like Chi-
                                 nese cake.'

                             Tā hǎusyàng búywànyi chyù.
                             'He doesn't seem to want to go.'

lyáng   FV: measure, measure out

                             Jwōdz dwó gāu? Yùng chř lyánglyang ba.
                             'How high is the table?' 'Better use a ruler
                                 and measure it.'

dìng   FV: order
dìngdzwò   FV: order made, have made to order
jywédìng   FV: decide

fàngdesyà   RV: have room for, can accommodate
fàngmǎn(le)   RV: fill up

bǐ   FV: compare
                             CV: as compared with (see Pattern B)

                             Byé cháng gēn byéren bǐ.
                             'Don't keep comparing yourself with others.'

                             Nèilyǎngge háidz, něige gāu? Wǒmen bǐyibǐ
                                 ba.
                             'Which of those two youngsters is the taller?'
                             'Let's compare them.'

                             Jèiběn shū bǐ nèiběn shū gwèide dwō.
                             'This book is much more expensive than
                                 that one.'

fēn(chéng)   FV: divide, share, divide into (parts)

                             Kéyi bǎ nǐkwai ròu fēnchéng lyǎngbàn, gěi
                                 yíge rén yíbàn.
                             'You might divide that piece of meat into two
                                 halves and give each person a half.'

jǎng	FV: grow
jǎngdà	FV: grow up

Tā jǎngde jēn hǎukàn.
'She has grown to be very good-looking.'

Háidz jǎngdàle jyou děi shàngsywé le.
'When a child grows up he must go to school.'

gēn	CV: with, and (see Pattern A)
yǒu	CV: comes up to, is as . . . as (see Pattern A-3)
yíyàng	SV: be alike, the same, similar

Nǐde màudz gēn wǒde wánchywán yíyàng.
'Your hat and mine are exactly alike.'

Yùbei gūngkè gēn yùbei fàn bùyíyàng.
'Preparing a lesson and preparing a meal
    are not the same.'

bùrú	FV: not be the equal of (positive form not used)
cháng	SV: be long
dwǎn	SV: be short
kwān	SV: be wide, broad
jǎi	SV: be narrow
mǎn	SV: be full, full of
pàng	SV: (of persons) be stout, obese
shòu	SV: be slender, thin (opp. <u>pàng</u>); lean (opp. <u>féi</u>)
féi	SV: (of meat) be fat; (of clothing) be loose; (of land) be rich, fertile

Particle (P)

-jī	(used in fractions; see Note 4-b)

Common Sayings

Hwèi-shwōde burú hwèi-tīngde; hwèi-tīngde burú hwèi-syíngde.	Talkers are inferior to listeners; listeners are inferior to doers.
Tyānsyàde lǎugwa yíyàng hēi.	Crows all over the world are equally black.
Syīn-jì burú mwò-jì.	A mental note is not as good as an ink-note.
Yíyàng hwà; bǎiyàng shwōfǎr.	A single utterance may be expressed in a hundred ways.
Yítswùn gwāngyīn, yítswùn jīn; tswùn jīn nán mǎi tswùn gwāngyīn.	An inch of sunlight, an inch of gold; the inch of gold can't purchase the inch of sunlight.

SENTENCE PATTERNS

A. Similarity and Dissimilarity

1. General Similarity

Jèige gēn nèige yíyàng.
'This one and that one are alike.'

Jūng gēn byǎu bùyíyàng.
'Clocks and watches are not alike.'

Tāde pǐchi gēn nǐde bùyíyàng.
'His temperament is not the same as yours.'

Wǒ péngyou dzwòde tsài gēn wǒ dzwòde buyíyàng.
'The dishes my friend cooks are not like what I cook.'

Jèige gēn nèige yíyàng ma? (or yíyàng buyíyàng?)
'Are this one and that one the same?'

To express general similarity, a coverbial expression consisting of the
CV gēn and its object is placed between the subject of the sentence and
the main stative verb yíyàng. The pattern is:

A	gēn	B	yíyàng.
'A	and	B	are identical.'

Jèige	gēn	nèige	bùyiyàng.
Jèige	bùgēn	nèige	yíyàng.

'This is not the same as that.'

The negative is prefixed to the CV gen only in categorical denial of a
statement already made. Pattern A-3 (below) is generally preferred in
negating equivalence.

2. Similarity in Specific Respects

Jèijang hwàr gēn nèijang hwàr yíyàng gwèi.
'This picture and that are the same price.'

Nǐ syěde gēn tā syěde yíyàng chīngchu.
'Your writing and his writing are equally clear.'

Tāmen yùbeide tsài gēn nǐmen yùbeide (tsài) bùyiyàng dwō.
'They are not as generous as you in the number of dishes prepared.'

Wǒ kāi chē kāide gēn nǐ kāide bùyiyàng kwài.
'I don't drive as fast as you do.'

To limit the similarity to a specific respect, an appropriate stative verb
is placed after yíyàng as a predicate complement. The negative bu- may
stand before either the coverb or yíyàng with no difference in meaning.
The pattern is:

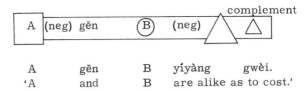

	A	gēn	B	yíyàng	gwèi.
'A	and	B	are alike as to cost.'

3. <u>Equivalence (with CV yŏu . . . nèmma SV)</u>

a. Jèige yŏu nèige nèmma dà.
  'This is as big as that.'

  Chìchē yŏu hwŏchē nèmma kwài ma?
  'Are cars as fast as trains?'

b. Jèige yĭdz chàbudwō yŏu nèige jwōdz nèmma jùng.
  'This chair is almost as heavy as that table.'

c. Hwŏchē méiyou fēijī nèmma kwài.
  'Trains are not as fast as planes.'

A coverbial expression with <u>yŏu</u> may be used in a sentence to indicate that A comes up to B (or, in negative, falls short of B) in respect to the quality expressed by the main stative verb. The adverb <u>nèmma</u> (or <u>jèmma</u>) often stands before the SV in the sense of 'so,' 'to that (or this) extent.' The negative particle always stands before the coverb <u>yŏu</u> not before the main verb. The pattern is:

Jèige   yŏu   nèige   nèmma dà.
'This is as big as that.'

Nèige gāngbǐ méiyou jèige   jèmma gwèi.
'That pen is not as expensive as this one.'

B. Comparison for Contrast (with CV bǐ . . . SV)

  1. <u>Simple Comparison</u>

  Jèige bǐ nèige dà.
  'This one is bigger than that one.'

  Nǐde yìsz bǐ wŏde hău.
  'Your idea is better than mine.'

  Jèmma dzwò bùyídìng bǐ nèmma dzwò rúngyi.
  'Doing it this way is not necessarily easier than doing it that way.'

  Wŏ sywé Jūnggwo hwà, sywéde bùbǐ tāmen kwài.
  'I'm not faster than the rest in learning Chinese.'

  To contrast persons or things which are different, the coverbial pattern with <u>bǐ</u> is used. The CV <u>bǐ</u> 'as compared with' and its object (B) with which the subject (A) is to be compared, stand before an appropriate stative verb. The negative bù- may stand before <u>bǐ</u> but not before the main verb. The pattern is:

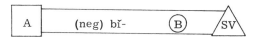

Byǎu   bǐ   jūng syǎu.
'Watches are smaller than clocks.'

Jèige gēer bùbǐ byéde gēer nánchàng.
'This song is not more difficult to sing than other songs.'

2. Degrees of Comparison

   a. Expressed Adverbially

Nín bǐ wǒ gèng máng.
'You are even busier than I.'

Tā pǎude bǐ wǒ pǎude hái kwài.
'He runs still faster than I.'

Certain adverbs, such as gèng and hái, may stand before the main verb to indicate degree.

   b. Expressed by a Predicate Complement

Gāngbǐ bǐ chyānbǐ gwèi dwōshau?	How much more expensive is a pen than a pencil?
(Gāngbǐ bǐ chyānbǐ) { gwèide dwō	much more expensive
gwèi yidyǎr	a little more expensive
gwèi yifēn chyán	one cent more

Jèige chwáng bǐ nèige gāu dwōshau?	How much higher is this bed than that?
(Jèige chwáng bǐ nèige) { gāu bàntswùn	higher by half an inch.
gāu háujitswùn	higher by several inches
gāu yíbàn	half again as high
gāu yíbèi	once again as high (twice as high)

In the degree complement, the interrogative of quantity, dwōshau?, may be used to ask a question, and an indefinite answer may take the pattern SV-de dwō 'much more'; otherwise a number-measure expression is used.

   c. In the Case of Functive Verbs

Tā bǐ wǒ dwō chřle sānwǎn fàn.
'He ate three more bowls of rice than I did.'

Wǒ bǐ nǐmen shǎu gěile ta shŕkwai chyán.
'I've given him ten dollars less than you folks did.'

Nín bǐ wǒ dzǎu dàu bànge jūngtóu.
'You arrive a half hour earlier than I.'

Wǒ bǐ nín wǎn dzǒu yíkè jūng.
'I leave a quarter of an hour later than you.'

Functive verbs may stand after the bǐ-pattern provided they are modified by an adverb such as dwō, shǎu, dzǎu, wǎn; the degree is indicated by a measure expression in the complement.

NOTES

1. <u>Uses of the Coverb</u> gēn

    a. <u>Gēn</u> was first introduced in Lesson 8 as a connective between two or more nominal elements, functioning like the English conjunction 'and.' In Lesson 9, <u>gēn</u> appeared as a coverb taking an object and functioning like an English preposition:

        Chén Syansheng gēn Chén Taitai dōu lái.
        'Mr. Chen and Mrs. Chen are both coming.'

        Wǒ gēn Chén Syānsheng sywégwo Jūngwén.
        'I have studied Chinese with Mr. Chen.'

    b. In this lesson <u>gēn</u> appears again as a coverb in the pattern for similarity. It stands between the two elements under consideration and takes the second as its object to form a coverbial expression qualifying the stative verb which follows. The nominal elements compared may be nouns, phrases or clauses:

        Tā gēn nǐ yíyàng.
        'He and you are alike.'

        Yīnggwo chyán gēn Měigwo chyán yíyàng ma?
        'Is English money the same as American money?'

        Tāmen gěi wǒ de gēn wǒ gěi tāmen de wánchywán yíyàng.
        'What they gave me is just like what I gave them.'

    c. Note that two or more nominal elements may be declared similar or dissimilar without contrasting one against the other:

        Bàu, dzájr̀ budōu yíyàng.
        'Newspapers and magazines are not all alike.'

        Nǐ, wǒ, tā wǒmen sānge rén chàbudwō yíyàng gāu.
        'The three of us are about the same height.'

    d. The adverb <u>chàbudwō</u> 'about,' 'almost,' 'approximately' may be placed immediately before <u>yíyàng</u> in the <u>gēn</u> pattern.

        Hwǒchē gēn chìchē chàbudwō yíyàng kwài.
        'Trains are almost as fast as cars.'

2. Indefinite Measures in Comparison

Expressions of indefinite measure or degree frequently appear as complements of the verb in the pattern of comparison with the coverb <u>bǐ</u>:

    syǎu yidyǎr   a little smaller
    hǎudwōle   much better
    dà hǎusyē   a good deal bigger
    gwèi dwōshau?   how much more expensive?
    gāude budwō   not much taller (or higher)
    cháng bushǎu   quite a little longer
    tsūngmingde dwō   much brighter (or smarter)
    ywǎnde hěndwō   very much farther

3. <u>Use of the Measure -bèi</u>

The Chinese measure -<u>bèi</u> has an English counterpart in the suffix '-fold' and is used similarly to indicate increase in geometric ratio— doubling, tripling, etc. It is commonly found in two patterns of comparison:

a. In comparisons with -<u>bǐ</u> it is used as a complement to the main verb:

Jèityáu hé bǐ nèityáu hé cháng <u>yíbèi</u>.
'This river is twice as long as that river.'

Logically, <u>cháng lyǎngbèi</u> should mean 'longer by twofold,' which would indicate 'three times as long,' but in Chinese as in English there is a common inclination to say 'tenfold' regardless of whether we mean 'ten times as large as' or 'larger by tenfold.' Hence the ambiguous usage:

cháng shŕbèi	usually indicates	eleven times as long or ten times longer than
dwō yìbǎibèi	usually indicates	100 times as much
gāu háujibèi	usually indicates	many times as high
dà háujishŕbèi	usually indicates	many tens of times as large

b. In expressions of similarity with <u>yǒu</u> (as well as equative statements with <u>shr̀</u>) no such ambiguity is involved because these are statements of equivalents:

Wǒde byǎu yǒu wo tàitaide (byǎude) lyǎngbèi nèmma dà.
'My watch is twice the size of my wife's.'

Tāde chyán shr wǒde (chyánde) háujibèi (nèmma dwō).
'He has many times as much money as I have.'

Bā shr sz̀de lyǎngbèi.
'Eight is two times four.'

4. <u>Use of Fractions in Comparison</u>

a. The Fraction yíbàn 'a half'

When <u>yibàn</u> is used in the CV <u>bǐ</u> pattern as a complement to stative verbs which express expansion in quality or degree (such as <u>gwèi</u>, <u>dà</u>, <u>cháng</u>, <u>dwō</u>, <u>ywǎn</u>, etc.), a half again this quality is indicated:

bǐ . . . gwèi yibàn	is half again as expensive (or one and one-half times as expensive)
dà yibàn	half again as big or large
cháng yibàn	half again as long
dwō yibàn	half again as much or many
gāu yibàn	half again as tall or high

When <u>yíbàn</u> follows stative verbs which express contraction in quality or degree the effect is reduction by one-half:

bǐ . . . pyányi yibàn	is cheaper by a half (or half as expensive)
syǎu yibàn	smaller by a half
dwǎn yibàn	shorter by a half
shǎu yibàn	fewer or less by a half

When yíbàn stands in the equivalence pattern before (nèmma) SV, only stative verbs expressing expansion are used:

yǒu . . . yíbàn nemma gwèi   is half as expensive
          yíbàn nemma dà   half as big or large
          yíbàn nemma cháng   half as long
          etc.

b. Fractions in the NU-fēnjr NU Pattern

NU-fēnjr NU is the common pattern for fractions other than yíbàn. The denominator being the larger number stands first in Chinese, followed by the numerator. The element -jr is the literary form of the particle -de. Sānfenjr yī literally means one part out of three, or one-third; sìfenjr sān means three parts out of four, or three-quarters; bǎifenjr bāshŕ, 80 parts out of 100, or 80 percent.

Fractions of this pattern stand in the same position as yíbàn in sentences expressing comparison. Compare the following:

Jèige jwōdz bǐ nèige gwèi sānfenjr-yī.
'This table is 1/3 more expensive than that one.'

Jīnnyande sywésheng bǐ chyùnyande dwō shŕfenjr-yī.
'There are 10 percent more students here this year than last.'

Jèige jwōdz yǒu nèigede sānfenjr-èr nemma cháng.
'This table is 2/3 the length of this one.'

Wǒde shū yǒu tāde bǎifenjr-yī nemma dwō.
'I have 1/100 the number of books that he has.'

Wǒde píbāu bǐ nǐde pyányi bǎifenjr-sānshŕ.
'My briefcase is 30 percent cheaper than yours.'

Wǒmen jīnnyǎn yùngde chyán bǐ chyùnyan shǎu wǔfenjr-èr.
'We are using 2/5 less money this year than last.'

5. Auxiliary Verbs in Comparisons

An auxiliary verb expression— with or without the verbal object— indicates a condition or status rather than an action. It is used in the plural.

An auxiliary verb indicates a condition or status rather than an action. Consequently an auxiliary verb, with or without its verbal object, may perform either of two functions in a comparison: (1) as complement to yíyàng, or (2) as main verb after a bǐ phrase or a yǒu phrase:

Tā gēn wǒ yíyàng ài chŕ Jūnggwo fàn.
'He and I are alike in enjoying Chinese food.'

Tā bǐ nǐ ài shwō hwà.
'He likes to talk more than you do.'

Tā yǒu nǐ nèmma syǐhwan chàng gēer ma?
'Does he like to sing as much as you do?'

6. Generalized Nouns of Measurement

Generalized nouns, indicating size, extent, weight, extent, weight, etc., are made by linking two opposite SV into a compound, as for example:

dàsyǎu	size	'large-small'
chángdwǎn	length	'long-short'
kwānjǎi	width	'wide-narrow'
kwàimàn	speed	'fast-slow'
gāudǐ	height	'high-low'

This treatment is limited to monosyllabic SV.

TRANSLATION OF THE INTRODUCTORY DIALOGUE AND SOME COMPARISONS

1. Having a Table Made

The day before yesterday I told my wife we ought to buy another book-case, because I'm always buying new books, but the bookcase we bought several years ago is already full and won't accomodate any more. So I went out to find a carpenter to make us a larger book-
5   case. I hunted quite a while before I found one.

I   :   You can make a bookcase, can't you?

Carp: We're always making them. Just yesterday a man came and ordered a couple of very large ones, foreign style. I assume you also would want Western style?

10 I   :   How did you know I'd want Western style?

Carp: When I saw that the clothes you wear are foreign style, I knew you'd probably like foreign style furniture too.

I   :   You guessed right. I do want foreign style, because our furniture is all foreign style, and if you put a Chinese style bookcase in, it won't
15   look too well.

Carp: Well then, how big a case do you want?

I   :   I haven't yet decided how big a one I want. Have you a finished book-case? May I take a look at it?

Carp: Yes, look at this one. If it were placed in your room, would the size
20   be right?

I   :   This one is much larger than what I was considering. I'm afraid it wouldn't go into that small study of mine. How high is this case?

Carp: It's seven feet five high and eight feet two long. Does it look too big to you?

25 I   :   I'm afraid it would have to be a little lower. The walls of our rooms are only seven feet high. Half as long as this one would be sufficient.

Carp: I'll tell you what! I'll draw a little sketch for you and put on it the measurements you have mentioned. Will you first take it home and measure how large your study is, and how large the space for the
30   bookcase is, and see if the measurements on this diagram of mine are satisfactory? If they are all right, I'll make it for you right away. It won't take but a couple of days.

I   : Good, I'll go back and measure the room. But if I order it, what
         will the price be?

35 Carp: That depends on what wood is used. There are inexpensive woods
         and expensive woods. If you are going to put it in the living room,
         it ought to be of a better wood. If it is to go in the study, you don't
         need to use as expensive a wood. The cheapest would be thirty-five
         dollars; for a better one, forty-eight dollars.

40 I   : All right, I'll go home and think it over. We'll discuss it further
         tomorrow.

    Carp: Won't you sit awhile?

    I   : I'll be going.

2. China and America Compared

China is larger than America, and there are more Chinese than Americans.

The mountains in America are high, but those of China are higher.

China's rivers are not as long as those of America.

If one speaks of customs, some are quite similar, others are very different.

5   There are quite a few large cities in China, but there are not as many as in
    the United States.

Shanghai's buildings are quite tall, but they are not as tall as New York's.
The world's highest building is in New York.

Chinese and Americans don't eat the same things. They don't eat in the
10 same manner either; but the times at which they eat do not differ much.

What Chinese and Americans drink differs too. Chinese ordinarily like to
drink tea. What Americans prefer to drink is coffee.

Chinese is extraordinarily easy to speak, easier than all other languages;
but Chinese characters are particularly difficult to write.

15 The Chinese national anthem is really beautiful, just as beautiful as Amer-
    ica's; but the American national anthem is harder to sing.

Lesson 19

SEPARATION AND DISTANCE

TWO DIALOGUES

1. Three Routes to China

Jyǎ : Wǒ syǎng syàywè dau Jūnggwo chyu. Jūnggwo lí Měigwo yǒu dwò ywǎn?

Yǐ : Kàn nǐ dzǒu něityáu lù.

Jyǎ : Něityáu lù dzwèi jìn?

5 Yǐ : Dzwèi jìnde lù shr jīnggwo Běijí.

Jyǎ : Nèityau lù dzěmma dzǒu?

Yǐ : Tsúng Nyǒuywē dzwò fēijī, yìjŕ wàng běi fēi, jīnggwo Jyānadà dau Běijí. Tsúng Běijí dzài wàng nán fēi, jīnggwo Ègwode dūngbù jyou dàu Jūnggwo le.

10 Jyǎ : Jèityau lù yǒu dwōshau yīnglǐ?

Yǐ : Yǒu chīchyāndwo-yīnglǐ.

Jyǎ : Dàu Jūnggwo méiyou bǐ jèityau gèng jìnde lù ma?

Yǐ : Méiyou. Jīnggwo Oūjōu yǒu yìtyau lù, kěshr nèityau bǐ jèityau ywǎn yidyǎr.

15 Jyǎ : Nèityau lù dzěmma dzǒu?

Yǐ : Yàu wàng dūng chyu, dzwò chwán gwò Dàsyīyáng dau Dégwo, dzài dzwò hwǒchē, jīnggwo Mwòszkē, búdau lyǎngge lǐbài jyou kéyi dàu Běijīng le.

Jyǎ : Jèityau lù bǐ nèityau ywǎn dwōshau?

20 Yǐ : Ywǎn lyǎngchyāndwo yīnglǐ.

Jyǎ : Wàng syī chyu dàubulyǎu Jūnggwo ma?

Yǐ : Dàudelyǎu, kěshr lù gèng ywǎnle. Yàushr dzǒu jèityau lù, děi syān dzwò hwǒchē dàu Jyòujīnshān, dzài dzwò chwán gwò Tàipíngyáng dàu Shànghǎi. Jèityáu lù dzwèi cháng dzǒu.

25 Jyǎ : Dwō syè, dwō syè!

Yǐ : Méi shemma!

(Note: Jyǎ and Yǐ are used in Chinese as A and B are in English to designate the first and second speaker.)

2. A North China Trip

Sānge rén yíkwàr tán hwà ne:

Chén: Nín shànglǐbài chyùde neige dìfang lí jer hěn ywǎn ba?

183

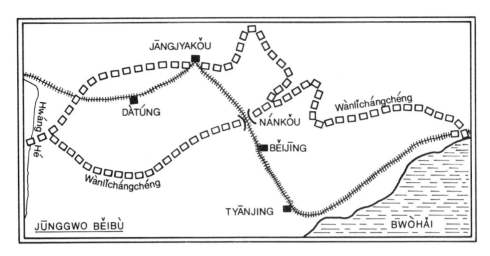

Lyóu: Nín shwōde shr shémma dìfang? Shr Dàtúng ba!

Chén: Wǒ jìbuchīng neige dìfang jyàu shémma míngdz— dàgài jyòu shr nín
        shwōde jeige Dàtúng ba?

5 Lyóu: Dàtúng yě bútài ywǎn— yěsyǔ yǒu wǔbǎi yīnglǐ.

Gwō :   Dàtúng yǒu nèmma ywǎn ma? Wǒ lyǎngnyán yǐchyán chyùgwo yìtsż.
        Wǒ jìde tsái yǒu sānbǎidwō yīnglǐ.

Lyóu: Tsái sānbǎi yīnglǐ! Wǒmen chyùde shrhou, dzwò hwǒchē dzǒule
        bājyǒuge jūngtóu.

10 Gwō :   Hwǒchē yíge jūngtóu yě jyou dzǒu sżshr yīnglǐ. Nèmma, báge jūng-
        tóu kéyi dzǒu sānbǎi-èrshr yīnglǐ. Nà jyou chàbudwōle.

Chén: Dàtúng jeige dìfang shr dzài Jūnggwode syīběibu, shr̀ bushr̀?

Lyóu: Aī, tsúng Běijīng wàng syīběi, jìnggwo Jāngjyakǒu.

Chén: Bǐ Jāngjyakǒu hái ywǎn ma?

15 Gwō :   Bǐ Jāngjyakǒu ywǎn dwōle. Jāngjyakǒu chàbudwó tsái yìbǎi yīnglǐ.
        Dàtúng lí jèr yǒu Jāngjyakǒu sānbèi nèmma ywǎn.

Lyóu: Dwèile, bǐ Jāngjyakǒu ywǎn èrbǎidwō yīnglǐ.

Chén: Jēn méisyǎngdàu yǒu nèmma ywǎn.

                        VOCABULARY

                        Nouns (N)

-lǐ(lù)   M: (for distance, about 1/3 of a mile)

-yīnglǐ   M: (for English miles)

(-)byār   N/M: side, edge, border, section (see Note 1)

jèibyar   PW: this side, over here
nèibyar   PW: that side, over there

něibyar?	PW:	which side? where?
shàngbyar	PW:	top
syàbyar	PW:	below
pángbyār	PW:	alongside

Nǐmen nèibyar yǒu hǎu fàngwǎr ma?
'Are there good restaurants over your way?'

Jèityáu lù lyǎngbyār dōu yǒu shwěi.
'There's water on both sides of this road.'

-bù	M·	part, section, area (M for regions, see Note 1)

Shànghǎi dzài Jūnggwode dūngbù.
'Shanghai is in eastern China.'

gūnglù	N:	highway (M: -tyáu) (lit. 'public road')
gūngywán	PW:	public park
tyānchi, tyār	N:	weather

Nyǒuywēde tyānchi hái bútswò.
'New York's weather is not so bad.'

Jīntyan tyānchi (or tyār) jēn hǎu.
'The weather today is fine.'

shr̀jyè(shang)	PW:	the world

Nèmma hǎude rén shr̀jyèshang budwō jyàn.
'One seldom sees people who are that good in this world.'

lyǔgwǎn	PW:	hotel
dàyī	N:	overcoat, topcoat (M: -jyàn)
hú	N:	lake
hǎi	N:	sea
dūng	N:	east ⎫
nán	N:	south ⎪ (indicators of direction, to which
syī	N:	west ⎬ -byar is added to indicate an area,
běi	N:	north ⎭ see Note 1)

Wàng dūng dzǒu!
'Go east!'

Běijīng syībyar yǒu gāu shān.
'West of Peking are high mountains.'

Adverbs (A)

yìjŕ	A:	straight on, straight ahead, directly

Tsúng jèr dzwò hwǒchē yìjŕ dàu nèr.
'Go from here by train straight there.'

Yìjŕ wàng syī dzǒu ba.
'Go directly west.'

Tsúng tā dzǒule yǐhòu, yìjǐ méiyou syìn.
'From the time he left, there's not been a
line from him.'

Verbs (V)

lí   CV: from (be separated or distant from) (see
                       Pattern A)

jīnggwò   FV: pass through, pass by

                       Dàu R̄běn chyu děi jīnggwo Tánsyāngshān.
                       'In going to Japan one must pass through
                       Honolulu.'

gwǎi   FV: turn (a corner)

                       Wàng běi gwǎi!
                       'Turn north.'

ywǎn   SV: be far away, distant
jìn   SV: be near, close

                       Sywésyàu lí wǒ jyā hěn jìn; lí tā jyā ywǎn
                       yidyǎr.
                       'The school is quite near my home, a little
                       farther from his home.'

lěng   SV: be cold
rè   SV: be hot

                       Jīntyan tyānchi jēn lěng.
                       'The weather today is quite cold.'

lyángkwai   SV: be comfortably cool
nwǎnhe, nwǎnhwo SV: be comfortably warm

shēn   SV: be deep, dark (in color), be deep (in meaning)
chyǎn   SV: be shallow

                       Hǎilǐde shwěi shēnjíle.
                       'The water in the ocean is extremely deep.'

                       Hwánghélǐde shwěi, yánsè shr shēn hwángde.
                       'The water of the Yellow River is deep yel-
                       low.'

                       Yìsz yàushr tài shēnle jyou buhǎudǔngle.
                       'If the meaning is too deep, it won't be easy
                       to understand.'

yǒumíng   SV: be famous, well known

                       Swūn Jūngshān Syansheng jeige rén hěn
                       yǒumíng.
                       'Sun Yat-sen is very famous.'

Common Sayings

Lěng shr yíge rén lěng;   When it's cold, one person is cold;
    rè shr dàjyā rè.   when it's hot, everyone is hot.

> Chāi dūng chyáng, Tear down the east wall
> bǔ syī chyáng. to patch the west wall.
> (Rob Peter to pay Paul.)

SENTENCE PATTERNS

A. Description of Distances with CV lí . . . ywǎn, or . . . jìn

Nǐ jyā lí sywésyàu ywǎn buywǎn? Bútai ywǎn.
'Is your home far from the school?' 'Not too far.'

Nyǒuywē lí Syīngǎng hěn ywǎn ba? Bújìn.
'New York is quite far from New Haven, isn't it?' 'It's not near.'

Wǒ jùde dìfang lí hwǒchējàn hěn jìn.
'The place where I live is quite near to the railroad station.'

Tāmen ner lí sywésyàu jìnjíle!
'Their place is extremely near the school!'

Wǒmen ner lí jèr yě tèbyé jìn.
'Our place is especially near too.'

Yǒu jǐwei syānsheng, tāmen jùde dìfang lí jèr tài ywǎnle!
'There are a few teachers whose living quarters are too far from here.'

Sywésyàu lí chénglǐtou bùdzěmma ywǎn.
'The school is not so far from downtown.'

1. To indicate the distance between two points, the coverbial pattern with lí 'be distant or separated from' is used. The coverbial expression stands before the stative verb ywǎn 'be far,' or jìn 'be near.' The negative bù- usually stands before the stative verb, not before the coverb lí.

2. Extent of separation is indicated (i) by an appropriate adverb (hěn, tài, fēicháng, etc.) standing before the stative verb; or (ii) by a complement (such as -de hěn, -jíle) standing after the stative verb. The patterns are:

(i)

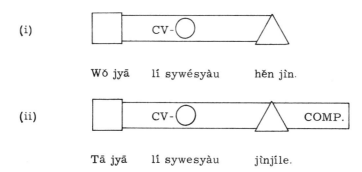

Wǒ jyā lí sywésyàu hěn jìn.

(ii)

Tā jyā lí sywesyàu jìnjíle.

B. Comparison of Distances with CV gēn, yǒu, and bǐ

1. Between Two Points and a Third Point

Lǐjyā (lí sywésyàu) gēn Mǎjyā lí sywésyàu yíyàng ywǎn ma? Chàbudwō.
'Are the Lǐ family and the Mǎ family the same distance from the school?'
'Just about the same.'

Sywésyàu lí chējàn yǒu wǒ jyā lí chējan nèmma ywǎn.
'The school is as far from the station as my home.'

Yīnggwo (lí Měigwo) méiyou Táiwān lí Měigwo nèmma ywǎn.
'England is not as far from America as Taiwan is.'

Jyānadà lí Měigwo bǐ Gūbā lí Měigwo jìn.
'Canada is nearer to America than Cuba.'

In describing relative distances between two points, A and B, and a third
point X, two identical coverbial expressions (preceded by their subjects)
are linked together by the coverbs gēn, yǒu, or bǐ, or their negated forms.
Because the two coverbial expressions are identical one or the other may
be dropped. The three patterns are:

a. A (from X) and B from X are the same.

b. A from X is as far as B (from X).

c. A from X compared with B (from X) is nearer.

2. Between Two Points and Two Other Points

Rběn lí Jūnggwo gēn Yīnggwo lí Fàgwo chàbudwō yíyàng ywǎn.
'Japan is about the same distance from China as England is from France.'

Nánjīng lí Shànghǎi yǒu Fèichéng lí Nyǒuywē lyǎngbèi nèmma ywǎn.
'Nanking is twice as far from Shanghai as Philadelphia is from New York.'

Wǒmen jyā lí nǐmen jyā bǐ chējàn lí sywésyàu jìnde dwō.
'Our home is much nearer your home than the station is to the school.'

In the case of comparing distance between two points, A and B, and two
different points, X and Y, the two coverbial expressions are not identical
so neither one may be dropped. The patterns are:

a. A from B and X from Y are equally distant.

b. A from B is twice as far as X from Y.

c. A from B compared with X from Y, is much nearer.

C. Use of yǒu in Measurement

Nǐ jyā lí sywésyàu yǒu dwō ywǎn? Méi dwō ywǎn.
'How far is your home from the school?' 'Not very far.'

Tsúng Syīngǎng dau Nyǒuywē yǒu dwō ywǎn? Yǒu chīshrwǔ yīnglǐ (ywǎn)
ma?
'How far is it from New Haven to New York? Is it 75 miles?'

Syānsheng, nín (yǒu) dwō dà swèishur? Wǒ lyòushrdwō le!
'How old are you, sir?' 'I'm over 60.'

Nǐmende syǎuhár (yǒu) jǐswèi le? Tā lyǎngswèibàn le.
'How old is your child?' 'He's two and a half.'

Jwōdz yǒu dwó cháng? Yǒu jǐchǐ cháng? Yǒu wǔchǐ cháng méiyou?
Chàbudwō.
'How long is the table? How many feet long? As much as five feet long?'
'Almost.'

Jūnggwo dzwèi chángde hé jyàu Chángjyāng. Chángjyāng yǒu yìchyāndwō yīnglǐ cháng ma? Yǒu.
'China's longest river is called the Chángjyāng.' 'Is it a thousand miles long?' 'Yes, it is.'

Shìjyè dzwèi gāude shān yǒu jǐwanchǐ gāu? Yǒu lyǎngwàn jyǒuchyān-dwōchǐ gāu.
'How many tens of thousands of feet high is the world's highest mountain?' 'It is 29,000 feet and over.'

Distance, age, length, height, etc., are measured by using the verb <u>yǒu</u> followed by a term of measurement. In this use, the verb <u>yǒu</u> is frequently omitted. (See Lesson 5 where the omission of <u>mǎi</u>, <u>mài</u>, <u>yàu</u>, and <u>shì</u> was noted.)

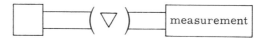

Tàishān   (yǒu)   dwō   gāu?
'How high is Taishan?'

(Tàishān   yǒu)   wǔchyandwō-chǐ (gāu).
'It is five thousand and some feet high.'

                Yǒu   nèmma gāu ma?
                'Is it that high?'

Yǒu, yǒu nèibyar neige shān nèmma gāu.
'Yes, it's as high as that mountain over there.'

NOTES

1. <u>The Measures</u> -byār <u>and</u> -bù

   a. The measure -<u>byār</u> means literally 'edge,' 'side,' 'border'; -<u>bù</u> means an area or section of territory. In some cases they may be used interchangeably:

   Nyǒuywē dzai Měigwode dūngbù (<u>or</u> dūngbyar).
   'New York is in the eastern part of the U.S.A.'

   Jūnggwode syībù gēn Měigwode syībù (<u>or</u> syībyar) dōu yǒu gāu shān.
   'There are high mountains in the west of China and of America.'

   Běijīng dzai Jūnggwode dūngběibù (<u>or</u> dūngběibyar).
   'Peking is in the northeastern portion of China.'

   b. The term <u>Měigwo nánbù</u> refers to the southern part of the U.S. — 'The South'; but <u>Měigwo nánbyar</u> may mean either 'the southern part of the U.S.' or 'south of the U.S.' Hence:

   Jřjyāgē dzai Měigwode jūngbù. (-<u>bù</u> only)
   'Chicago is in the central region (district) of America.'

   Dàsyīyáng dzai Měigwode dūngbyār. (-<u>byār</u> only)
   'The Atlantic Ocean is east of America.'

c. The measure -byār may also be compounded with other directional terms:

Chyánbyar yǒu chìchē. Shéi láile? (-byār only)
'There's a car out front. Who's come?'

Tā pángbyār jànjede neige rén shr shéi? (-byār only)
'Who is the person standing at his side?'

Kèren shr dzwòdzai jūrende dzwǒbyar, háishr dzwòdzai yòubyar? (-byār only)
'Should a guest sit on the host's left or right?'

d. Note that the terms jèr and nèr, introduced in Lesson 8, are actually shortened forms for jèibyar and nèibyar.

Wǒmen nèibyar (or ner) yǒu shān yě yǒu shwěi.
'Over where we are, there are mountains, lakes, and rivers.'

2. Chinese Forms of Foreign Place Names

a. In some cases the meaning is translated into Chinese:

Tàipíngyáng 'the ocean of great peace'	Pacific Ocean
Dìjūnghǎi 'the sea in the midst of land'	Mediterranean Sea
Syīngǎng 'new port' or 'haven'	New Haven
Dūngjīng 'eastern capital'	Tokyo
Běijí 'northern extremity'	North Pole

b. In some cases a Chinese descriptive term is applied:

Dàsyīyáng 'the great western ocean'	Atlantic Ocean
Tánsyāngshān 'the mountain fragrant with sandalwood'	Honolulu
Jyòujīnshān 'old golden mountain'	San Francisco

c. In some cases the pronunciation is approximated in Chinese:

Nyǒuywē	New York
Hwáshèngdwùn	Washington
Jřjyāgē	Chicago
Sānfānshr̀ (or Jyòujīnshān)	San Francisco
Syàwēiyí	Hawaii
Bwōshrdwùn	Boston

d. In some cases, long names are abbreviated, with or without the addition of a purely Chinese ending:

Fèichéng (Fèi-city)	Philadelphia
Yǎjōu (Yǎ-continent)	Asia
Oūjōu (Oū-continent)	Europe
Fēijōu (Fēi-continent)	Africa
Měijōu (Měi-continent)	America
Aùjōu (Aù-continent)	Australia
Běiměi	North America
Nánměi	South America

3. Meaning in Chinese Geographic Names

(Standard map spelling)	(Chinese pronunciation)	(Literal meaning)
Peiping	Běipíng	northern peace (or plain)
Peking	Běijīng	northern capital
Nanking	Nánjīng	southern capital
Shantung	Shāndūng	east of the (Taihang) mountains
Shansi	Shānsyī	west of the (Taihang) mountains
Honan	Hénán	south of the (Yellow) river
Hopeh	Héběi	north of the (Yellow) river
Hunan	Húnán	south of the (Tungting) lake
Hupeh	Húběi	north of the (Tungting) lake
Yunnan	Yúnnán	south of the clouds
Kiangsi	Jyāngsyī	west of the (Yangtze) river
Kwangtung	Gwǎngdūng	east of Kwang (ancient Hukwang province)
Kwangsi	Gwǎngsyī	west of Kwang
Yangtze River	Chángjyāng	long river
Yellow River	Hwánghé	yellow river
Taiwan	Táiwān	terraced bay
Taipei	Táiběi	(in) northern Taiwan
Far East	Ywǎndūng	distant east
Southeast Asia	Dūngnán Yǎ	east-south Asia*
Middle East	Jūngdūng	middle east (including Near East)
Northeast	Dūngběi	east-north*
Northwest	Syīběi	west-north*
Great Wall	Wànlǐ-chángchéng	10,000 lǐ long wall†

* Note that east and west (not north and south) are used in China as focal points in reckoning points between, and that the four points of the compass start from the east and work around to the north (dūng, nán, syī, běi). In fact, the compass is called a 'south-pointing needle.'

† Note that the expression wànlǐ '10,000 lǐ,' indicates a very great distance, rather than an accurate measurement of length. Wàn in this indefinite sense is found in a number of expressions in common use. (The Chinese measure -lǐ is about one-third of an English mile.)

4. <u>Grammatical Use of the Directions</u>:

The indicators of direction, including the points of the compass and the opposite pairs <u>dzwǒ/yòu</u>, <u>chyán/hòu</u>, may stand alone after the coverb <u>wàng</u>
but after <u>dzài</u>, <u>dàu</u>, and <u>tsúng</u> they must be compounded with such endings
as <u>-byār</u> and <u>-bù</u> which indicate an area, not just a direction. Hence:

Tsúng nèr wàng běi dzǒu.	From there go north.
Chǐng nín dzai dzwǒbyar jànje.	Please stand on the left.
Wàng chyán dzǒu.	Move forward.
Dàu chyánbyar chyu.	Go to the front.

TRANSLATION OF THE INTRODUCTORY DIALOGUES

1. <u>Three Routes to China</u>

A : I'm thinking of going to China next month. How far is China from
America?

B : It depends on which route you take.

A : Which is the shortest route?

5 B : The nearest route is via the North Pole.

A : How do you travel by that route?

B : From New York you fly by plane straight north, across Canada to
the North Pole. From the North Pole you fly south, cross the eastern part of Russia and you reach China.

10 A : What is the length of this route?

B : More than seven thousand miles.

A : Isn't there a shorter route to China than this one?

B : No. There is a way through Europe, but that route is a little longer
than this one.

15 A : How do you go by that route?

B : You must go east by ship, crossing the Atlantic Ocean (Great Western Ocean) to Germany. Then you go by train via Moscow, and in
less than two weeks you can reach Peking.

A : How much longer is this route?

20 B : It's more than two thousand miles longer.

A : Can't you reach China by going west?

B : You can, but it is still longer. If you travel this route, you must
first go by train to San Francisco, then by boat across the Pacific
Ocean to Shanghai. This is the most commonly traveled route.

25 A : Much obliged!

B : Not at all!

2. A North China Trip

(Three people are conversing.)

Chén: I suppose that place you visited last week is quite far away?

Lyóu: What place are you talking about? Dàtúng?

Chén: I can't quite recall the name of the place— probably it is the Dàtúng you mention.

5 Lyóu: Dàtúng isn't very far— possibly five hundred (English) miles.

Gwō : Is Dàtúng that far? I went there once two years ago. As I recall it, it was around three hundred miles.

Lyóu: Only three hundred miles! When we went, we traveled by rail for between eight and nine hours.

10 Gwō : A train makes only something like forty miles an hour. So in eight hours you can cover 320 miles. That's about it.

Chén: This Dàtúng is in the northwestern part of China, isn't it?

Lyóu: It is. You go west from Peking via Jāngjyakǒu.

Chén: Is it farther than Jāngjyakǒu?

15 Gwō : Much farther than Jāngjyakǒu. Jāngjyakǒu is only about a hundred miles. From here, Dàtúng is three times as far as Jāngjyakǒu.

Lyóu: Right, it's over two hundred miles farther than Jāngjyakǒu.

Chén: I never realized that it was so far away.

Lesson 20

COVERBS OF AGENT

DIALOGUE

The Lost Invitation

Húng : Lǎu Èr, nǐ dzěmmale? Wèishemma jèmma jāují a?

Hwáng: Yǒurén chǐng wo chr̄ fàn, kěshr wǒ bujìde shr shéi chǐng wo le.

Húng : Nèmma nǐ wèishemma búdzài kànkan syìn ne?

Hwáng: Nèifeng syìn ràng wo syǎu dìdi gěi rēngle. Hòulai wǒ jǎule bàntyān
5   méijǎujáu.

Húng : Hài, nǐ wèishemma busyǎusyīn ne?

Hwáng: Kěbushr̀ma! Kànwánle yǐhòu, wǒ bǎ neifēng syìn fàngdzai shūjwōr-
          shang, méisyǎngdàu syǎu dìdi pǎudau wo shūfángli chyu wár chyule.

Húng : Hǎu, wǒ bāngju ni syǎng ba! Shr̀ bushr Lyóujyā?

10 Hwáng: Búshr. Búshr syìng Lyóu de.

Húng : Nèmma yěsyǔ shr Tángjyā.

Hwáng: Yě búshr Tángjyā. Wǒ burènshr shemma syìng Táng de rén.

Húng : Yàuburán, yěsyǔ shr syìng Tswēi de.

Hwáng: Yě búshr syìng Tswēi de.

15 Húng : Nèmma, tā hái chǐngle byérén le ma? Syìnshang shwōle meiyou?

Hwáng: Shwōle. Tā budàn chǐngle wǒ, hái chǐngle jige túngsywé, kěshr shr
          shéi wǒ bùjrdàu.

Húng : Nǐ jeige rén! Nǐ syǎngbuchilái shr shéi chǐng ni, dàgài lyán něi-
          tyān yě bujìde le ba?

20 Hwáng: Wǒ jìde shr něityān. Shr hòutyān, kěshr wǒ wàngle shr něige
          fàngwǎr le.

Húng : Où, hòutyan wǎnshang Chén Déhwèi Syansheng chǐng wǒ chr̄ fàn.
          Shr̀ bushr̀ tā?

Hwáng: Kěbushr̀ma! Jyòushr tā! Nèmma, tā gēn ni shwōle meiyou, shr
25   dzai něige fàngwǎr chr̄ fàn ne?

Húng : Shwōle. Tā chǐng chī-báge rén dau Dūng Lái Shwùn chyu chr̄ fàn.
          Shr lyòudyǎnbàn jūng chr̄ fàn.

Hwáng: Nà tài hǎule. Dūng Lái Shwùn lí wǒ jyā kě bújìn. Wǒ hái bùjrdàu
          dzěmma dzǒu ne.

30 Húng : Nǐ kéyi fàngsyīn. Wǒ yǒu chē. Lyòudyǎn jūng wǒ kāi chē lái jyē
          ni. Wǒmen yíkwàr chyu, hǎu buhau?

Hwáng: Hǎujíle! Wǒ jēn bùjrdàu yīngdāng dzěmma syèsye nín.

Húng : Byé kèchi le!

194

VOCABULARY

Nouns (N)

jīhwei

N: opportunity, chance

Wǒ jèijityān méi jīhwei chyu kàn nǐmen.
'I've had no time the last few days to go to
see you.'

Wǒmen tīng Jūnggwo hwà de jīhwei tài shǎu.
'We have too little chance to hear Chinese!'

túngsywé

N: schoolmate, fellow student

Adverbs (A)

chíshŕ

MA: actually, in fact

Tā shwō ta méichyù; chíshŕ tā chyùle.
'He said he didn't go there, but actually he
did.'

Paired Adverbs (see Pattern B and Note 2)

hwòshr . . . , hwòshr . . . , yàuburán (jyoushr) . . .	either (it is) . . . , or . . . ; or else (it is) . . .
búdàn . . . , yě (or hái) . . .	Not only . . . , but also . . .
búdànshr . . . , lyán . . . dōu	Not only . . . , but even . . .
swéirán . . . , kěshr . . .	although . . . , yet . . .
hǎusyàng . . . , kěshr . . .	it seems as if . . . , but . . .
yàubúshr . . . , jyòushr . . .	if it isn't . . . , then . . .
chúle . . . yǐwài, (lìngwài) hái . . .	in addition to . . . , . . . also

Verbs (V)

ràng

FV: let, permit
CV: by (introduces agent; see Pattern A)

Tā fùchin búràng ta chyù.
'His father won't let him go.'

Ràng wǒ tì nín dzwò ba.
'Let me do it for you.'

jyàu

FV: tell or require (someone to do something);
call out to; cause, make

Fùchin jyàu háidz lái, kěshr háidz bulái.
'The father told the child to come, but he
didn't come.'

Fùchin jyàule bàntyān, kěshr háidz shwō tā
méitīngjyàn.
'The father called for a long time, but the
child said he didn't hear.'

Háidz lǎu bulái, jyàu fùchin hěn bugāusyìng.
'When the child never came, it made the
father unhappy.'

CV: by (introduces agent of an action; see Pattern A)

bìyè   VO: graduate, be graduated (from a school)

Nǐ něinyán bìyè?
'When do you graduate?'

Nǐ dzai shémma sywésyàu bìde yè?
'From what school did you graduate?'

fàngjyà   VO: have a vacation (lit. 'release for holiday')

Wǒmen míngtyan fàngjyà bufàng?
'Do we have a holiday tomorrow?'

Nǐmen syàlǐbài fàng jǐtyan jyà?
'How many days holiday do you have next
week?'

fàngsywé   VO: let out school, close school (session)

Wǒmen jeige sywésyàu syàtyan fàngsywé,
fàngde hěn wǎn.
'Our school closes very late in the summer.'

Nǐmen měityan syàwǔ jǐdyǎn jūng fàngsywé?
'What time each afternoon do you get out of
school?'

swéibyàn   VO: do as one pleases; (do) as one wishes (lit.
'follow one's convenience')

Swéibyàn, něige dōu kéyi.
'As you like, either will do.'

Háishr swéi tāde byàn ba!
'We'd better do as he wishes, after all.'

Chǐng swéibyàn chr̄, byé kèchi!
'Please help yourself, don't stand on ceremony!'

hwéidá   FV: reply to, answer (someone's question)

Nǐ wèishémma buhwéidá tā ne?
'Why don't you answer him?'

Wǒ hwéidá tāde wèntí le, kěshr hwéidáde
budwèi!
'I answered his question, but incorrectly!'

jyějywé   FV: solve (a problem)

Wǒ yǒu jǐge wènti. Kéyi bukéyi chǐng nín
bāng wǒ jyějywé?
'I have a few problems. Will you please
help me solve them?'

jāují	FV: worry, worry about
fàngsyīn	FV: rest assured, feel easy about (lit. 'relax the mind')
bufàngsyīn	FV: be uneasy, anxious about

Nǐ dzěmma nèmma ài jāují ne? Jāují méiyùng. Fàngsyīn ba!
'Why do you like to worry so much? There's
no use in worrying. Relax!'

Wǒ bútài fàngsyīn nèige rén.
'I don't feel too easy about that person.'

syǎusyīn	SV/FV: be careful; take care; look out for

Kāi chē děi syǎusyīn!
'Be careful when driving!'

Syǎusyīn nèige rén!
'Watch out for that man!'

Syǎusyīn yidyǎr!
'Take care!'

jyē	FV: to go and get (someone), to meet (at the train)

Expressions

Hāi!	Say!
Jyòushr tā.	That's he.

Common Saying

Mùjyang dwōle, gàiwāile fáng.	When there are many carpenters, the house is built crooked. (Too many cooks spoil the broth.)

SENTENCE PATTERNS

A. The Passive Construction with Coverbs of Agent

Táng jyàu háidz chřle.	The candy was eaten by the children.
Tāde jyòu shǒubyǎu ràng ta tàitai gei màile.	His old wristwatch was sold by his wife.
Tā syěde syìn jyàu wǒ dōu gěi rēng chuchyule.	All the letters he wrote were thrown away by me.
Tāde džsyíngchē ràng ta dìdi chídau sywésyàu chyule.	His bicycle was ridden to school by his younger brother.
Hǎibyārshang fángdz dōu jyàu dà fēng gěi gwāhwàile.	All the houses on the seashore were blown down by a high wind.
Wǒde gāngbǐ ràng ta jyèle hǎujihwéile.	My pen has been borrowed by him several times.

In each of the above sentences the receiver of the action becomes the subject. The doer of the action is introduced by a coverb of agent— either jyàu or ràng (interchangeable)— which is the equivalent of the English preposition 'by.' The main verb is followed by the particle le or other complement:

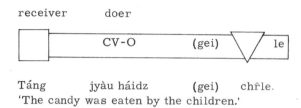

receiver   doer

Táng   jyàu háidz   (gei)   chřle.
'The candy was eaten by the children.'

(See Note 1 where the passive construction with ràng or jyàu is contrasted with the active construction with bǎ.)

B.   Connective Adverbs in Multi-Clausal Sentences (see Note 2)

    1. Coordinate Clauses

      Hwòshr wàng dūng gwǎi, hwòshr yìjŕ dzǒu, dōu dàudelyǎu.
      'Whether you turn east or go straight ahead, you'll get there all the same.'

      Hwòshr nǐ chyù, hwòshr wǒ chyù; yàuburán jyòushr tā chyù.
      'Either you go or I go; or else he goes.'

      Nèige sywésheng búdàn hwèi kàn Jūnggwo shū, tā yě hwèi syě Jūnggwo dž.
      'That student not only can read Chinese, but he can write characters as well.'

      Tāmen búdàn(shr) yǒu lyǎngge chìchē, lyán syǎu fēijī dōu yǒu.
      'They not only have two cars, but even a small plane.'

      Wǒ hǎusyàng jyàngwo ta, kěshr bugǎn shwō yídìng.
      'It seems as if I had met him, but I can't say for certain.'

      Nèige sywésheng hǎusyàng hěn bèn, chíshŕ yìdyǎr dōu búbèn.
      'That student seems stupid, but he isn't a bit.'

    2. Subordinate Clause and Main Clause

      Yàubúshr nǐmen lyǎngge rén bāngmáng, wǒ jyou méi fádz bànle.
      'If it weren't for you two helping out, I would have been in a fix.'

      Yàubúshr tā shwōde, jyòushr nǐ shwōde, yàuburán shr Lǎu Lǐ shwōde.
      'If it wasn't he that said it, it was you, or else it was Lǐ.'

      Wǒmen swéirán jùde hěn jìn, kěshr wǒ bucháng kànjyan tāmen.
      'Although we live very near (each other), still I don't see them often.'

      Chúle nǐ yǐwài, méiyou byéde rén.
      'Except for you, there is no one else.'

      Chúle tā yǐwài, (lìngwài) hái yǒu sānge rén kéyi gēn nǐ chyù.
      'Besides him, there are three others who can go with you.'

The coordinating adverbs hwòshr, búdàn, hǎusyàng, kěshr and yàuburán coordinate independent statements, any of which may stand alone. Yàuburán is unique in that it assumes that one or more suggestions have already been made and rejected, as is the case with its English counterpart, 'otherwise.'

The subordinating adverbs yàushr, yàubúshr, swéirán, and chúle introduce not independent statements but contingent conditions. The main clause after these subordinates is usually introduced by jyou(shr) (unstressed) or kěshr.

C. Sentence-Subjects

1. Subject Is a Stative Verb:

Tài syǎule bùhéshr̀.	If it's too small, it will not be satisfactory.
Lyángkwai yidyǎr hǎu, tài rèle busyíng.	A little cooler is better, too hot won't do.
Búpàng búshòu dzwèi hǎukan.	It is most handsome to be neither stout nor thin.

2. Subject Is a Functive Verb:

Dzǒuje busyíng.	It won't do to walk.
Nèmma shwō budwèi.	It's wrong to say it that way.
Tsúng jèr dzǒu jìn.	It's shorter to go this way.

3. Subject Is a Verb-Object Combination:

Shwō hwà rúngyi; dzwò shr̀ nán.	It's easy to say and hard to do. (proverb)
Dzwò hwǒchē tài màn.	It's too slow going by train.
Gěi ta chyán méiyùng.	It's no use giving him money.

4. Subject Is a S-V-O Sentence:

Jèige màudz, nǐ dài buhǎukàn.	This hat doesn't look well on you.
Wàigwo rén sywé syě Jūnggwo dz̀ butài rúngyi.	It's not too easy for foreigners to learn to write Chinese characters.
Nǐ dzài gěi ta syě syìn yě méiyùng.	It's no use your writing to him again.

In Lesson 4 it was shown that verbs such as shwō, gàusung, jr̄dau, wèn, etc., may be followed by sentence-objects. In each of the above examples a sentence (or clause) stands before the main verb as a subject. It will be noticed that the main verb is usually a stative verb or the verb shr̀.

NOTES

1. The passive construction with ràng or jyàu contrasted with the active construction with bǎ.

Situation: Wǒ mǎile yìdyǎr táng, gěile syǎuhár le.
             'I bought some candy and gave it to a youngster.'

Active: Wǒ bǎ táng gěile syǎuhár le. Syǎuhár bǎ táng chřle.
             'I gave the candy to the child; the child ate it up.'

Passive: Táng dōu ràng háidz gei chřle.
             'The candy was all eaten up by the child.'

The active sentence starts with the actor; the object is transposed by means
of the coverb bǎ to a position in front of the verb.

The passive sentence starts with the thing acted upon, after which the actor
is introduced by a coverb of agent— either jyàu or ràng.

In a sentence containing a coverbial phrase with bǎ, jyàu, or ràng, the main
verb is often preceded by a gěi which is not readily translatable. This gěi
may originally have been a coverb followed by a pronoun indicating the person affected by the action of the main verb. A comparable situation in col-
loquial English is the remark 'Sorry, but I've gone and scratched up your
car for you.' More proper English would omit the final prepositional phrase;
in Chinese the object has been dropped but not the coverb.

In both constructions the main verb is never left 'exposed': it is followed
by le or other complement.

The adverb dōu may stand before either the coverb or the main verb, but
not between gei and the main verb.

2. Adverbs in Associated Pairs:

Several associated pairs of connecting adverbs have been introduced in previous lessons. They should be reviewed in connection with the new pairs
introduced in the current lesson:

a. Coordinating Adverbs

yě . . . yě . . .	both . . . and . . .	(Lesson 4)
yě bu- . . . yě bu- . . .	neither . . . nor . . .	(Lesson 4)
yòu . . . yòu . . .	both . . . and . . .	(Lesson 14)
yòu méi . . . yòu méi . . .	neither . . . nor . . .	(Lesson 14)
(hái)shr . . . háishr . . . ?	is it . . . or is it . . . ?	(Lesson 20)
yěsyǔ . . . yěsyǔ . . .	perhaps . . . perhaps . . .	(Lesson 15)
ywè . . . ywè . . .	the more . . . the more . . .	(Lesson 18)

b. Subordinating Adverbs

yīnwei . . . swóyi . . .	because . . . therefore . . .	(Lesson 8)
. . . jyou . . .	when . . . (then) . . .	(Lesson 11)
. . . tsái . . .	when . . . (then and only then)	(Lesson 12)
	(not until then)	(Lesson 13)
yì . . . jyou	as soon as . . . (then) . . .	(Lesson 13)
syān . . . dzài . . .	after first . . . , then . . .	(Lesson 16)

TRANSLATION OF THE INTRODUCTORY DIALOGUE

The Lost Invitation

Húng : Lǎu Èr, what's the matter with you? Why so upset?

Hwáng: Someone invited me to dinner, but I don't remember who it was that invited me.

Húng : Well, why don't you look at the letter again?

5   Hwáng: The letter was thrown away by my kid brother. I looked a long time for it afterwards but didn't succeed in finding it.

Húng : Say, why don't you be more careful?

Hwáng: Isn't that the truth! When I finished reading it, I put the letter on my desk, never thinking that my kid brother would run into my study
10   to play.

Húng : Well, let me help you think. Was it the Lyóus?

Hwáng: No, it wasn't anyone by the name of Lyóu.

Húng : Then maybe it was the Tángs.

Hwáng: Nor was it the Tángs. I don't know anyone by the name of Táng.

15 Húng : Or else, maybe it was someone by the name of Tswēi?

Hwáng: No, it wasn't anyone by the name of Tswēi either.

Húng : Well, did he invite anyone else? Did the letter mention anyone?

Hwáng: Sure, it did! He not only invited me, but several schoolmates in addition, but who they were I don't know.

20 Húng : What a man! You can't recall who invited you, so you probably don't remember for what day you were invited.

Hwáng: I remember what day it was; it was day after tomorrow; but I've forgotten which restaurant.

Húng : Oh! Day after tomorrow evening Mr. Chén Déhwèi has invited me
25   to dinner. Is he the person?

Hwáng: Of course he is! Precisely he! So, did he tell you at what restaurant it is to be?

Húng : Sure! He has invited seven or eight people to Dūng Lái Shwùn for dinner. And we eat at six-thirty.

30 Hwáng: That's wonderful! But Dūng Lái Shwùn is not very near to my home. I don't even know how to get there.

Húng : Take it easy! I have a car. At six o'clock I'll drive over here for you. We'll go together, right?

Hwáng: Grand! I really don't know how to thank you.

35 Húng : Forget it! (Don't stand on ceremony.)

INDEX

A

a   P: (semi-interrogative, used in greetings)   2

ABBREVIATIONS   xix

ACTION
  and attendant circumstances contrasted   112
  completed, -le   102
  contingent, -je   138
  continuing, -ne   57, 101
  incomplete   103

ADJECTIVE (see Stative Verbs)   6

ADVERBS   6
  totalizing adverb dōu   12
  movable adverbs   23
  yě and kěshr in compound sentences   20
  paired adverbs yòu . . . yòu and yě . . . yě   138
  connective adverbs in multi-clausal sentences   198
  in associated pairs   200
  coordinating adverbs   200
  subordinating adverbs   200
  movable adverbs wèishémma, yīnwei, swóyi   76
  nouns of time as adverbs   110
  stative verbs as adverbs   6
  in commands and requests   138

AGENT, coverbs of   197

āi!   P: oh! yes! my goodness!   55

ǎi   SV: be short, low   2

ài   FV/SV: like/like to; love/love to   30

ALTERNATIVE CHOICE QUESTIONS   4
  (hái)shr . . . háishr . . .   136
  shr . . . shr . . . ?   136
  shr bushr?   32, 36

AMBIGUITY
  ambiguous reference of dōu   36
  ambiguous clauses   65

AMOUNT per unit   46

ānjing   SV: be quiet, peaceful   72

ANSWERS to questions   6
  alternative — either/or   136, 198
  inclusive — both/and   198
  exclusive — neither/nor   200

'ANY' and 'SOME'   48

'APIECE' how expressed   46

APPOSITION   36

APPROXIMATION, using dwō   47

ARTICLE
   definite   49
   indefinite   22, 49

ASPECT, time and tense   101
   change of status with le   101
   completive with le   99, 102
   contingent with je   138
   continuing with ne   101
   customary   101
   experiential with gwo   126

'AS SOON AS' expressed by yī . . . jyou . . .   103

ATTENDANT CIRCUMSTANCE stressed by shr . . . de   112

AUXILIARY VERBS   12, 14
   in comparisons   180
   Questions and answers   12

B

BA, use of particle   65

ba   P: (indicating suggestion or probability)   63

bā   NU: eight   17

bǎ   M: (for chairs)   17

bǎ   CV: (for treatment)   151

BǍ CONSTRUCTION   154
   CV bǎ and its object   155
   translating a bǎ sentence   155
   uses of the bǎ construction   156
   contrasted with passive construction (ràng and jyàu) 199

bái   SV: be white, fair   109
   báityān   MA/N: daytime, during the day   107

-bǎi   NU/M: hundred   26

bān   FV: move (something), transport (goods)   143
   bānchuchyu   FV: move (things) out   143
   bāndau   FV: move to   143
   bāngwolai   FV: move (something) across   143
   bānjyā   VO: move (one's residence)   143

bàn   FV: manage, carry out   161
   bànfǎ(r)   N: way to handle a problem, solution 160
   bànshr̀   VO: handle a matter of business   161

bàn-M   NU: half a M   40
   -bàn   M: half, one half   40
   NU-M-bàn   NU: NU and a half   41
   bàntyān   MA: for a long time, for quite a while 98
   bànyè   N/MA: midnight   107

bāng(ju)   FV: help, assist (someone)   152
   bāngmáng   VO: render assistance   152

bǎu   SV: be satisfied (after eating)   163

bàu   N: newspaper   2

'BE,' translating into Chinese   75

-bēi   M: glass of, tumbler of   79
  bēidz   N: glass, tumbler, cup   80

běi   N: north   185

-BÈI, use of the measure   179

-bèi   M: (for number of times)   171

Běijīng   PW: Peking   119

-běn   M: (for books), volume   17

bèn   SV: be stupid, clumsy   63

bǐ   N: pen, pencil, writing instrument   2

BǏ, CV of comparison for contrast   176
  comparison of distances   187

bǐ   FV: compare   173
                             CV: as compared with   173
  bǐjyǎu   A: comparatively, relatively   172

bìng   N: illness, sickness, disease (M: tsż)   108
  bìng(le)   FV: be ill, be sick   109
  bìngrén   N: sick person, patient   108

bìyè   VO: graduate, be graduated (from a school)   196

BOUND FORMS   36

BU, tones   5

bu, bù, bú   A: not   2
  -bu-   P: verbal infix   163
  búbì   AV: need not, not have to   43
  búdà   A: not very   53
  búdàn . . . yě   not only . . . but also . . .   195
  búdànshr . . . ,
    lyán . . . dōu . . .   not only . . . but even . . .   195
  budōu   A: not all (of)   11
  búdàu   SV: be less than, not as much as   153
  Búdwèi!   Wrong!   xx
  búfàngsyīn   SV: be uneasy about, anxious about   197
  Bùgǎndāng.   EX: You flatter me (lit: I don't dare assume
                                 the honor).   144
  bùjyǒu   A: before long   108
  Búkèchi.   EX: You're welcome.   11
  bùrú   FV: not be the equal of   174
  bushǎu   SV: a good many, quite a few   44
  bútswò   SV: be not bad, quite good   30, 82
  butúng   SV: be unlike, dissimilar, different   163
  búyaujǐn   SV: be unimportant; never mind! don't worry!   109
  bùyidìng   MA/SV: not certain about, not necessarily   89
  búyùng   AV: need not, be unnecessary to   80

-BÙ and -BYĀR, use compared   189

-bù	M:	part, area, section	185
-byār	M:	side, edge, border, section	184
byǎu	N:	watch	9
byé	AV:	don't (imperative)	10
byéde	N:	another (person or thing)	97
byéren	N:	other people	97

C

CALENDAR TIME		125
inquiring the year, month, week, day, and hour		125
previous and succeeding time units		115
time of an action		101
CEASING ACTION (See CHANGE OF STATUS)		56

chá	N:	tea (brewed)	53
chágwǎr	PW:	teahouse	71
cháhú	N:	teapot	80
cháwǎn	N:	teacup	80
cháyè	N:	tea leaves	53
CHÀ			128

chà	V:	differ by; lack, (by clock time) be before	121
chàbudwō	MA:	almost	121
chàyidyǎr	EX/MA:	almost	121
chàyidyǎr méi-V	EX:	barely, escape V-ing	121
CHÀBUDWŌ			128
CHÀYIDYǍR			128

chādz	N:	fork	80
cháng	SV:	be long	174
chángdwǎn	N:	size (in length)	172
cháng(cháng)	A:	often, frequently	18
chàng	FV:	sing	54
chàng gēer	VO:	sing (songs)	54
CHANGE OF STATUS WITH LE			56
in condition or quality			56
in interrogative sentence			58
starting or ceasing action			56
CHANGE OF TONE ON NU AND BU			23

chǎu	SV:	be noisy, clamorous	72
chē	N:	vehicle (with wheels)	89
chējàn	PW:	station, shop (for vehicles)	89
chéng	N:	city	71
chéngchyáng	N:	city wall	151
chī	NU:	seven	17
chí	FV/CV:	ride (straddle)	90

chìchē	N:	automobile, car (lit. gas vehicle)	89
chǐlai	FV:	arise, get up	121
chǐng	FV:	invite, to ask to, please . . .	29
Chǐng!	EX:	Please!	2
Chǐng fānyi.	EX:	Please translate.	45
Chǐng gěi wo shū.	EX:	Please give me the book.	11
chǐng kè	VO:	invite guests	61
Chǐng nyàn.	EX:	Please read.	45
Chǐng wèn?	EX:	May I ask?	19
chīngchu	SV:	be clear, distinct	134
chíshŕ	MA:	actually, in fact	195
chìshwěi	N:	carbonated drink	53
chŕ	FV:	eat	54
chŕbǎu	RV:	eat to satiety, get enough to eat	163
chŕ fàn	VO:	eat (a meal)	54
chŕdz (sháur)	N:	spoon	80
-chŕ	M:	foot (measure)	171
chŕ	N:	ruler, foot rule	172
chŕtswùn	N:	measurement, size	172
chū	FV:	exit	142
chūchyu	FV:	go out	142
chūlai	FV:	come out	142
chūmén(r)	VO:	leave the house, go out	142
chúfáng	J:	kitchen	141
chúle . . . yǐwài, (lingwài) hái . . .		in addition to . . . , . . . also	195
chwān	FV:	wear (clothes, shoes), put on	62
chwán	N:	boat, ship	89
chwáng	N:	bed	141
chwānghu	N:	window	131
chwūntyān	N:	springtime	107
-chyān	NU/M:	thousand	26
chyán	PW:	front	89
chyántou	PW:	front, in front of	71
chyántyan	MA/N:	day before yesterday	107
chyán	N:	money	10
chyǎn	SV:	be shallow	186
chyānbǐ	N:	(lead) pencil	10
chyáng	N:	wall	151
chyōutyān	N:	autumn, fall (time)	107
CHYÙ and LÁI after wàng			94

    coming and going   92
    sequence of CV expressions with   94
    verbs of movement compounded with   144

chyù   FV: go (there)   89
  -chyù   BF: (verb ending)   142

chyùnyán   MA/N: last year   106

CIRCUMSTANCES STRESSED   112

CLAUSES
    clausal expressions become nouns   67
    general and specific   65
    modification by   64, 67
    multi-clausal sentence   198

CLOCK
    amounts of clock time   122
    time when by the   122
    what time is it?   125

COMING and GOING   92
    purpose of   92

COMMANDS and REQUESTS   136
    involving manner   138

COMPARISON
    AV in   180
    -bèi (M), use   179
    degrees of   177
    for contrast   176
    fractions in   179
    indefinite M in   178
    similarity and dissimilarity   175
    use of CV gēn   178

COMPLETED ACTION
    aspect of completion   99
    completion of action and time   99
    expressing purpose   102
    negative méi   100
    question forms   102
    use of tsái   116
    with le   99

COMPOUND SENTENCES   7
    with jyou   124
    with yé and kěshr   20

COMPOUND VERBS
    compounds with -dàu   145, 147
    compounds with -dzài   145, 147
    compounds with -gěi   145, 147
    compound verbs in bǎ construction   156
    ending in -dzài, -dàu, -gěi   145
    ending in lái and chyù   144
    ending in lái and chyù compounds   145
    resultative compounds   164, 167

CONNECTIVES
   adverbs in associated pairs   200
   connective adverbs in multi-clausal sentences   198
   connective use of gēn   72
   coordinating adverbs   200
   subordinating adverbs   200

CONTINUITY or SUSPENSE, use of ne   57

CONVEYANCE
   CV of means of conveyance   93
   stressed with shì . . . de construction   115

COORDINATING ADVERBS   200

COORDINATION OF NOUNS   14, 35

COUNTING   30, 31

COUNTRIES, NAMES OF
   Dégwo   28
   Fàgwo   28
   Jūnggwo   10
   Meǐgwo   10
   Řběn   108
   Yìgwo   28
   Yìndù   119
   Yīnggwo   18

COVERBS   75, 85
   bǎ and its object   155
   general pattern   84
   of agent (jyàu, ràng)   197
   of comparison (bǐ, yǒu, gēn)   176, 178
   of conveyance (dzwò, chí)   93
   of direction (wàng)   93
   of interest (gēn, gěi, tì, yùng, dwèi)   83, 85
   of location (dzài)   72, 74
   of movement (tsúng, dàu)   92
   of separation (lí)   187
   sequence   94

D

dǎjàng	VO: fight, make war	109
dǎkai	FV: open (containers, boxes, etc.)	132
Dǎkai shū.	EX: Open (your) books.	45
dǎswan	N: intention, plan	80
	AV: plan to, expect to, intend to	81
dà	SV: be large, big	10
dàgài	MA: probably, most likely	141
dàjyā	N: everyone	119
dàren	N: adult	27
dàsyǎu	N: size (in mass)	172
dàsywé(syàu)	N: college or university	161
dàyī	N: overcoat, topcoat (M: -jyàn)	185

dài		FV: lead, accompany, take bring, bring along	144
	dàidau	FV: take (something) to	144
	dàihwéi	FV: take (something) back to	144
dài		FV: wear (on head, neck, wrists), put on	62
dāngjūng		PW: middle, in the middle of	71
dāngrán		MA: of course, naturally	132

DATES, INQUIRING YEAR, MONTH, ETC.   125

-DÀU   92
    verbs of movement compounded with   146

dāudz		N: knife	80
dàu		FV: arrive, reach a destination	90
	-dàu	BF: (verb ending) to, as far as	143
	dàu	CV: to (a place)	90
dàu		FV: pour	81
	dàule	FV: pour out, discard	81

DAYS OF THE WEEK   116

DE (particle)
    two distinct uses of de   137
    use in modification   64

de		P: (added to nouns, phrases, and clauses to indicate modification)	45, 63
	-de-	P: (verbal infix indicating positive potential result)	163
	-de	P: (verb ending indicating manner)	134
	. . . de shŕhou	MA: while . . . , at the time when . . .	120

DEGREE
    degrees of comparison   177
    manner and degree   135

Dégwo		N: Germany	28
děi		AV: must, have to	43
dēng		N: lamp, light	131
děng(je)		FV: wait, wait for	133

DESCRIPTION
    descriptive use of shŕ   85
    of distances   187

DESTINATION AND STARTING POINT   92

DÌ, ORDINAL SP, AND TÓU-   126

dì-		SP: (ordinalizing prefix to numbers)	97
	Dìjĭkè? Dìyíkè.	EX: Which lesson? Lesson one.	45
dì		N: ground, land	151
	dìsya	N: floor	151
dìdi		N: younger brother	41
dìfang		N: place, position, location	70
dìng		FV: order	173

dìngdzwò   FV: order made, have made to order   173

DIRECTION with CV wàng   93
    grammatical use of the directions   192

DISSIMILARITY   175

DISTANCE AND SEPARATION   187
    comparison of distance   187
    description of distance (with ywǎn or jìn)   187

dǐsya   PW: underside, underneath   71

DŌU, use of   12
    ambiguous reference   36
    in inclusive expressions   82
    relation to subject   12
    relation to transposed object   32

dōu   A: all, both   11
    dōu bu-   A: none   11

dūng   PW: east   185

dǔng   FV: understand   19

dūngsyi   N: thing   28

dūngtyān   MA/N: winter   107

dwǎn   SV: be short   174

dwèi   SV: be correct, right   xx, 19
    dwèi   CV: to, toward (lit. face)   81
    Dwèibuchǐ!   EX: I beg your pardon!   19
    Dwèibudwèi?   EX: Correct?   xx
    Dwèile.   EX: (That's) right.   19

DWŌ in approximation   47
dwō   SV: be many, be much, be more   44
    dwō   A: more   42
    -dwō   NU: plus, and more, over   41
    (NU-M)-dwō   NU: (plus less than another full M)   41
    NU-dwō-M   NU: (plus an additional full M)   41

dwōjyǒu?   A: how long?   108

dwōma (dwó(ma))?   MA: how? to what extent or degree?   141

DWŌSHAU as NU   34

dwōshau?   N/NU: how many? how much?   28

-dyǎn   M: (measure for hours on the clock)   119

dyǎnsyin   N: cake, cookie, light refreshment   53

dyàntī   N: elevator (lit. electric ladder)   141
    dyànyǐng(r)   N: moving picture, movies (lit. electric
                            shadow) (M: -chǎng)   108
    dyànyǐngrywàn   N: movie house   108

dyōu   FV: lose, misplace, discard   161

dž   N: Chinese character (ideograph)   61

DZÀI indicating location   72
    verbs of position compounded with   145

dzài   FV: be (located) at   72
                              CV: at   72
  -dzài   BF: (verb ending) at, on, in   143
  dzài wǒ kàn   EX: in my opinion, as I see it   144

DZÀI (A), TSÁI, JYÒU, uses compared   127

dzài   A: then (in the future; contrast yòu)   120

dzài   A: again, additionally, more   42
  dzàijyàn   EX: goodbye (See you again!)   2
  dzàishwō   EX: further, what's more, moreover   144
  Dzài shwō!   EX: Say it again!   19
  Dzài shwō yítsż!   EX: Say it once more!   30

dzájr̀   N: magazine (M: -běn)   42

dzāng   SV: be dirty   82

dzǎu   SV: be early   98
  Dzǎu   EX: good morning   2
  dzǎufàn   N: breakfast (lit. early meal)   97
  dzǎushang   (MA)N: morning   97

dzěmma?   A: in what way? by what means? how?   89
  Dzěmma bàn?   EX: What's to be done about it?   164
  Dzěmma hwéi shr̀?   EX: How come? How did this happen?   134
  Dzěmmale?   A: What's the matter?   89
  dzěmmayàng?   QW: in what manner? how?   171
  Dzěmmayàng?   EX: How about it? What do you think?   171

dzèmma   A: in this way, thus   89

dżjǐ   N: self, oneself   119

DZǑU after CV wàng   93

dzǒu   FV: walk, go, depart   90

dżsyíngchē   N: bicycle (lit. self-propelled vechicle)   89

dzwěi   N: mouth   161

dzwèi   A: the most, -est   61

dzwǒ-   PW: left   89

DZWÒ, CV to sit (conveyance)   93

dzwò   FV: sit, be seated   90
                              CV: by (a conveyance with seats)   90
  dzwòsya   FV: sit down   90

dzwò   FV: do, make, engage in   54
  dzwò fàn   VO: cook, prepare food   54
  dzwòlǐbài   V: (engage in) worship   109
  dzwò mǎimai   VO: engage in business   54
  dzwò shr̀   VO: work, engage in an occupation   54
  dzwò yige lìdz   EX: make (give) an example   45

dzwótyan   (MA)N: yesterday   97

E

è   SV: be hungry   163

EQUATIVE SENTENCES with shr̀   32
  question patterns for equative verbs   36

EQUIVALENCE in comparison   176

ÈR, use of èr and lyǎng   22

èr	NU:	two	17
Èrywè	N:	February	107
ěrdwo	N:	ears	161
érdz	N:	son	61

EXCLUSIVENESS, intense   83

EXISTENCE in a place with yǒu   73

EXPERIENTIAL VERB ENDING -GWÒ   126

F

fádz	N:	way, method, plan	160
Fàgwo	N:	France	28
fān	FV:	translate	162
fānchéng	FV:	translate into	162
fānyi	N/FV:	translation; translate	162
fàn	N:	food, meal, cooked rice	53
fàngwǎr	PW:	restaurant	71
fànjwō(r)	N:	dining table	141
fàntīng	PW:	dining room	141
fànwǎn	N:	rice bowl	80
-fáng	BF:	combining form indicating a house, building, or room (M: -jyān, room)	140
fàng	FV:	put (something somewhere) (lit. let go of)	151
fàngdesyà	FV:	can accommodate, have room for	173
fàngdzai	V:	put (something) in a place	151
fàngje	V:	lie, be lying (of inanimate objects)	151
fàngjyà	VO:	have a vacation (lit. release for holiday)	196
fàngmǎn(le)	RV:	fill up	173
fàngsya	FV:	put (something) down	151
fàngsyīn	SV:	rest assured, feel easy (about) (lit. VO release the mind)	197
fàngsywé	VO:	let out school, close school (session)	196
fāngbyan	SV:	be convenient	153
fángdz	N:	house, building (M: -swǒ)	71
fāngfǎ	N:	way, method, plan	160
fāpíchi	VO:	get angry, lose one's temper	161
fēi	FV:	fly	91
feījī	N:	airplane, plane (lit. flying machine)	89
feījichǎng	PW:	airfield	89
feīcháng	A:	unusually, extraordinarily	131

féi	SV: be fat (of meat); be loose (of clothing); rich, fertile (of land)	174
fēn(chéng)	FV: divide, share, divide into	173
-fēn	M: (tenth, part, used in fractions)	171
-fēn	M: (measure for minutes)	119
-fēn	M: (measure for cents)	40
fěnbǐ	N: chalk	10
-fēng	M: (for letters, correspondence)	79
fēng	N: wind	141
-fèr	M: copy (M for newspapers)	40

FOREIGN PLACE NAMES, Chinese forms for   94, 190

FRACTIONS
bàn, half   41
in comparison   179
in the NU-fēnjr-NU pattern   180

fùchin	N: father	41
fùmǔ	N: parents	41

FUNCTIVE SENTENCE   2

FUNCTIVE VERBS   6

G

gǎi	FV: change, revise, correct	161
gǎn	AV: dare to, venture to	141
gāng(gāng)	A: just this minute, just now	98
gāngtsái	MA: a short while ago, just now, just a few minutes ago	53
gāngbǐ	N: pen (writing instrument with metal point)	10
gānjing	SV: be clean	82
gāu	SV: be tall, high	2
gàusu(ng)	FV: tell, inform	29
gāusyìng	SV: be happy, pleased	110
-ge	M: (general measure)	17
gēer	N: song	53
gēge	N: older brother	41

-GĚI, compounds   146

gěi	FV: give (to)	10
-gěi	BF: (verb ending) for, for the benefit of, to	143
gěi	CV: for, on behalf of, to	81

GĒN (coverb)   84
use in comparison   178

gēn	CV:	together with	81
gēn	Connective:	and (between nominal elements <u>only</u>)	72
gēn	CV:	with, and (used in pattern of similarity)	174
gēn . . . jyè	CV/V:	borrow from	152
gèng	A:	more, still more, even SV-er	131
GEOGRAPHIC NAMES, meaning of			191
GOING AND COMING			92
gòu	SV:	be enough, sufficient	44
	A:	enough, sufficiently	42
gūngfu	N:	(free or leisure) time	79
gūngkè	N:	lessons	89
gūnglù	N:	highway (M: -tyáu) (lit. public road)	185
gūngywán	PW:	public park	185
gùshr	N:	story, tale	61
gwā	FV:	blow (of wind)	141
gwāfēng	VO:	blow (lit. blow-wind)	141
gwà	FV:	hang (an article), hand from (a position)	152
gwàdzai	FV:	hang (in a position)	152
gwàje	FV:	be hanging	152
gwǎi	FV:	turn (a corner)	186
gwān	FV:	close (doors, windows)	132
gwānshang	FV:	close (up)	132
gwānsyi	N:	relation, connection, relevance	160
gwèi	SV:	be expensive	2
gwèigwó	EX:	your (honorable) country or nationality	28
gwèisyìng	EX:	your (honorable) surname	29
gwógēer	N:	national anthem	53
GWÒ, experiential particle			126
gwò	V:	pass, exceed; cross over; past (by the clock)	121
-gwò	P:	(verb ending, indicates experience)	122

H

Hāi!	EX:	Say!	197
hái	A:	still, yet (continuing)	53
hǎi	N:	the sea	185
hǎibyār	N:	seashore	151
háidz	N:	child, children	27
HǍU			
as prefix to verbs			55
as resultative ending			165
-hàu	M:	(measure for day of month, number of house, room, etc.)	79

hău	SV:	be good, well	2
hău-V	SV:	(hău before an FV forms a compound which functions as a SV)	55
hăubuhău?	EX:	How about it? (Is that a good idea?)	19
hăuhăurde	A:	properly, nicely	132
háuji	SP:	several, many	40
háujyŏu	A:	for a long time	108
hăukàn	SV:	be good looking	11
hăutīng	SV:	be good to listen to, tuneful	63
hăuyùng	SV:	be easy to use	80
Hău shr hău.	EX:	That's true enough.	45
hăusyē	NU:	many, a lot of	40
hăusyàng . . . , kěshr	MA-MA:	it seems as if . . . , but . . .	195
hăusyàng . . . (shrde)	FV/MA:	seemingly, seem like, look like	173
hē	FV:	drink	54
hé	N:	river (M: -tyáu)	172
hédz	N:	box (smaller than syāngdz)	151
hēi	SV:	be black (oppos. bái); dark (oppos. lyàng)	109
hēibăn	N:	blackboard	141
hěn	A:	very, quite, very many	2
hěndwō	SV:	be many, a lot	44
hěnjyŏu	A:	for a long time	108
héshang shū	VO:	close the book	45
héshr̀	SV:	be suitable, fitting; fit (as clothes)	134
hòu-	PW:	back	89
hòulái	MA:	later, afterwards (referring to time past)	53
hòutou	PW:	rear, back of	71
hòutyan	MA/N:	day after tomorrow	107
-hú	M:	pot (for tea, water, wine, etc.)	79
hú	N:	lake	185
húng	SV:	be red	134
hwā	FV:	spend	98
hwā chyán	VO:	spend money	98
hwāfei	N:	expense	97
hwà	N:	language, (spoken) words (M: -jyù)	17
hwà	FV:	paint, draw	30
hwài	SV:	be bad, spoiled, broken	55
hwán	FV:	pay back, return (a loan)	153
hwángei	FV:	return (something) to, give back to	153
hwáng	SV:	be yellow	134
hwàr	N:	picture, painting	28
hwéi	FV/A:	return to, go back to	90

-HWÉI (M) and tsz̀   126

-hwéi	M:	times (occurrences, repetitions)	119
hwéichyu	FV:	return (there), back	90
hwéidá	FV:	reply to, answer (someone's question)	196
hwéilai	FV:	return (here), come back	90
hwéisyìn	N/VO:	letter in reply, reply to a letter	79

hwèi   N: meeting, gathering (of people)   131

hwèi   AV: can (in sense of 'know how to')   19

hwǒchē   N: (railroad) train (lit. fire-wagon)   89
  hwǒchējàn   PW: railroad station   89

hwòshr . . . ,   either (it is) . . . , or . . . ; or else
  hwòshr . . . ,   (it is) . . .
  yàuburán   195

I

INCLUSIVES, question word as   85

INDEFINITES, question word as   85
  indefinite M in comparison   178
  indefinite specification   49

INDIRECT OBJECTS   11, 13

INQUIRING
  name and nationality   34
  time and date   125

INTERROGATIVE
  particle ma   3
  sentences with no, lo   58
  use of ne particle   137

J

jǎi   SV: be narrow   174

jàn(je)   FV: stand   133

-jāng   M: sheet (for paper, tables, paintings)   17, 26

jǎng   FV: grow   174
  jǎngdà   FV: grow up   174

jǎu   FV: look for, hunt for   161
  jǎujáu   RV: find   161
  jǎulái jǎuchyù   RV: hunt here and there, hunt everywhere   161

jǎu   FV: give in change   44

jāují   FV: worry, worry about   197

JE, uses of particle   138

-je	P: (verb ending; indicating continuance)	134
jèi	SP: this	16
jèibyar	PW: this side, over here	184
jèige jyùdz	EX: this sentence	45
jèisye	SP-M: these	40
jèmma	A: in this way, by this means, like this	89
jèmma hwéi shr̀	EX: it happened this way	134
jèmmayàng	MA: in this manner, in this case	171
jēn	A: really, quite	11
Jēn kěsyī!	EX: That's too bad! It is greatly to be regretted.	56
jèng(dzai)	MA: just in the midst of	131
jèr	PW: here	71
JǏ- and DWŌSHAU compared		34
jǐ-?	NU: how many? (under ten)	17
jǐ- (ji-)	NU: a few (up to ten), some	40
jì	FV: transmit mail	162
jìsyìn	VO: mail letters	162
jì(de)	FV: remember, keep in mind	152
jīhwei	N: opportunity, chance	195
-jíle	P: (ending to SVs, indicating an exaggerated degree)	134
jìn	FV: enter	142
jìnchéng	VO: go into town	142
jìnchyu	FV: go into	142
jìnlai	FV: come in	142
jìn	SV: be near, close	186
jīnggwò	FV: pass through, pass by	186
jīngshen	N: spirits, vivacity	172
jīnnyan	MA/N: this year	107
jīntyan	MA/N: today	97
-jr̆	P: (used in fractions)	174
-jr̆	M: (for pencils)	40
jr̆	N: paper	28
jr̆dau	FV: know, know of, know that	29
jù	FV: live, reside	72
jūng	N: clock	9
jūng	N: o'clock	119
jūngtóu	N: an hour (60 minutes of time)	119
jūngfàn	N: lunch (lit. middle meal)	97
Jūnggwo	PN: China	10
jūngnyánren	N: middle-aged persons	172
jūngsywé(syàu)	N: secondary school, high school	161

jūngwǔ	MA/N:	noon	97
jǔren	N:	host, hostess	61
jūròu	N:	pork	80
jwōdz	N:	table	17
jyā	PW:	at home	71
	N/M:	home, family, a family of	71
jyājyu	N:	furniture	141
jyāsyìn	N:	home letter (M· -fēng)	79
jyātíng	N:	family, home	131
jyàchyán	N:	price, cost	161
jyāhwo	N:	utensil, implement, tool	80
jyàn	FV:	meet, see, interview (more formal than kàn)	121
jyǎndān	SV:	be simple, concise	163
jyǎng	FV:	talk, explain, discourse	161
jyǎngyijyang	VO:	explain	161
jyānglái	MA:	in the future	121
jyāu	FV:	teach	62
jyāu shū	VO:	teach school	62

JYÀU and RÀNG   197
   use of ràng and jyàu contrasted with bǎ   197

jyàu	FV:	tell or require (someone to do something);	
		call out to; make, cause	195
	FV:	call for, order (food in a restaurant)	98
	FV:	be (given) named, called, call, summon	29
	CV:	by (introduces agent of action)	196
jyàutàng	PW:	church	71
jyē	FV:	to go and get (someone), to meet (at the train)	197
jyē	N:	street (M: -tyáu)	71
jyè	FV:	borrow, lend	152
jyègei	FV:	lend to	152
gēn . . . jyè	FV:	borrow from	152
jyějye	N:	older sister	41
jyějywé	FV:	solve (a problem)	196
jyèshaù	FV:	introduce	121
jyou	A:	then (introduces subsequent action)	53
jyǒu	NU:	nine	17
jyǒu	N:	liquor, wine	53
jyǒubēi	N:	wineglass, winecup	80
-jyǒu	BF:	for a long time, long since	108

JYÒU (then)
   compound sentences and jyòu   124
   distinguishing jyòu ' immediately' and jyòu ' then'   103

introducing a second clause			58
jyòu, tsái, dzài uses compared			127
jyòu	SV:	be old (worn), used	62
jyòu	A:	only, just	28
jyòu(yau)	A:	immediately, right away	98
Jyòu jèmma bàn!	EX:	Do it this way. So be it!	164
Jyòushr tā.	EX:	That's he.	197
-jyù	M:	(for hwà) sentence, expression	61
jyùdz	N:	sentence, phrase	61
jywédìng	FV:	decide	173

K

kāfēi	N:	coffee	53
KĀI, used with wàng (CV)			94
kāi	FV:	operate (a car); start, leave (trains, boats)	91
kāi(kai)	FV:	open (up)	132
kāi hwèi	VO:	open a meeting, hold a meeting	132
KÀN, used with wang (CV)			94
kàn	FV:	look, look at, read	2
kàn	FV:	visit, see	91
kàn(kan)	FV:	consider, regard, think	121
kàn	CV/FV:	depending on; it depends on	173
kànjyan	FV:	see	98
kǎu	FV:	take or give an examination	91
kǎushr̀	VO:	take or give an examination	91
	N:	examination, test	91
kě	SV:	be thirsty	163
kě	A:	but	18
Kěbushr̀ ma!	EX:	Why, of course! Now isn't that the truth!	134
-kè	M:	lesson (measure for lessons)	96
	M:	(measure for quarter-hour)	119
kè(ren)	N:	guest	61
kèchi	SV:	be polite, courteous	30
kètīng	PW:	living room	141
kěn	AV:	be willing to	163
kěnéng	AV/SV:	be possible, may, maybe	121
KĚSHR in compound sentences			20
kěshr	MA:	but, however	18
kěsyàu	SV:	be laughable, amusing	134
kéyi	AV:	may, can (in sense of 'be permitted to')	19
kǒudàr	N:	pocket; (soft) bag	150

kū	FV: cry, cry about	133
kǔngpà	AV: fear that, be afraid that, probably, perhaps	91
kwài	SV: be fast, quick	133
kwàikwārde	A: quickly, hurry up and . . .	132
kwài(yàu)	A: soon, quickly	98
-kwài	M: piece, lump (M: for dollars)	40
kwàidz	N: chopsticks (M: -shwāng, pair)	80
kwàilè	N/SV: happiness, be happy, joyful	133
kwān	SV: be wide, broad	174
kwùn	SV: be sleepy	55

L

LÁI		92
compounds		145
after CV wàng		94
lái	FV: come (here)	89
-lái	BF: (verb ending)	142
lán	SV: be blue	134
lǎn	SV: be lazy	55
lǎu	SV: be old, elderly (cannot mean antique)	54
	A: always, ever, (with negative) never	151
lǎunyánrén	N: elderly persons	172
LE, particle		56, 58
change of status		56
completed action with le		99
in a bǎ construction		156
in interrogative sentences		58
verbs of action with le		99
verbs with simple objects and le		99
with measured objects		100
with quantified objects		114
with question forms		102
le	P: (indicating change of status)	55
lèi	SV: be tired	2
lěng	SV: be cold	186
LÍ, CV of separation, distance		187
lí	CV: from (be separated or distant from)	186
lǐ	PW: in	89
-li	PW: in (localizing suffix to PW)	71
lǐtou	PW: inside, inside of, among	71
-lǐ (lu)	M: (measure for distance—1/3 mile)	184
lǐbài	N: week	107
Lǐbaityān	N: Sunday	107
Lǐbaisān	N: Wednesday	107

lìdz   N: example   161

lìhai   SV: be fierce, severe   109

lìkè(jyou)   MA: immediately   120

líng   NU: zero   17

LOCATION   72
    coverbs of location   75
    existence in a place   73
    localizers   74
    place words   74
    positional nouns   75
    two ways of expressing   146
    with dzài and a place word   72

lóu   N: building (of more than one story)
                                (M: -tséng, a story)   71
    lóushàng   PW: upstairs   71
    lóusyà   PW: downstairs   71
    lóutī   N: stairs, stairway   141

lù   N: road, path; way, route (M: -tyáu)   131

lyán   DV: even (including)   81

lyǎn   N: face (lit. or fig.)   150

lyáng   FV: measure, measure out   173

lyángkwai   SV: be comfortably cool   186

LYĂNG and ÈR, use of   22

lyǎng-   BF-NU: two, a couple of   17

lyàng   SV: be light, bright   109

lyànsyí   N/FV: practice, drill   97, 98

lyòu   NU: six   17

lyǔgwǎn   PW: hotel   185
    lyǔsyíng   N/FV: travel; take a trip   153

lyù   SV: be green   134

M

ma   P: (interrogative sentence particle used
                                to form simple questions)   2

mǎi   FV: buy   2
    mǎimai   N: business (lit. buying and selling)   53

mài   FV: sell   2
    mài   FV: sell for (so much)   44
    màigei   FV: sell to   44

màn   SV: be slow   133
    mànmārde   A: slowly   132

mǎn   A: be full, full of   174

máng	SV: be busy	2
MANNER and degree of an action or condition		135
commands and requests		136
-máu	M: (measure for dimes)	40
máubǐ	N: Chinese brush pen	80
màudz	N: hat, cap	61
MEANS of conveyance		93
with coverbs <u>dzwò</u> and <u>chí</u>		93
MEASUREMENT		
generalized nouns of measurement		180
use of <u>yǒu</u> M		188
MEASURES		21
general and specific		22
-<u>bèi</u>		179
-<u>byār</u> and -<u>bù</u>		189
in comparison		178
polite		35
quantification of N		21
-<u>tsż</u> and <u>hwéi</u>		126
MÉI		103
negated and suspended action with <u>méi</u>-		100
méiyǒu, use of		14
méi	A: not (negative for <u>yǒu</u>)	11
méi(you)	A: (negates completion of action)	97
méichyán	SV: be poor, destitute	63
méifádz	N: no way out, no way to manage	160
méigwānsyi	SV: be irrelevant, unimportant	163
Méi nèmma hwéi shr̀!	EX: There's no such thing!	134
Méi shemma!	EX: It's nothing!	45
méiyou	FV: has not, have not	10
méiyìsz	SV: be dull, uninteresting	63
méiyǒu, méi(you)	FV: (impersonal) there isn't, there aren't	43
méiyùng	AV: be useless	80
méi . . . méi . . .	A: neither . . . nor . . .	132
měi-	SP: each	106
Měigwo	(PW)N: America	10
mèimei	N: younger sister	41
mén	N: door	131
ménkǒu(r)	N: doorway, gateway, entrance	141
mén pyàu	N: admission ticket	141
míngbai	FV: comprehend, understand (clearly)	62
míngdz	N: name, given name	27
míngnyan	(MA)N: next year	107
míngtyan	(MA)N: tomorrow	97

MODIFICATION   60
  by clauses   64
  by clauses with de   67
  by phrases with de   66
  by PN and N   64
  by SV   64
  general and specific modifying clauses   65
  of N indicated by de   64, 66
  use of SV to modify N   14, 68

MONETARY EXPRESSIONS   45
  amount per unit   46
  concise forms   45
  higher numbers   50
  monetary measures   45, 47
  use of dwō in approximations   47

MOVABLE ADVERBS   23
  wèishémma, yīnwei, and swóyu   76

mǔchin   N: mother   41

mùjyang   N: carpenter, woodworker   172

mùtou   N: wood, lumber   172

N

ná   FV: take, grasp, hold, carry   151
  náchilai   FV: take or pick up (with the hand)   151
  náje   FV: hold, be holding (in the hand)   151
  náhwéi   FV: take back   151

nà   A: in that case   89

NAMES
  Chinese forms for foreign place names   190
  foreign proper names   94
  inquiring name, nationality   34
  meaning in Chinese geographic names   191
  name with title   35
  surnames and given names   35

nán   SV: be difficult, hard to do   63

nán   PW: south   185

nán-   BF: male (of persons)   27
  nánde   N: man, male (person)   27

nǎr?   PW: where?   71

Nǎrde hwà?   EX: Where did you get such an idea?   153

NATIONALITY, inquiring   34

ne   P: (indicating continuing state or action)   55

NE
  abbreviated questions   137

    alternative questions   137
    continuity or suspense   57
    interrogative uses of particle ne   58
    Nǐ ne?   137
    Shr̀ . . . háishr . . . ne   136
NEGATIVE
    negated and suspended action with méi   100
    negated verbs before yǐchyán   127
    in manner pattern   136
    notes on bù   5

něi-?   SP: which?   17
    něibyar?   PW: which side, where?   185
    něigwó?   SP-N: which country, nationality?   28
    něisyē?   SP-M: which ones?   40

nèi   SP: that   16

nèibyar   PW: over there   184
    nèibyar?   PW: which side? where?   185

nèisye   SP-M: those   40

nèmma   A: in that way, by that means, so   89

němma?   A: in which direction?   89

nèmmayàng   MA: in that way, in that case   171

néng   AV: can   19

nèr   PW: there   71

nǐ   PN: you (singular)   1
    nǐde   N: your, yours   10
    nín   PH: you (polite)   1
    nǐmen   PN: you (plural)   1
    nǐmende   N: your, yours (plural)   10
    nínde   PN: your, yours (polite)   10
    Nǐ dwèi ta shwō   EX: You say to him   45
    Nǐ hwéidá.   EX: You answer.   45
    Nín hǎu a?   EX: How are you?   2
    Nǐ shwōtswòle.   EX: You said it wrong.   30

NOUNS   5
    Modification by clauses   67
    Modification by SV   14, 68
    Modification indicated by de   66
    Quantification of   19
    Relation to each other   13
    Specification of   20

NUMBERS   21
    Below 10,000   33
    Higher numbers   50

nwǎnhé, nwǎnhwo   SV: be comforable warm   186

nyán   M: (for years)   106
    nyánnyán   A: year by year, yearly   108
    nyánchǐng rén   N: youth, young person   172

| nyàn | FV: read (aloud) | 61 |
| nyàn shū | VO: study | 61 |

| nyóuroù | N: beef | 80 |

nyǔ	BF: female	27
nyǔde	N: women, female	27
nyǔer	N: daughter	61

O

OBJECT   3
   direct and indirect   13
   in the shr̀ . . . de pattern   83
   indirect   11, 13
   sentence object   20, 34
   transposed   83

ORDINAL SPECIFIERS dì and tóu contrasted   126

OTHER, translating   103
   another (byéde)   103
   the other (nèige)   103

Ou!   P: Oh!   55

P

pà   AV/FV: be afraid to, be afraid of   91

pàng   SV: be stout, obese (of persons)   174

pángbyār   PW: alongside   185

PART, whole before the part   48

PARTICLES   6
   aspect   100
   ba!   65
   de (subordinating particle)   64, 137
   gwo   126
   je   138
   le   56
   ma?   3
   ne   57, 137

PARTICULARIZED VERBS   94

PARTS OF SPEECH— defined   5
   adverbs   6
   auxiliary verbs   12, 14
   functive verbs   6
   nouns   5
   particles   6
   pronouns   5
   stative verbs   6
   verbs   5

PASSIVE construction with CV of Agent   200
    with ràng and jyàu   199

pău   FV: run   133

péngyou   N: friend   26

píbāu   N: leather case, briefcase, billfold   150

píchi   N: temperament, disposition   160

píngcháng   SV/A: be ordinary, common; ordinarily   133

písyé   N: leather shoes   150

PLACE NAMES, FOREIGN   94, 190

PLACE WORDS   73

POSITIONAL NOUNS   74

PRESTATEMENT of topic   32
    in manner expressions   138
    transposed order   155
    with resultative compound verbs   167

PRONOUNS   5
    modifying nouns   50
    omission of tone marks on PN objects   14

PRONUNCIATION
    Chinese sounds with English counterparts   xi
    consonant clusters   xiii
    checklist of syllables   xv
    final consonants   xii
    four tones   xiii
    paired initial consonants   xii
    retroflex sounds   xii
    sibilants   xii
    sounds ts- and dz   xii
    umlaut yu (-yw-)   xiii
    zero final sounds   xiii

PROPER NAMES
    foreign   94, 190
    geographic   191
-pù   BF: (ending for stores)   71
    pùdz   N: store   71

PURPOSE, expressing   102
    of coming and going   92

pyányi   SV: be cheap, inexpensive   44

pyàu   N: ticket (M: -jāng)   141

Q

QUALITY, change in   56
QUANTIFICATION   31

of nouns   19
quantified objects and <u>le</u>   114

QUESTIONS
  alternative choice Q with <u>shr</u> . . . <u>háishr</u>   136
  alternative choice Q with <u>shr</u> . . . <u>shr</u>   36
  choice-type   4
  more choice-type questions   13
  question and answer with AV   12
  question forms with <u>le</u>   102
  question patterns for equative verbs   36
  question with <u>shrbushr</u>   36
  question-word question   4
  simple questions with <u>ma</u>   3
  three types   3

QUESTION WORDS
  intense exclusiveness — with <u>lyán</u> and <u>dōu</u>   83
  <u>jǐ</u>- and <u>dwōshau</u>   34
  question-word questions   4
  used as inclusive before <u>dōu</u>   82
  used as indefinites   82

R

ràng   FV: let or permit (someone to do something)   195
  ràng   CV: by (introduces agent of action)   195

Ìbĕn   N: Japan   108

rè   SV: be hot   186

REDUPLICATION
  reduplicated verbs   48
  reduplicated verbs in <u>bǎ</u> construction   154
  reduplication of nouns   115

RELATIVE TIME, expressions of   123
  general expressions of relative time   123
  specific expressions of relative time   124

rén   N: man, person, people   17
  rénren dōu   EX: everyone   110

rēng   FV: throw   153
  rēngdzai   FV: throw into   153
  rēngle   FV: throw away   153

rènshr   FV: know, recognize, be acquainted with   121

RESULTATIVE COMPOUND VERBS   164, 167
  actual resultative compounds   165
  potential resultative compounds   165
  resultative verb endings   165, 166

ròu   N: meat, flesh; pork   80

rúngyi   SV: be easy, simple (to do)   63

S

sān	NU: three	17
sàn hwèi	VO: close a meeting, dismiss	132

SAYINGS, COMMON

Búpà màn, jyòu pà jàn.		92
Bujǐng yishr̀, bujǎng yijr̀.		122
Chāi dūng chyáng, bǔ syī chyáng.		187
Chyántou yǒu chē, hòutou yǒu jé.		72
Dwèi nyóu tán chín.		82
Dzài jyā chyān r̀ hǎu, chū wài shŕshŕ nán.		72
Dzǒutswòle lù hwéidelái, shwōtswòle hwà hwéibulái.		164
Gwàje yángtóu mài gǒu roù.		135
Gwò ěr jr̄ yán bùkě tīng.		122
Gwò hé chāi chyáu.		122
Hǎu jyè hǎu hwán, dzài jyè bunán.		153
Hwā chyán rúngyi, jèng chyán nán.		99
Hwèi shwōde burú hwèi tīngde		174
Hwódau lǎu, sywédau lǎu		164
Jèi shān wàngje, nèi shān gāu.		135
Jr̄li bāubujù hwǒ.		164
Jyòude búchyù, syǐnde bùlái.		92
Jyòu rén, jyòudau lyǎur, sùng rén, sùngdau jyā.		144
Kàn shr̀ rúngyi, dzwò shr̀ nán.		64
Lěng shr̀ yíge rén lěng, rè shr̀ dàjyā rè.		186
Méiyou gāu shān, busyǎn píng dì.		153
Mùjyang dwōle, gàiwāile fáng.		197
Nánde búhwèi, hwèide bunán.		64
Pàngdz búshr̀ yìkǒu chr̄de.		110
Rén dwō hǎu dzwòhwó, rén shǎu hǎu chr̄fàn.		55
Sāntyān dǎ yú, lyǎngtyān shài wǎng.		110
Shǎu shwōhwà, dwō dzwò shr̀.		56
Shwōdau nǎr, bàndau nǎr.		144
Shwōdau Tsáutsau, Tsáutsau jyou dàu.		144
Shwō yī shr̀ yī, shwō èr shr̀ èr.		30
Syǐn jǐ burú mwò jǐ.		174
Tsǎudǐli shwōhwà, lùshang yǒu rén tīng.		99
Tyānsyàde lǎugwā yíyàng hēi.		174
Yǎn bujyàn, syīn bufán.		99
Yǎn jyàn shr̀ shŕ, ěr tīng shr̀ syū.		99
Yǐhwéi shēng, èrhwéi shú.		122
Yìjr̄ budùng, bǎijr̄ buyáu.		122
Yìjr̄ shǒu pāibuchū bājang.		164
Yìrén nán chèn bǎirén yì.		110
Yítswùn gwāngyīn, yítswùn jīn		174
Yíyàng hwà, bǎiyàng shwōfǎ.		174
Yǒu yìjyù, shwō yìjyù.		64

SENTENCE OBJECT, verbs taking		20
more verbs taking sentence object (wèn and gàusung)		34

SENTENCE SUBJECTS	199

SENTENCES

bǎ construction	155

    compound sentences   7
    compound sentences with <u>yě</u> and <u>kěshr</u>   20
    equative sentences with <u>shr̀</u>   32
    simple functive sentence   2
    simple stative sentence   3
    three types of sentence structure   154

SEPARATION (see DISTANCE)

shān	N:	mountain, hill	141

shàng-	FV:	ascend, mount	142
-shàng	PW:	on (localizing suffix to PW)	71
shàng	PW:	up	89
shàngbān	VO:	go to work	142
shàngbyar	PW:	top	185
shàngchē	VO:	board a car or train	142
shàngchyu	FV:	go up	142
shàngjyē	VO:	go shopping	142
shàngkè	VO:	go to class	91
shànglai	FV:	come up	142
shànglǐbài	N:	last week	107
shànglóu	VO:	go upstairs	142
shàngshān	VO:	climb a mountain	142
shàngsyīngchī	N:	last week	107
shàngsywé	VO:	go to school	142
shàngtou	PW:	top, on top of, above	71
shàngwǔ	MA/N:	forenoon, A.M., morning	119
shàngywè	N:	last month	107

Shànghǎi	PW:	Shanghai	119

sháur	N:	spoon	80

shǎu	SV:	be few, scarce of	44
	A:	less	42

shéi?	N:	who? whom?	2
shéide?	N:	whose?	10

shémma?	N:	what?	2
shémmade	EX:	and so forth, etc.	144
shémmayàng(de)?	QW:	what sort of?	171
Shémma yìsz?	EX:	What is the meaning?	45

shēn	SV:	be deep, dark (in color), deep (in meaning)	186

shēngchì	VO:	get angry, be angry	109

shēngdż	N:	new word, vocabulary (lit. unfamiliar word)	151

shōu	FV:	receive, collect, put away	162
shōuchilai	RV:	store away	162
shōuhweilai	RV:	get back, recover	162
shōushr	FV:	put in order, repair	72

shǒu	N:	hand	150

shòu	SV:	be slender, thin (opp. <u>pang</u>) lean (opp. <u>fei</u>)	174

shŕ	NU:	ten	17
-shŕ	M:	a unit of ten	26

shŕhou   N: time   108

-shŕ   BF: style, fashion   171

SHR̀, equative verb   32
   alternative choice questions with shŕ   136
   descriptive use   85
   distinction between yǒu and shŕ   86
   equative sentences   32

SHR̀ . . . DE CONSTRUCTION   112
   alternative position of object   114
   descriptive shŕ   85
   compared with nominal clause   115

shŕ   EV: be (am, is, are)   29
   shŕ . . . (hái)shr   (see Sentence Pattern C, p. 136)   132

shŕ(ching)   N: affair, matter, business   52

Shŕde!   EX: That's right!   99

shŕjyè(shang)   PW: the world   185

shū   N: book   2
   shūfáng   N: study, den, office   141
   shūjwō(r)   N: desk (M: -jang)   17
   shūjwōdz   N: desk   17
   shūjyà(dz)   N: bookcase   172
   shūpù   N: bookstore   71

shūfu   SV: be comfortable, feel well   54

shwěi   N: water   53

shwèi   N: tax   42

shwèi   FV: go to sleep, sleep   162
   shwèijyàu   VO: sleep for a period   162

shwō   FV: say, speak; say that   xx, 18
   shwōfǎ(r)   N: way to say a thing   160
   shwō gùshr   VO: tell a story   61
   shwō hwà   VO: speak   18

SIMILARITY AND DISSIMILARITY   175
   comparison for contrast   176
   degrees of comparison   177

'SOME' and 'ANY'   48

SPECIFICATION   22
   definite and indefinite specification   49
   of nouns   20
   ordinal specifiers dì and tóu   126
   SP-NU-M   22, 65

STARTING POINT AND DESTINATION   92
   with coverbs tsúng and dàu   92

STATIVE SENTENCE   3

STATIVE VERBS   6
   as modifiers of nouns   14

of restricted function			47
used to modify nouns			68
sùng	FV:	send, deliver (goods); escort, see off (persons); present (gifts)	143
sùngdau	FV:	send to, escort to	143
sùnggei	FV:	present to	143
sùngsyìn	VO:	deliver the mail	143
súyŭ	N:	common saying, proverb	61
swàn	FV:	figure, calculate	43
swànyiswan	FV:	figure, calculate	43
swéibyàn	VO:	do as one pleases; do as one wishes (lit. follow one's convenience)	196
swéiràn . . . , kĕshr . . .		although . . . , yet . . .	195
-swèi	M:	(measure for years of age)	106
swèishu(r)	N:	age (lit. age-count)	172
SWÓYI			76
swóyi	MA:	therefore, and so	71
swŏ	N:	lock	162
swŏ(shang)	FV:	lock up, secure	162
-swŏ	M:	(for houses)	71
swŏyŏude	N:	all, every, all there are	151
syà	FV:	descend	142
syà	PW:	down	89
syàbyar	PW:	below	185
syàchyu	FV:	go down	142
syàkè	VO:	dismiss class	91
syàlai	FV:	come down	142
syàlĭbài	N:	next week	107
syàsyāng	VO:	go to the countryside	142
syàsyīngchī	N:	next week	107
syàsywĕ	VO:	snow	142
syàtou	PW:	bottom, at the bottom of, below	71
syàwŭ	MA/N:	afternoon, P.M.	119
syàyŭ	VO:	rain	142
syàywè	N:	next month	107
syān . . . dzài	A-A:	first . . . and then . . .	120
syàndzài	MA:	now, at the present time	53
SYĂNG			48
syăng	V:	think	42
syăng(yàu)	AV:	intend to, wish to, be thinking of doing	43
syăng(yi)syăng	FV:	think it over	43
syàng	FV:	resemble, be like	173
syàng . . . shrde	FV:	seems as though, seems like	173
syàngdāng	A:	fairly, rather	172
syàngdz	N:	suitcase, trunk, box, case	150

Syānggǎng	PW: Hong Kong	89
syāngsya	N: countryside, rural area	71
syānsheng	N: gentleman, teacher, husband, Mr., sir	27
syàtyan	N: summer(time)	107
syǎu	SV: be small, little	10
syǎuháidz	N: (small) child	27
syǎuhár	N: child, children	27
syáujye	N: young lady, girl, daughter	27
Syaujyě	N: Miss	27
syǎushwō(r)	N: novel	131
syǎusyīn	SV/FV: be careful, take care of, look out for	197
syǎusywé(syàu)	N: primary school	161
syàu	FV: laugh, smile; laugh at	133
syàuhwa(r)	N/FV: joke, humorous anecdote; laugh at	133
syàuhwar	N: joke, funny story	131
-syē-	M: (suffix indicating quantity, number)	40
syé	N: shoe (singular: jr; pair: shwang)	61
syě	FV: write	62
syě dz	VO: write, (character or words)	62
Syèsye!	EX: Thank (you)! Thanks!	11
syī	PW: west	185
syīshr̀	N: foreign style	171
syīgwā	N: watermelon	161
syígwàn	N: habit, custom	160
syǐ	FV: wash	81
syǐhwan	FV/AV: like, prefer, enjoy; like to	10
syīn	SV: be new	62
syìn	N: letter (mail) (M: -fēng)	79
syìnfēng(r)	N: envelope	79
syìnjǐ	N: letter paper	79
syíng	SV: satisfactory, all right	63
syíngle	EX: (that's all right, O.K.)	63
syíngli	N: baggage	150
syǐng	FV: wake up (from sleep)	162
syìng	N: surname	27
	FV: be surnamed	29
syīngchī	N: week	107
Syīngchi-r̀	N: Sunday	107
Syīngchisż	N: Thursday	107
Syīngchilyòu	N: Saturday	107
syīwang	N: hope, expectation	108
	AV: hope that, hope for, expect that	109
syōusyi	FV: rest	121
sywé	FV/AV: study/learn (how) to	61

sywésheng	N:	student, pupil	27
sywésyàu	PW:	school	71
sywě	N:	snow	141
sż	NU:	four	17

T

tā	PN:	he, him, her, she	1
tāde	N:	his, her, hers	10
tāmen	N:	they, them	1
tāmende	PN:	their, theirs	10
tài	V:	too, excessively, too much	11
Táiběi	PW:	Taipei	89
tàidu	N:	attitude, manner	160
tàitai	N:	(married) lady, wife, Mrs.	27
tán	FV:	converse, chat, talk over	80
tán hwà	VO:	converse, chat	80
tāng	M:	soup (M: -wǎn)	80
táng	N:	sugar, candy (M: -kwài)	42
tǎng	FV:	lie, recline	144
tǎngje	FV:	lie down	144
tǎngsya	FV:	lie down	144
tèbyé	SV/A:	be special, distinctive	133
tì	CV:	for (in the place of)	81

TIME
amounts of clock time	123
completion of time and action	102
jyòu, tsái, dzài after time expressions	127
lapse of time before negative verbs	114
previous and succeeding time units	115
relative time	123
sequence of time units	125
shr̀ . . . de construction	112
time as a measure of action	111
time clauses	114
time of an action	100
time meanings	101
time when	110
time when by the clock	122
time words	113
types of time when expressions	113
types of time expressions which measure action	114

tīng	FV:	listen to, hear	xx, 62
tīng . . . shwō		hear . . . say	62
tīngjyan	FV:	hear	98
tīngshwo	FV:	hear it said, hear tell	62

TONES
   on the negative <u>bu</u>-   5
   omission of tone marks on pronoun objects   7, 14
   successive low tones   5
   change on certain numbers and <u>bu</u>-   23

TOPIC, prestatement of   32

tóu   N: head   150
   tóu-   SP: first (in a series)   119

TRANSLATING
   <u>bǎ</u> sentences   155
   English verb 'be'   75
   'other'   103

TSÁI, use in incomplete and completed action   116
   <u>jyòu</u>, <u>tsái</u>, <u>dzài</u>, uses compared   127

tsái   A: only, just, merely   120
                            A: then and only then, not until   108

tsài   N: dish (menu item) (M: -<u>ge</u>) (lit. vegetable)   80

tséng   M: (for floors of a house, stories)   84

TSÚNG   92

tsŭngming   SV: be intelligent   63

tsúng   CV: from (a place or position)   90
   tsúngchyán   MA: formerly, previously, once   53
   tsúnglái   MA: heretofore, in the past   121

tswòle   EX: wrong   30

-tswùn   M: inch (measure)   171

-TSẒ (M)   126

-tsẒ   M: times, repetitions   119

tú   N: map, diagram   172

túngsywé   N: schoolmate, fellow student   195

-tyān   M: (measure for days)   106
   tyānchi   N: weather   185
   tyāntyān   A: day by day, daily   108

-tyáu   M: (for streets)   71

V

VERBS   5
   auxiliary   12, 14
   compound verbs   144
   coverbs   75
   equative   32
   functive   6
   reduplicated   48

resultative verb compounds   164
stative   6, 47
taking sentence object (wèn and gausùng)   20, 34

VERB-OBJECT COMBINATIONS   58

W

wài-	PW:	out	89
wàigwo	N:	foreign country	10
wàitou	PW:	outside, outside of	71
wánchywán	A:	completely, entirely	172
wǎn	SV:	be late	98
wǎnfàn	N:	dinner, supper (lit. late meal)	97
wǎnshang	(MA)N:	evening	97
-wǎn	M:	cup of, bowl of (see wǎn N below)	79
	N:	bowl, cup	80
-wàn	M:	(tens of thousands)	40
-wànwan	M:	(hundreds of millions)	40
wàng	FV:	forget	55
wàngle	FV:	forget	55
WÀNG, coverb of direction			93
particularized verbs which may follow a wàng phrase			94
wàng	CV:	toward (in a given direction)	90
wán(le)	SV/RVE:	be finished (finished doing something)	163
wár	FV:	play, play at or with	30
-wèi	M:	(polite M for persons)	26
WÈISHÉMMA?			76
wèishémma?	MA:	why?	71
wēnsyi	FV:	review, brush up on	91
-wén	BF:	language (as in Jūngwén, Yīngwén, etc.)	28
wèn(wen)	FV:	ask, inquire (a question)	19
wèntí	N:	problem, question	17
WHOLE BEFORE THE PART			48
wǒ	PN:	I, me	1
wǒde	N:	my, mine	10
wǒmen	PN:	we, us	1
wǒmende	N:	our, ours	10
wǒ yíge ren	EX:	I alone, singlehanded	99
wòfáng	PW:	bedroom	141
wūdz	N:	room (M: -jyan)	71
wǔ	NU:	five	17
wǔfàn	N:	noon meal (like jungfan)	97

Y

-yàng(r)	M:	kind, sort, type	171
yàngdz	N:	style, pattern	171
yǎnjing	N:	eyes	161
yàu	FV/AV:	want, want to, going to	10
yàu	FV:	demand, request	153
gén . . . yàu CV . . . V:		ask (someone) for (something)	153
yàu(shr)	A/MA:	if, in case	120
yàuburán	MA:	or else, otherwise	195
yàubúshr . . . jyòushr		if it isn't . . . then it is . . .	195
yàujǐn	SV:	be important	109
YĚ in compound sentences			20, 138
yě	A:	also, too	18
yě bù	A:	and . . . not, not . . . either, neither	18
yě . . . yě	A:	both . . . and	28
yě bu- . . . yě bu- . . .		neither . . . nor	28
yěsyǔ	MA:	perhaps, maybe, possibly	141
-yè	M:	(measure for nights)	106
yèli	MA/N:	nighttime, during the night, at night	107
yī	NU:	one	17
yī . . . (jyòu)	A:	just as soon as . . . (then)	120
yíbàn	NU-M:	one half, half of	41
yídìng	A:	definitely, certainly	89
yìdyǎr	NU-M:	a little	41
yígùng	A:	altogether, totaling	42
yìhwěr	NU-M:	a little while	119
yìhwěr . . . jyou	MA:	shortly, a moment, a little while	120
yìjŕ	A:	straight on, straight ahead, direct	185
yíkwàr	A:	together	72
	PW:	(in) one place	72
yílù píngān	EX:	a pleasant journey (to you)	134
yíyàng	SV:	be alike, the same, similar	174
	A:	similarly, equally	172
Yīywè	N:	January	107
YĪ . . . JYOU, 'as soon as'			103
YǏCHYÁN, negated verbs before			127
yǐchyán	MA:	previously, formerly (like tsúngchyán)	120
. . . yǐchyán	MA:	before . . . , . . . ago	120
yǐdz	N:	chair	17
yǐhòu	MA:	thereafter, afterwards (like hòulai)	120
. . . yǐhòu	MA:	after . . .	120
YIGE (unstressed)			22
Yìgwó (Yìdàlì)	PW:	Italy	28
yǐjing	A:	already	53

Yìndù	PW: India	119
yīngdāng	AV: ought to, should	81
Yīnggwo	N(PW): England	18
-yīnglǐ	M: (measure for English miles)	184
Yīngwén	N: English language	18

YĪNWEI 76

yīnwei	MA: because	71
yīshang	N: clothing (M: -jyan)	61
yìsz	N: meaning, intention	61
yìsz shr	EX: the meaning is	45

YǑU

existence in a place		73
méiyou		14
use of yǒu in measurement		188

yǒu	FV: have, has	10
	CV: comes up to, is as . . . as	174
	FV: (impersonal) there is, there are	43
yǒuchyán	SV: be rich, affluent	63
yǒude . . . , yǒude	EX: some . . . , some . . .	42
yǒude	verbal N: some, there are those which (who)	42
yǒugwānsyi	SV: be relevant	163
yǒumíng	SV: be famous, well known	186
yǒurén	N: some people	42
yǒusyē	N: (there are) some, several (who)	79
yǒuyìsz	SV: be meaningful, interesting	63
yǒuyùng	SV: be useful	80
yǒu shr yǒu	EX: that's so, but . . .	92

yòu	PW: right	89
yòu	A: again (in the past)	98
yòu . . . yòu	A: both . . . and; (neg.) neither . . . nor . . .	132

YÒU . . . YÒU 138

yú	N: fish	80
yǔ	N: rain	141
yùbei	AV/FV: prepare, get ready for	91
yùng	FV: use, employ	80
	CV: with, using	81
yùnggūng	SV: be studious, work hard (at studies)	110
ywándzbǐ	N: ball-point pen	10
ywǎn	SV: be far away, distant	186
ywàndz	N: courtyard	71
ywànyi	AV: wish to, want to	19
ywè	N: month	107
ywèywè	N: month by month	108
ywè . . . ywè	A: the more . . . , the more . . .	172
ywèlái . . . ywè	A: more and more	172